FROM THE
KLONDIKE
TO
BERLIN

MICHAEL GATES

FROM THE
KLONDIKE
TO
BERLIN

THE YUKON IN WORLD WAR I

Lost Moose is an imprint of Harbour Publishing Co. Ltd.
P.O. Box 219, Madeira Park, BC VON 2H0
www.harbourpublishing.com

Front cover photos: Hemera Technologies/PHOTOS.com/Thinkstock (top);
Yukon Archives George Black fonds 81/107 #163 (bottom)
Edited by Pam Robertson
Indexed by Kyla Shauer
Cover design by Brianna Cerkiewicz
Text design by Setareh Ashrafologhalai
Printed and bound in Canada

Harbour Publishing acknowledges the support of the Canada Council for
the Arts, which last year invested $153 million to bring the arts to Canadians
throughout the country. We also gratefully acknowledge financial support
from the Government of Canada through the Canada Book Fund and from
the Province of British Columbia through the BC Arts Council and the Book
Publishing Tax Credit.

LIBRARY AND ARCHIVES CANADA CATALOGUING IN PUBLICATION

Gates, Michael, 1949-, author
   From the Klondike to Berlin : the Yukon in World War I / Michael Gates.

Includes bibliographical references and index.
Issued in print and electronic formats.
ISBN 978-1-55017-776-3 (softcover).—ISBN 978-1-55017-777-0 (HTML)

   1. World War, 1914–1918—Yukon. 2. World War, 1914-1918—War work—
Yukon. 3. Soldiers—Yukon—Biography. 4. Heroes—Yukon--Biography.
5. Yukon—Biography. 6. Yukon—History--20th century. I. Title.

D547.C2G38 2017   940.3'7   C2017-900599-5
                                          C2017-900600-2

This book is dedicated to all the men and women who volunteered for service, especially those who were injured or died while serving their country in this brutal conflict. I want their sacrifices to be remembered.

TABLE OF CONTENTS

1919 AND BEYOND

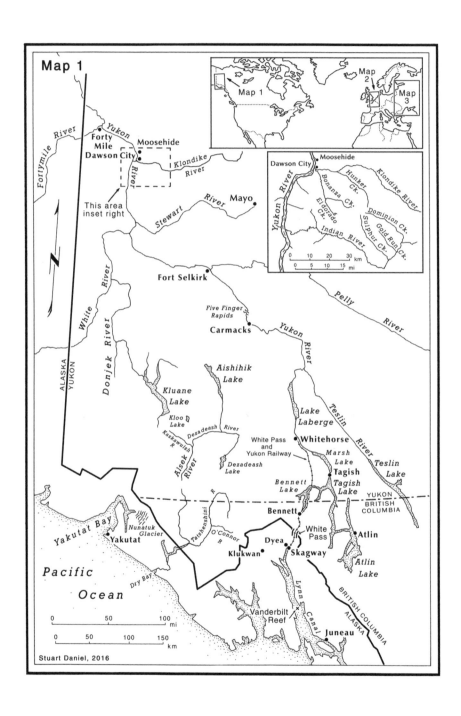

Map 1

Map 2
Map 1
Map 3

Fortymile River
Yukon River
Forty Mile
Dawson City
Moosehide
Klondike River
This area inset right

Dawson City
Moosehide
Yukon River
Bonanza Ck.
Hunker Ck.
Klondike River
El Dorado Ck.
Dominion Ck.
Sulphur Ck.
Gold Run Ck.
Indian River
0   10   20   30 km
0   5   10   15 mi

Stewart River
Mayo

White River

Donjek River

ALASKA
YUKON

Fort Selkirk

Pelly River

Five Finger Rapids
Carmacks
Yukon River

Aishihik Lake

Kluane Lake
Kloo Lake
Kaskawulsh R.
Dezadeash River

Lake Laberge
Teslin River

White Pass and Yukon Railway
Whitehorse

Marsh Lake

Alsek River
Dezadeash Lake

Teslin Lake

Bennett Lake
Tagish
Tagish Lake

YUKON
BRITISH COLUMBIA

Tatshenshini R
O'Connor R

Bennett

Atlin

Yakutat Bay
Nunatuk Glacier
Yakutat

White Pass
Dyea
Klukwan
Skagway

Atlin Lake

Pacific Ocean

Dry Bay

Vanderbilt Reef

Lynn Canal

BRITISH COLUMBIA
ALASKA

Juneau

0   50   100 mi
0   50   100   150 km

Stuart Daniel, 2016

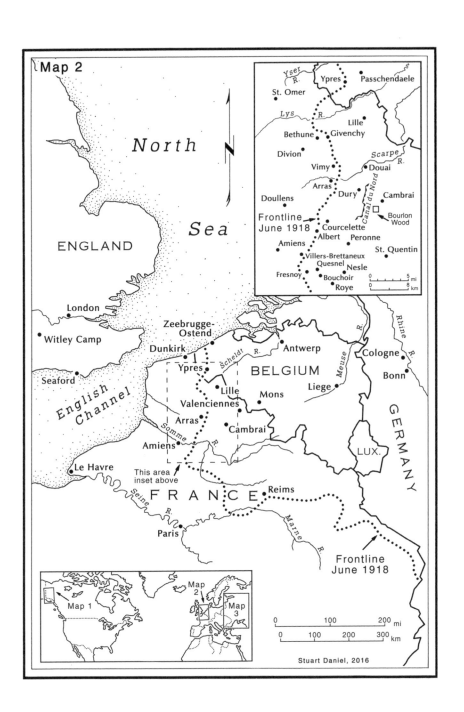

Map 2

North Sea

ENGLAND

London
Witley Camp
Seaford

English Channel

Le Havre

Zeebrugge-Ostend
Dunkirk
Ypres
Lille
Valenciennes
Arras
Cambrai
Amiens

Somme R.

This area
inset above

F R A N C E

Seine R.

Paris

BELGIUM

Scheldt R.

Mons
Liege

Antwerp

Meuse R.

Reims

Marne R.

Rhine R.

Cologne
Bonn

GERMANY

LUX.

Frontline
June 1918

Map 1
Map 2
Map 3

0   100   200 mi
0   100   200   300 km

Stuart Daniel, 2016

Inset (upper right):

Yser R.

St. Omer
Ypres
Passchendaele

Lys R.

Bethune
Givenchy
Lille

Divion
Scarpe R.

Vimy
Douai

Arras
Dury
Cambrai

Doullens

Canal du Nord

Bourlon Wood

Frontline
June 1918
Courcelette
Albert
Peronne

Amiens

Villers-Brettaneux
Quesnel
Nesle
St. Quentin

Fresnoy
Bouchoir
Roye

0   5 mi
0   8 km

Map 3

Petrograd

Reval

Map 1   Map 2   Map 3

Riga

Dvina R.

Moscow

R U S S I A

Vilna

Minsk   Mogilev

Treaty of
Brest-Litovsk

Bug R.

Brest-
Litovsk

Kiev

Kharkov

Armistice Line
Oct. 1917

Dnieper R.

Lemberg

Khmerinka

Tarnopol

Dniester R.

AUSTRIA-
HUNGARY

Kishina

Jassy

Bikaz

Cotofanesti

Odessa

Sebastopol

Sulina   Yalta

ROMANIA   Black   Sea

Bucharest

Danube R.

| 0 | 100 | 200 mi |
| 0 | 100 | 200 | 300 km |

Istanbul

Romanian expansion 1918

From Russia -
Bessarabia

From Austria-Hungary -
Transylvania,
Bukovina, Crisina, and Banat

Stuart Daniel, 2016

PREFACE

FROM THE KLONDIKE TO BERLIN germinated from seeds planted unexpectedly by my wife, Kathy, who was compiling volumes of information about a Yukoner named George Black. He is more commonly referred to as Martha Black's husband, because his wife is better known than he is. Awareness of his accomplishments as a gold rush stampeder, a lawyer and a politician is essential to understanding the evolution of this sparsely populated district in the far northwest of Canada.

Flooded with information, Kathy asked me if I would help compile material from his wartime experiences. I obliged, and my journey through time and place began.

The Yukon has had an interesting history, yet there are many untold stories. Although the First Nations had lived there for millennia, the Yukon in its modern form was born as a result of the sudden surge of humanity in search of Klondike gold. The gold rush era has been well documented in thousands of books, magazine accounts, diaries, photographs and oral histories. So too has the construction of the Alaska Highway. Yet there are other periods of the Yukon's history that remain unexplored. The period during World War I (1914–1919) is one of them. Except in passing, there was little reference to the Yukon published during the period known as the Great War, and that is why I felt compelled to write this account.

During the Great War, Yukoners by the hundreds flocked to enlistment offices to volunteer their services in aid of king and country. The reason for doing so varied from one individual to another, but I suspect it was because of a number of factors, including patriotism, a strong sense of empire, a thirst for adventure and peer pressure. How would they have felt had they known the terrible conditions they would endure once they reached the battlefields? There is no doubt that their romantic ideals about war were shattered. Frequently, their spirits were shattered as well.

Writing about what happened to hundreds of Yukon men and women during World War I was not an easy undertaking. The graphic descriptions of trench warfare, of the inhuman conditions experienced by millions of soldiers on both sides in the trenches and No Man's Land, were very disturbing. Accounts that I read of the constant bombardment, the rats, the rotting corpses and the stubborn determination of arrogant military commanders to shed every last drop of other men's blood had a profound effect on me. Frequently, I had to lay them down to take a break and walk our dog in the abundant green spaces found everywhere around my northern home. Only these unspoiled wooded areas could return the calm after reading about the waste of human lives and the desolation of the battlefields of Belgium and France.

This account follows what happened to Yukoners at home and overseas, year by year, between 1914 and 1919, and later. The sources that I relied upon include the local newspapers. Alaska historian Preston Jones has noted that Alaskan newspapers during this period were a rich source of information. The Yukon's *Dawson Daily News* and *Whitehorse Star* were too. Published letters, sent home from those overseas, were extremely valuable sources of information.

I relied upon military records to help fill in the details. Attestation papers and military service files tracked the individual courses of the volunteers of the Canadian Expeditionary Force. Records from the navy and the air force were much less abundant. The war diaries of two units that were made up primarily of Yukon enlistees were particularly useful in plotting the day-to-day activities. These units were the Yukon Motor Machine Gun Battery and the 2nd Canadian Motor Machine Gun Brigade.

Accounts of Canada's involvement in the Great War by military historians provided me with the greater context of the war. Of these, the writings of Canadian authors/historians Tim Cook and G.W.L. Nicholson, among others, were very helpful. Specialized references about machine guns and snipers filled in details important to the story.

Some Yukon participants in the war stood out from the rest, either by what they wrote or by what others wrote about them. George and Martha Black and Howard Grestock fit into the former category. Joe Boyle and James Murdoch Christie fit into the latter. Although many displayed individual acts of bravery, these latter two men stand out for their heroic accomplishments. The efforts of the women who remained at home in the Yukon to raise funds for patriotic purposes also demanded attention.

I have woven together these disparate accounts into what I hope is a compelling and informative overview of what happened to people of the Yukon during World War I. I hope that it opens doors to the past that others will choose to enter. I do not consider myself an expert in the history of war, but I think that I share that with the hundreds of brave souls who volunteered for what they saw as a noble purpose.

INTRODUCTION

IT WAS IMPOSSIBLE for the men and women of the Yukon to imagine what
lay before them when they answered the call to war between 1914 and 1918.
The Yukon was not the most distant region of the British Empire, but it was
certainly the most isolated. Spawned by the Klondike gold rush that started
in 1896, the Yukon came into existence on June 13, 1898. Dawson City, its
capital, rose almost fully formed from the swampy land at the confluence
of the Yukon and Klondike Rivers, only a short distance from the Arctic
Circle, in the span of two years. At the peak of the gold rush, it was said to
be the largest city west of Winnipeg, and it had all the conveniences of any
modern city of that time period. In fact, it came to be known as the "Paris
of the North."

Dawson City wasn't easy to get to. During the gold rush, it would take
months for a man to haul his year's supplies over the rocky trails of the
mountainous Pacific coast and down the system of rivers and lakes, more
than 900 kilometres into the heart of a wilderness. This journey was shared
by tens of thousands of northern Argonauts. Even after the community had
settled into Victorian respectability, it was subject to the tenuous chain of
transportation links that started with ocean liners travelling from Vancouver, Victoria or Seattle to Skagway, Alaska, followed by a train ride on the
White Pass and Yukon Route railway through the mountains to Whitehorse,
and concluded with a two-day journey downriver by sternwheel riverboat.
The winters were worse. Once the Yukon froze up in the subarctic autumn,
all transportation ceased until the ice on the rivers was safe to cross and the
snow was deep enough to allow sleighs to be drawn by horses through the

arctic half-light at temperatures reaching fifty degrees below zero. It was a place where you could get away from it all, as many did.

The Yukon, long inhabited by First Nations people, had remained undisturbed by European intrusion until the mid-nineteenth century. Then gold was discovered. The earliest prospectors first came into the Yukon River valley in 1873, but it was another decade before they started to trickle into the region in any significant numbers. Buoyed up by optimism that the great find would someday be discovered, these hardy individualists moved from one promising prospect to another, looking for the pay streak.[1]

Gold was discovered on the Fortymile River in 1886, and the following year, the small town of Forty Mile grew up and served as the centre of mining in the region for the next decade. More gold was discovered on the nearby creeks of the Sixtymile River, and then at Birch Creek in Alaska. By 1896, sixteen hundred prospectors and miners had come into the Yukon River valley to search for the yellow metal.

All of this changed dramatically when Keish (a First Nation man from Tagish, also known as Skookum Jim), the brother-in-law of an American prospector named George Washington Carmack, discovered gold on Rabbit Creek, a tributary of the Klondike River, in August 1896. Rabbit Creek was quickly renamed Bonanza Creek. This was the gold discovery that everyone had been waiting for, and thousands more hopeful prospectors flocked to the Yukon with dreams of becoming rich.

Gold was found in incredible quantities on Bonanza Creek; Eldorado Creek, its main tributary, was even richer. The first two dozen claims on Eldorado Creek made their owners millionaires. Gold was found on Hunker Creek, and many other streams radiating out from a central peak, that was named King Solomon's Dome, like the spokes on a giant wheel. Gold was even found in the gravels on the hillsides above Bonanza, Eldorado and Hunker Creeks. Everywhere they turned, the prospectors seemed to find more of it. Production of the precious yellow metal peaked four years later, when more than a million troy ounces of gold were washed out of the frozen gravels of the Klondike.

At the peak of the gold rush, the Yukon had a population of thirty thousand, centred on the metropolis of Dawson City, and the satellite communities and mining operations of the surrounding goldfields. A few hundred lived in the tiny village of Whitehorse, which was, at that time, a place to pass through, rather than a destination. An even smaller number inhabited the millions of hectares of wilderness that surrounded these places. The original occupants of the land, the First Nations of the Yukon, numbering perhaps fifteen hundred individuals, were completely overwhelmed by this flood of humanity. Dawson became a vibrant city of dirt streets and boardwalks, electric lights and running water. Yet only a short distance away, grayling abounded in the streams and moose, bears and caribou were abundant in the hills and valleys. The region had yet to be explored and mapped by the new arrivals.

Within a few years, the countless claims at first mined by hand labour and sweat of brow were being operated by steam hoists, pumps and mills; these in turn were displaced by massive floating gold-digging machines called dredges, run by mining companies based thousands of kilometres away. The result was depopulation, and a stabilization of the community, which became dominated by the corporate giants operating there. In addition, thousands of miners were drawn away to mining camps in Alaska. The population of the Yukon was only about five thousand by 1914.

Throughout this period, however, Dawson City remained an active and dynamic Victorian town, and its inhabitants never lost the optimism that the next big find was just around the corner. Through the Yukon Order of Pioneers, the first fraternal organization in the Yukon, the old-time miners of the gold rush began to celebrate Discovery Day, turning it into one of the biggest events of the summer. It was symbolized by the individual prospector and miner who had mucked for gold for a quarter of a century before the big strike was made. The prospector crouched over his pan looking for gold became the iconic image that characterized the mining industry of the time, as it still does today. And it was with that in mind, that the community of Dawson was starting to think of the August 17 celebration in the summer of 1914.

Now imagine a landscape that is as barren as the moon. The trees are gone, or if they still survive, they are mere skeletal stumps, devoid of branches and leaves. They provide no shade, nor do they harbour songbirds.

Dawson City, which had exploded in population in 1898, was in slow decline by the time of the Great War, but still displayed some of the grandeur of the Klondike gold rush. YUKON ARCHIVES CLAUDE AND MARY TIDD FONDS 008360

The ground is littered with long rows of barbed wire ready to entangle anything or anyone who attempts to pass. They call it No Man's Land, and never was there a better description.

On either side of No Man's Land are opposing sets of trenches zigzagging across northern France. Along this line are thousands of machine gun nests, ready to spray a deadly rain of lead across the enemy lines. To attempt to approach is a death sentence for anyone who dares.

Behind each line of trenches are rows of howitzers and mortars that lay down a constant barrage of explosives, shrapnel and gas in No Man's Land—and the opposing trenches. Unlike conventional warfare, where soldiers die in hand-to-hand combat with their enemy, here they can be wounded, gassed or killed while hunkered down in a trench, without ever seeing their foe.

The Yukon and the Western Front were as far apart in distance and in contemplation as it was possible to be, yet during the Great War of 1914–1918, these two places were linked by bonds of patriotism and the British Empire as though bound by strands of steel. This is the story of how the men and women of the North came to travel halfway around the globe from a world of isolation and natural beauty, clear blue skies, untrampled wilderness and streams filled with pure, clean water, a land of hard work and opportunity, to one of death, desolation, pollution and conflict. This is the story of the Yukon and World War I.

1914–1916

WAR IS DECLARED

WINTER COMES EARLY in Canada's Far North. The weather had been dull grey and cool with a spot of rain in early August. It was the first warning that the summer of 1914 would soon be over in Dawson City. A large contingent of Shriners of the Gizeh Temple from Victoria, BC, was visiting the Yukon capital, and the ladies who had accompanied their husbands on this long journey were received on the afternoon of August 4, 1914, at the home of Mrs. Gus Johnson. They were, as of yet, unaware of events unfolding in Europe. This would be the last social event in the Klondike for five years that was innocent of the shadow of war.[2] The Auditorium Theatre (better known today as the Palace Grand) had just opened for the season to present silent movies to Dawsonites. Advertised for the silver screen in early August were *The Honeymooners, Prisoner of War, Red Saunders' Sacrifice, The Signal of Distress* and *The Contortionist.* Miss Zella Goodman was the pianist.

There were two other theatres also offering the newest in silent film productions. The Dawson Amateur Athletic Association (DAAA), at the corner of Queen Street and Fifth Avenue, was presenting a drama (*Two Daughters of Eve*), two comedies (*Two Gay Dogs* and *Chumps*) and a weekly Pathé newsreel. The admission was twenty-five cents, and for the reserved seats, fifty. Professor Carpenter provided musical accompaniment on the piano. Meanwhile, the Orpheum Theatre on Front Street was presenting three dramas and two comedies.

When the visiting Shriners' wives met for a garden party at the home of Mrs. Gus Johnson on August 4, 1914, they had little idea that Canada would be at war by the end of the day. YUKON ARCHIVES ROY MINTER FONDS 92/15 # 314

That evening, the Shriners were present at a special program of entertainment at the DAAA, which included, in addition to films, the singing of Miss Hazel Hartshorn, and a monologue and dancing by Danny Green. Just as the performance was ending at the DAAA, news reached the patrons that the British fleet had sunk six German ships. Mr. Walter Creamer, the manager of the theatre, projected a slide of the king on the screen, and Professor Carpenter struck the introductory chords to "Rule, Britannia!" The audience rose as one and sang "until the house shook."[3] That was followed by "God Save the King." When a picture of Queen Mary was projected on the screen, the crowd sang "The Maple Leaf Forever."

The same happened at the other theatres. The Auditorium Theatre was filled to capacity. During an interval, a telegram was passed to George Black, the commissioner of the Yukon Territory. Upon reading it, he went to the stage and, after a perceptible pause, eloquent with suppressed emotion, read the cable. The message was from the federal undersecretary of state, saying that England was at war with Germany.

In silence, men and women looked at each other aghast, trying to absorb the significance of the announcement. According to Martha Black, wife of the commissioner:

> In the centre of the house about twenty scarlet-coated members of the Royal North West Mounted Police occupied seats. Two of the men, brothers, were former members of the Coldstream Guards, well over six feet in height, and both with fine voices. They looked at each other, whispered to other members of the force with them, rose to their feet and commenced singing "God Save the King." The effect was electrical; with one move the audience was on its feet and never in the world . . . was the national anthem sung with greater fervour or more depth of feeling than that night in this tiny mining village on the edge of the Arctic.[4]

As they filed out of the theatres onto the twilit streets of Dawson, men and women, young and old were abuzz with earnest discussion. Although it was not yet officially stated, the community understood what this meant: that Canada, too, was at war alongside Britain. The Yukon was now at war.

The following evening, at the end of their stay in Dawson City, the visiting Shriners were feted at a grand ball in the Arctic Brotherhood (AB) Hall (today known as Diamond Tooth Gertie's). The hall was colourfully decorated with Union Jacks and flags of other nationalities, Shriner emblems, pennants and bunting. Evergreens and a myriad of potted flowers and swinging baskets adorned the room. The festivities were interrupted when the Yukon's member of parliament, Dr. Alfred Thompson, read out news bulletins just received by the *Dawson Daily News*. Mounting the rostrum, Thompson read out the first announcement, which called for parliament to convene on August 18. The announcement was greeted by cheers and the singing of the national anthem. The second message announced a major naval victory, after which the orchestra played "Rule, Britannia!" According to the account published in the *Dawson Daily News* of August 7, "from every throat welled the chorus till the house shook. Then followed 'God Save the King,' and three cheers and a tige[r]. Commissioner Black was present on the platform and joined heartily in the demonstration."[5]

"We all had read skimpy reports of European troubles in the *Dawson Daily News*," wrote Laura Berton, wife of the mining recorder, "but Europe, really, seemed a planet or so away."[6] A month earlier, the *Dawson Daily News* of June 30 carried a brief article noting the assassination of Archduke Franz Ferdinand, heir to the Austro-Hungarian throne. It consisted of only sixty-seven words.

This was an inauspicious way to herald the coming of a global Armageddon. The headlines in the *Dawson Daily News* devoted more space to the events surrounding the Mexican Revolution, and upheaval in Ireland, but by the end of July, reports from Europe became increasingly ominous.

On July 25, the *News* stated that Austria-Hungary and Serbia were engaged in open hostilities. Russia was sympathetic with the Serbian cause. If it became involved, Germany would stand behind the Austro-Hungarian position. Britain, though not in a state of war with Germany over the "Pan-Servian question," placed its fleet on a war basis on July 27.

By July 30, the headlines in the *Dawson Daily News* declared that Britain might not be able to remain apart from the conflict. Across the country, Canadians were abuzz with discussions about the latest developments. Crowds gathered outside of newspaper offices in small towns and large cities in the hope of seeing new reports as soon as they were posted. At that time, people thought that the conflict would be over by Christmas.

It is unclear how these events affected people in Dawson City. There was no commentary in the newspaper regarding public stirrings of concern, yet the *News* was well supplied with images of all the key players in the conflict by the end of July. "WAR EXTRA" declared the *Dawson Daily News* in a headline that filled one third of the front page of the August 1 edition: "Germany Declares War on the Russians."[7]

THE VOLUNTEERS

OFFICIAL NOTICE FROM the Canadian government of Britain's declaration of war against Germany reached Commissioner George Black on August 6. Subsequent declarations of war against the Austro-Hungarian Empire

(August 13) and Bulgaria (October 15) would follow within weeks. Black immediately wired the secretary of state that a force of volunteers would be raised in the Yukon. The day after the official notification of war arrived, Black placed advertisements in the newspaper calling for volunteers.[8] He and Dr. Alfred Thompson, Yukon's member of parliament, were the first to sign their names in a ledger laid out in the lobby of the Territorial Administration Building, which stood in a prominent location on Fifth Avenue, on land set aside for government use. Sixty-seven others followed their example; by war's end, most of them had signed up and shipped to Europe. Of the men who signed the ledger, only two identified themselves as Canadian—the rest, nearly half of whom were born in Canada, listed their nationality as British. Dr. Thompson said: "Our Empire and our Dominion now face the greatest crisis in their history, and I feel it is my duty to be in Ottawa when such momentous matters are to be discussed."[9] A large notice placed by the commissioner appeared in the *Dawson Daily News* on August 9 calling for volunteers. Veterans and servicemen, British subjects who were less than thirty-five years of age and capable of passing a rigid medical examination, were preferred.

Men immediately stepped forward to sign up. Most believed that the conflict would not last very long. Many of the first to volunteer in support of the empire were born in Britain. Howard Grestock, a Londoner and veteran of the Boer War, was the first. Within days of the declaration, he was aboard the steamer *Dawson*, heading Outside—out of the Yukon—to enlist. He signed his papers on September 22 at Valcartier, Quebec, and shipped out with his old regiment, the Lord Strathcona's Horse. His letters from France would be published in the *News* for years to come. With him was Jack Maitland. During the Boer War, Maitland was with the Royal Scots Greys and was wounded twice. A large crowd of friends and well-wishers massed at the waterfront to see the two men off. Aboard the riverboat with them were the Shriners from the Gizeh Temple, who had concluded their visit to Dawson City.

Thomas Corville, a miner working at Coal Creek, also decided to enlist. Unfortunately, he did not have the fare to book passage on the riverboat for Whitehorse, and he could not get anybody to loan him the money for travel, so he put some hardtack into a pack, threw it to his shoulders and walked more than 600 kilometres overland to Whitehorse.[10] Ironically, he was rejected because of flat feet! Jack Morgan from Mayo was also quick to respond, as was Kenneth Currie from the Fortymile district, a long-time miner who was "prominent on many a platform in stirring meetings of the camp."[11] Neither knew what was to come.

All twenty-five members of the Royal Northwest Mounted Police in the Dawson City detachment were quick to volunteer. Nine of the fifteen officers in the Whitehorse detachment offered their services, including Inspector Arthur Acland, who was the first to step forward. Acland, who served as a constable on the Dalton Trail during the Klondike gold rush, quickly rose through the ranks, and would eventually retire from the Mounted Police as assistant commissioner in 1933.[12] Those who were British Army reservists were called upon to join their regiments in England, including Constables Harvey, Dooley, Hull, King and Greenaway. Greenaway reached London by November 1 and joined the Coldstream Guards. He was on the battlefront by the middle of the month.[13]

Sam Steele of the North-West Mounted Police, who had guided the stampeders safely through the great gold rush sixteen years earlier, joined and took a senior command position. Other former Mounties were commissioned officers in the British or Canadian Expeditionary Forces. Malcolm "Scotty" Morrison had served in the Yukon for thirteen years. Corporal Ward, who led the annual patrol from Dawson to Fort McPherson, and had left for the coast in the spring, joined the 68th Battalion of field artillery the day he arrived. Weston Burrell, formerly with the Whitehorse detachment, joined the 83rd Battalion. Constable George Pearkes, who was born in Watford, England, on February 26, 1883, came to Canada in 1906 and joined the Royal Northwest Mounted Police. In 1915, he enlisted in the Canadian Expeditionary Force, later rising to command the 5th Canadian Mounted Rifles.

By August of 1918, 101 former and current Mounties from the Yukon had enlisted for service overseas. Most tragic of all may have been a former constable named Spreadbury, who, after leaving the Mounted Police, worked for the White Pass and Yukon Route. Spreadbury had a good character reference with the force but was despondent after being rejected because of his age. In a fit of despair, he killed himself with a gunshot to the chest.[14]

Volunteering for military service quickly reached a fever pitch and continued during the protracted conflict overseas. For some, it was a family affair. Dr. P.F. Scharschmidt of Whitehorse and his two sons, Guy, a surveyor, and Howard, signed up.[15] Three sons of Fred Maclennan, the collector of customs in Dawson, enlisted. Eldest son James found himself on a patrol boat in the Atlantic. Fred Jr. eventually left with a large contingent accompanying George Black. Son Jack was accepted by the British Columbia School of Aviation and trained in the flying corps.[16] Frank Slavin, an Aussie pugilist and former empire heavyweight champion, signed up, followed by nineteen-year-old Frank Jr. a year later. The aging boxer would survive the war, but his son would not.

Elliott and Alfred Totty, and Kenneth and Hugh McDonald, all sons of Anglican missionaries and First Nation mothers, enlisted and served with distinction. Hugh was married and studying law in Winnipeg when he enlisted January 4, 1915. Kenneth joined the Royal Navy. First Nation men from the Yukon, however, found it difficult, or impossible to volunteer for service in the early stages of the war. According to military historian Timothy Winegard, "John Campbell, an Eskimo from the Yukon Territory, made a 3,000-mile journey by trail, canoe and river-steamer to enlist at Vancouver. He had previously tried to enlist in the Yukon with three Indians. They were all accepted by the recruiting depot and passed the medical exam; however, after complaints from men in the Yukon contingent, they were all summarily released from the unit. No Indian or Eskimo was accepted for service in the Yukon itself prior to conscription."[17]

Several women enlisted for service. One was Mrs. L.G. Bennet, whose husband, a Dawson City lawyer, had enlisted as an officer on November 28, 1916. A few months later, in the spring of 1917, she was selling their Seventh Avenue Dawson home, hoping to close the deal by the breakup of the Yukon River.[18] She then planned to go overseas as a nurse. Marie Thompson, daughter of Dr. and Mrs. W.E. Thompson of Dawson, served as a nurse in France and Flanders. Zowitza (Zo) Nicholas, second daughter of Mrs.

Jennie Nicholas of Dawson, and later Mayo Landing, joined the U.S. Army Nurse Corps and eventually left with a Seattle contingent.[19]

In addition to the Scharschmidt family, Whitehorse residents Jack Taylor, W.L. Breese, James Salvatore, Harold Newton and Frank G. Wilson, a nineteen-year-old student at the University of British Columbia, all joined up. By war's end, the Whitehorse volunteers would number ninety-six. Volunteers also came from Atlin, Mayo, Carmacks, Carcross and Fort Selkirk.

The news of the war filtered through the territory. Nevill Armstrong, a tall hardy Englishman, was returning with a hunting party after a trek to the south fork of the Macmillan River in search of large game. In the mid-afternoon of September 22, 1914, they encountered an old friend of Armstrong's, a French Canadian by the name of Tom Jeffreys, who was hauling out the hindquarters of a moose onto a gravel bar in the river. When he saw them, Jeffreys became agitated; he had important news to convey to the party. According to Armstrong, Jeffreys told him: "The War—half the world fighting!... there 'was one hell of a war going on on land.' Thousands of Germans killed, in some places piled thirty feet high, the bodies being used as breastwork! Although it was impossible to obtain any coherent explanation of what was actually happening in Europe, it was only too painfully evident that the whole of Europe was up in arms, and it was our duty to get back as soon as possible and offer our services."[20]

Within weeks, Armstrong was an officer in the 50th Regiment (Gordon Highlanders of Canada). Armstrong survived the war and left the military with the rank of captain and an Order of the British Empire (OBE) five years later.

Two men, William Annett and Walter Keddy, were on Herschel Island, the most northerly point in the Yukon, when they answered the call. They mushed by dog team hundreds of kilometres over ice and snow to Fort Yukon, near the mouth of the Porcupine River, then came up the Yukon to Dawson City, on the first boat of the season, to enlist. William Forbes came all the way from the Liard River in Dease Lake country to sign up in Whitehorse.[21] Several members of the territorial assembly left their seats to serve king and country, as did sixty-seven members of the Fraternal Order of Eagles.[22]

They came from all walks of life: lawyers, bankers, dockworkers and ships' crews. There were miners in large numbers. George Chapman was the son of the man who ran the steam power generating plant in Dawson. Alfred Cronin worked as a clerk for the Northern Commercial store in Whitehorse. Jack Taylor was the son of the magistrate in Whitehorse. Rowland Bourke, son of Dr. Isadore Bourke, formerly of Dawson City, was rejected from all three branches of the Canadian military, so he booked passage overseas and enlisted in the Royal Naval Reserve. Other Yukoners, like Selwood Tanner, who joined the 11th Hussars when he got to England, did the same.[23]

The Yukon volunteers were of various nationalities. The United States was not at war with Germany until 1917, but Americans in the Yukon signed up to fight with the Canadian forces, and a number of impatient citizens from Alaska came to Dawson to enlist with the Canadian Expeditionary Force. Seventeen men of American birth joined the George Black contingent, which went overseas in early 1917. Russians, Italians and those from the Balkan states who were not called up from the reserves by their own countries joined the Canadian forces. Aside from volunteers from the countries of the British Empire, those from the Balkans formed the next-largest group of Yukon volunteers. A number of French citizens in the Yukon departed for France at the beginning of the conflict, including August Brun, who was working for C.P. Dolan at Granville; Charles Troceasz, Julius Barbe and Gustav Espenon.

They joined up singly, or in groups. Nearly two dozen Whitehorse men volunteered in Victoria together, their regimental numbers falling in sequential order. Most of them ended up serving in the 67th Canadian (Pioneer) Battalion. A year later, fourteen Dawson men joined the 231st Battalion (Seaforth Highlanders of Canada), along with a number of men from Atlin.[24]

One of the most remarkable volunteers of all was "Grizzly Bear" Jim Christie. James Murdoch Christie was born in Perthshire, Scotland, on October 22, 1867. When he joined the stampede to the Klondike in 1898, he had been farming in Carman, Manitoba. Christie remained in the Yukon after the gold rush, later becoming a guide and professional hunter, but his extraordinary story began in late October 1909, when he and partner George Crisfield were trapping on the Rogue River, a remote tributary of the Stewart River. Christie had been tracking a large grizzly bear that had disturbed one of their caches. A marauding grizzly bear at that time of year is never good news. The bear surprised him as he climbed up a snow-covered riverbank, and at a range of 30 metres, he got off one shot from his Ross rifle, which hit the bear in the chest, and a second round to the head, just before the bear was upon him. Christie tried to escape the charging grizzly, but to no avail.

The grizzly took Christie's head into his powerful jaws and began to crush his skull. Christie's jaw and cheekbone were crushed, his skull was fractured and his scalp was ripped away from his head, drenching the snow with his blood. One eye was blinded. To protect himself, Christie thrust his right arm into the angry bear's maw, and it too was crushed. Christie might not have survived had the bear continued its attack, but the bullets finally took effect and the beast rolled over, lifeless.

Christie was in terrible shape. He was bleeding profusely, and his broken jaw hung open. He wrapped his jacket around his head to hold the fractured jawbone in place and staggered half-blinded toward his cabin, which was 11 kilometres away. By force of will, he overcame the impulse to give up and lie down in a snowbank and freeze to death. Leaving a trail of blood behind him, he struggled forward. It took him an hour to stagger and crawl the last kilometre to the cabin. Crisfield was not there, so Christie kept a fire going despite being half-delirious, until his partner returned. Crisfield barely recognized his mutilated partner at first. After a couple of days' rest, Crisfield strapped Christie into a sled and headed to Lansing, the nearest trading post, on the Stewart River. Wrapped in his blood-soaked clothing, Christie endured in silence the pain from every bump and jolt on the four-day journey.

For two months, J.E Ferrell, the trader, and his wife (a former nurse) tended to Christie, slowly nursing him back to health. Ferrell even trimmed the jagged edges of Christie's scalp wounds as the flap of skin began to heal.

Jim "Grizzly Bear" Christie was one of the heroic figures of the Yukon. He survived a vicious bear attack in 1909 to become a decorated hero during World War I. PPCLI MUSEUM AND ARCHIVES

Eventually, Christie was fit enough for the journey to Dawson by dog team. He, Ferrell and Crisfield left Lansing on New Year's Day. Christie even insisted on doing much of the physical work on the journey to Mayo, and then on to Dawson City, where he arrived in mid-January.

By this time, his jaw had healed improperly, so he could not chew solid food and was reduced to consuming a liquid diet. The staff of St. Mary's Hospital in Dawson could do nothing for him, so he went to Victoria, where surgeon Dr. C.M. Jones reset his arm and his jaw, and reconstructed his face over the course of several operations. Dr. Jones told Christie: "You have no business to be alive." Much of the credit for Christie's recovery goes to the Ferrells, who tended him for so many weeks.[25] Within months, he was back in the Yukon.

When war was declared August 4, 1914, Christie knew he wanted to serve, and signed up in Ottawa only three weeks later. The doctor's physical examination noted the scars on his head from the grizzly attack five years before. If he had not lied about his age, he would never have been accepted into the Canadian Expeditionary Force. He listed his age as thirty-nine years, ten months, but in fact he was seven years older than that.[26] He joined Princess Patricia's Canadian Light Infantry (PPCLI) and saw considerable action as a scout and sniper in France.

The federal government made a commitment to provide a force of Canadian soldiers to aid the British, so the need for volunteers was urgent. It quickly established procedures by which civil servants could enlist, with a job guarantee when they returned after the war. Notice was received that a new war tax would be imposed on tobacco products, alcohol, coffee, sugar and confections containing sugar. Commissioner Black received a letter from a miner on Independence Creek pointing out that miners and prospectors who enlisted for overseas duty would be unable to fulfill their annual assessment to keep their claims in good standing, and would thus lose their claims. Although this was beyond the powers of the commissioner to rectify, Dr. Thompson introduced the issue in parliament and was able to confirm, just six weeks later, that he had been successful in getting the government to consent to the proposal that: "In case of mining leases in the West, including Yukon, held by men who are enlisting to go to the front, they shall be exempt from payment of the leases while absent at war."[27]

The territorial government also placed restrictions on the actions of German and Austro-Hungarian nationals, who were required to register with the Royal Northwest Mounted Police. The collector of customs was instructed to compile names, occupations, places of employment, ages and religions for these individuals. Note was made of any of those expressing pro-German sentiments, and restrictions were placed on their movement. None expressing pro-German sentiments would be employed in the public service in the territory, and any German attempting to leave the territory would be arrested. Superintendent Moodie of the Mounted Police hastily added that while Germans remained where they were and were neutral, they would be afforded the same protection under the law as any other person in Canada.[28]

Joe Boyle, the manager of the Canadian Klondyke Mining Company, posted a notice stating that any employees expressing pro-German sentiments, or those who failed to report anyone doing so, would be fired.[29] The territorial government later instituted a similar policy. Pro-German magazines and newspapers were banned from the mail. Germans on the American side of the border in the nearby Fortymile district continued to voice their pro-German sentiments, as long as America remained neutral, but doing so often led to a "rap on the nose."

ON THE HOME FRONT

WHILE PATRIOTIC MEN were lining up to volunteer, the entire community geared up to support the war effort. The Imperial Order Daughters of the Empire (IODE) would become the pivotal organization for raising funds for the war effort. The purposes of the IODE were, among others, to "foster a bond of union among the women and children of the [British] Empire," and "to provide an efficient organization by which prompt and united action may be taken ... when such action was desired."[30] In other words, the IODE

Martha Black (seated far right) and ladies of the IODE in the sun room in Government House, making pyjamas for the soldiers serving overseas. HOWARD FIRTH

was meant to do good deeds but honour the British Empire, and its history, as well.

The first chapter of the order was established in the Yukon on March 6, 1913, when Martha Black formed the George M. Dawson chapter at a meeting in Government House in Dawson City. Until the war started, the activities of the order were mostly social, along with hosting a few charity events and handing out prizes for essays written by the public school children. After the war began, the student essays were written on patriotic subjects.

A second chapter, the Fitzgerald chapter, was created less than a year later, on January 17, 1914. It was named in honour of a member of the Mounted Police who perished on a patrol from Fort McPherson to Dawson in 1911.[31]

Three more chapters followed: the Klondike chapter on January 29, 1915; the Martha Munger Black chapter, of Dawson City, on February 1, 1916; and a chapter in Whitehorse, established on October 21, 1914, with Mrs. Phelps, wife of Willard Phelps, lawyer and member of the territorial council, as its first regent. All were active in organizing events and raising funds for patriotic purposes during the war.

As soon as war was declared, the national IODE organization vowed to raise $100,000 for the purchase of a hospital ship. On August 7, Martha Black, the regent of the George M. Dawson chapter, received a telegram requesting the aid of the local IODE in raising the money. She quickly responded that they had already set themselves to the task and announced a special fundraising meeting of both local chapters at Government House on August 9 at three o'clock in the afternoon. Even women who weren't members attended the meeting to offer their assistance. The *Dawson Daily News* started the ball rolling by donating $100, and hundreds more soon followed.

By August 10, the hospital ship fund had grown to $1,800; the next day it had reached $3,000. A day later, that amount had doubled. Of that amount, a contribution of $2,500 was made by entrepreneur Joe Boyle. This was just the beginning of Boyle's patriotic giving. Boyle was an active member of the British Empire Club and reportedly "never turned down any request to raise money for the despatch of parcels to Yukon volunteers serving in his company or any other Canadian units overseas."[32]

The IODE wasn't the only community group rallying to fund the hospital ship. On August 14, the Daughters of Nippon added another $85 to the quickly growing bank account. Other women's groups, including the Order of the Eastern Star and the Women's Patriotic Service League, began raising funds for the ship as well.

On September 1, Commissioner Black received a telegram from the Governor General asking him to become a vice-president of the Canadian Patriotic Fund, and he agreed to do so. The purpose of this campaign was to raise a national fund to provide for the dependents of Canadian soldiers, British reservists and others going to the front. He approached Martha, as regent of the George M. Dawson chapter of the IODE, asking that their organization manage the collection of money for the fund. The chapter agreed and they commenced immediately, stationing members at the government administration building, Scougale's Mercantile and the post office to collect donations.[33]

In support of their effort, the *Dawson Daily News* pounded the patriotic drum in an editorial dated September 7: "Not a man, woman or child lives in Yukon who cannot give a golden nugget... The gold harvest here contains hundreds of thousands of nuggets. It will be a simple thing for those who have no nuggets at home to toss in their dollars or their quarters, and later for the committee to purchase the equivalent in raw gold direct from the miners, the dredge companies or the banks... Open the pokes—roll up the nuggets."[34]

Whitehorse also responded to the call. Within days of the announcement, $2,170 had been raised, with the largest donation, $100, having come from Taylor Drury Pedlar & Company. The number continued to rise slowly through September and October. By early November, they had raised nearly $3,000.[35] This prompted the *Dawson Daily News* in its October 5 editorial to report that the total raised to date in the territory was $10,000. They went further to point out that if the rest of the country were to contribute on the same per capita basis, the sum raised nationally would be $16 million. By Christmas, the total raised in the Yukon had risen to $20,000.

The community gave money to many charitable causes during the war. Early on, there was the fund for the hospital ship, the Canadian Red Cross Society, the British and the Serbian Red Cross societies, Belgian relief, Polish relief, the Duchess of Connaught Hospital Fund and the Queen's Canadian Military Hospital at Shorncliffe, England. The number of funds multiplied. There was the Yukon Comfort Fund, which was administered by Martha Black when she was stationed in London, England. There was the Field Comfort Fund, and money given to both Dawson hospitals. There was a disablement fund, a Serbian relief fund and the Queen Mary Christmas Box fund.

In November 1914, the George M. Dawson chapter of the IODE decided to open a fund for Christmas presents for the soldiers at the front. The war office in Ottawa wanted to provide each man in active service with a pound of chocolate, a pound of tobacco and a pack of cards. Subscriptions to this fund were to be sent to Mrs. Frank Osborn, treasurer of the chapter. The ladies also planned an informal tea party at Government House (until they went overseas, Commissioner and Mrs. Black were generous in making their spacious mansion available for a variety of patriotic activities). A pair of wolf/Belgian cross puppies were raffled off at fifty cents a ticket, to raise another hundred dollars.[36] When not busy with her IODE duties, Mrs. Black helped form another organization for wartime purposes: the Women's Patriotic Service League, which also raised funds for the war effort. Before Christmas of 1914, they had ordered the material to produce hospital garments to be sent overseas. "Everything is for the war," said Martha Black. "Any festivity arranged has a war fund for the motive; everyone is enthusiastic, and no sacrifice is too great."[37]

Society in the Yukon was heavily invested in patriotic activities and all social organizations took part in the cause. Yukon women were prolific joiners, and during the war, a number of patriotic clubs and organizations were formed to provide support in one way or another. In 1915, the Sunshine Club put on a lawn party, and the money raised from the sale of handkerchiefs, jellies and candies went to the patriotic fund.

The First Nation people of the territory also pitched in. Reverend Totty at the Moosehide settlement reported that his congregation gave their church offerings to the Canadian Patriotic Fund. Those located at the village of Big Salmon sent nine pairs of moccasins and a cash donation to the IODE in Whitehorse.[38]

Even children became involved, both in school and out, with wartime activities. In November 1914, the Dawson Boy Scouts were picking up bundles of clothing assembled by Dawsonites for the relief of Belgians. On May 24 of the following year, the children of Dawson City raised $596.25 holding an "entertainment" at the Dawson public school.[39] As for the girls, said Mrs. Black:

And the girls? I must tell you about our Girl Guides, who are very sorry they can't be soldiers. Three years ago we organized the Guides with Mrs. Frank Osborn as Scout Mistress, and Miss Hilda Potter and Miss Hazel McIntyre as Lieutenants. Mrs. Osborn is also the Regent of the Martha Munger Black Chapter of the I.O.D.E. and President of the

Women's Auxiliary of the Church of England. Each summer the Girl Guides spend two weeks in camp about twenty miles above Dawson, on Klondike River. Lately sixteen of the Guides passed the Tenderfoot Test, and are now wearing trefoil pins.

They are being drilled too. Major Knight, the Commandant of the Royal North-West Mounted Police in Dawson is drilling the Girl Guides, the Boy Scouts, and two hundred Dawson Men who are ineligible for active service overseas, yet feel they want to be ready in case Canada calls for men for home defence.[40]

If there was an event honouring the new volunteers, the children were there to help with the celebrations. As Christmas approached, the Daughters of the Eastern Star put on a fundraising event to a full house at the DAAA (one hundred people had to be turned away). One of the features of the evening was a series of tableaux involving young schoolboys. For years to come, both the Boy Scouts and the Girl Guides played a significant role in any event that was sponsored in the communities of Dawson City and Whitehorse.[41]

Just before Christmas 1914, Mrs. Black stated in an article in the *Dawson Daily News*, "Dawson, the most northerly capital of the British Empire, realizes that, though far from the motherland, she, too, must do her duty, nor will the Yukon be found lacking for her people are united in their determination that their portion shall be One Flag, One Throne, One Empire, and that the British."[42] It was quite a pronouncement for an American who first came to the Yukon during the gold rush!

Mrs. Black concluded: "Yukon is proud of the fact that sixty-five of her stalwart sons have given themselves for the defense of the Empire, fifty of whom are yet in training with the second Canadian contingent at Hastings Park, Vancouver."[43]

Fundraising activities continued at a hectic pace in 1915. The women of the Yukon found countless opportunities to open purses and wallets. One of the most powerful tools at their disposal was the publication of donors' lists in the newspaper, which were aimed at shaming those unwilling to contribute to the war effort. Social pressure was a powerful tool to loosen purse strings. The civil servants of the territory were subject to special scrutiny, as they were in salaried positions of privilege. Later in the year, the Whitehorse chapter of the IODE received one hundred copies of the pamphlet *Why Don't You Wear a Uniform?* for local distribution.

The theatres of Dawson became common venues for patriotic events. Included in the nightly film screenings were newsreels with war content carefully edited to produce patriotic stirrings while concealing the tragic horror of the battlefields. The DAAA announced that viewers would be treated to scenes like the Russian bombardment of Turkish coastal towns, and "marvellous realism depicting scenes of the battlefields" were advertised, promising that the weekly Pathé newsreels were "brought directly from the front and are well worth seeing."

In Whitehorse in February, five reels were shown as part of a program sponsored by the IODE, supplementing an evening that featured singing by both children and adults. Several compositions had been specially prepared for the event (people were regularly penning patriotic songs, whose lyrics were often published in the newspapers).[44] The films included a two-reel Italian love story, the weekly Pathé newsreel, a reel with four comedies and the film titled *High Tide*. The program was followed by dancing, and the management charged admission for all the men who tried to slip into the dance after the films were shown.[45]

In April 1915, Martha Black received a package containing battlefield souvenirs from Walter Greenaway, a former Mountie who served in the Dawson detachment, now stationed overseas with the Coldstream Guards. The noses from a couple of German artillery shells and a spiked German helmet, which contained inside it the name of the soldier and the unit he belonged to, were placed on display in the front window of Charles Jeanneret's jewelry store.[46] Mrs. Black could be counted on to give a wholehearted contribution to any event she attended. In July, she gave a speech at the annual session of the Anglican Church women's auxiliary. "There are but few of us in this most northerly bit of British territory possessing large means," she said, " but what we can afford we can give cheerfully and regularly."[47] One of these ladies, Marie Joussaye Fotheringham, published a book of poetry titled *Anglo-Saxon Songs*, and the proceeds were donated to various causes, including the local war veterans association.[48]

In the past year, Mrs. Black noted, they had raised more than $20,000 for various causes. And the fundraising would continue apace in Dawson City. A couple of days later, at the Discovery Day event at Minto Park beside the administration building, the IODE sold refreshments for the patriotic cause. Money from a fundraiser at the Auditorium Theatre on Labour Day was contributed to the machine gun fund. The ladies achieved their goal, and the money was sent off; Sam Hughes, the minister of militia and defence sent a letter of thanks to Commissioner Black, acknowledging their contribution.[49] Another event sponsored by the IODE in late November at the DAAA included Pathé newsreels and other films. Everybody joined in with songs or recitals; Charlie MacPherson sang "It's a Long Way to Tipperary," and Mrs. Frank (Laura) Berton sang Kipling's immortal "Recessional." This event raised another $250.[50]

America may not yet have entered the war, but in Dawson City, the American Women's Club threw themselves wholeheartedly into fundraising. The club held a Fourth of July picnic in 1916, and the White Pass Company provided them with the steamer *Casca* and a barge for the purpose. Lunch was served on the *Casca*, and ice cream on the barge. Lemonade and cigars were sold to the revellers. They also organized a patriotic fundraising ball at the Arctic Brotherhood Hall. The event was a grand affair attended by the acting commissioner George Williams and his wife, as well as Judge Macaulay. Their Fourth of July picnic alone brought in $1,100, and other events raising thousands more dollars followed over the course of the war.[51]

The most high-profile IODE event of 1916, Alexandra Rose Day, was sponsored by the George M. Dawson chapter at Government House on July 20. Charming matrons circulated on the grounds selling roses handmade by children with disabilities in England. No one could say no to them. People played bridge in the drawing rooms and circulated throughout the main floor rooms, smoking and talking. The rooms were filled with a profusion of cut flowers taken from the government greenhouse. Ice cream, cake, sandwiches and coffee were served on the lawn, while people played various games, the most popular being "Swat the Kaiser." Likenesses of Kaiser Wilhelm II and the crown prince were placed on hinged boards in front of a canvas backstop, and three tennis balls could be thrown at them for twenty-five cents. Winners received a fancy cigar or other gift. Meanwhile, an orchestra played on the verandah, where there was also enough room for dancing the waltzes and one-steps.[52]

One of the most creative money-raising schemes for the patriotic fund came from the Duchess of Connaught. Mrs. Black got her to knit six pairs of socks on her knitting machine. When she received them, Mrs. Black raffled three pairs for $25 and sold the other three pairs for the same amount. The winner of the raffle returned the socks, and the IODE raffled them a second time, making $100 more.[53]

By the end of 1915, the total amount paid out to various funds and societies in the Yukon for war purposes was more than $53,000.[54] By March 1916, that amount had risen to $62,000. An article in the *Dawson Daily News* estimated that Yukoners had donated often and generously at a rate of $12 per capita, compared with $1 per person in the rest of the country. "It is doubtful," the article concluded, "if anywhere in the world a larger per capita contribution is given any war fund."[55] This was a recurring theme in newspaper articles and speeches until the end of the war.

FIFTY BRAVE MEN

THE YUKON'S EXCEPTIONAL support for the war was not limited to fundraising. Yukon men volunteered to serve in numbers that dwarfed the rates of enlistment in other parts of Canada. Nearly one thousand men, from a population of four to five thousand, enlisted before the end of the war. Most notable among the first to step forward was a group of men who joined a machine gun unit sponsored by local mining millionaire Joe Boyle.

If anybody was to fit the mould of heroic figure, it was Joe Boyle, whose exploits were filled with the sort of bravery, leadership and adventure that inspire books and movies.

Boyle was born in Woodstock, Ontario, in 1867. Always an independent spirit, he went to sea as a deckhand while in his teens. By the time he left the seafaring life three years later at age twenty, he had been promoted to ship's quartermaster. Next, he ran a lucrative feed- and grain-shipping business in the United States, but his dreams of expanding into a nationwide chain of grain elevators fell through, so he moved on. He went on an exhibition tour, promoting fights for Australian heavyweight boxing champion Frank Slavin, who was known as the "Sydney Cornstalk."

In Seattle, in the early summer of 1897, Boyle and Slavin caught wind of the opportunities in the Klondike. They headed north before the full stampede began, and Boyle soon found himself working on claim number 13 on Eldorado Creek, where he became friends with its owner, the notorious "Swiftwater" Bill Gates.[56] They forged a partnership of sorts and headed out of the Yukon just about the time the Yukon River was starting to freeze up in the fall. Fighting through ice floes and bitter arctic weather, they made their way up the Yukon River to Carmacks Post, where they joined forces with another party that was attempting to make their way out of the Yukon over the Dalton Trail.

Fighting snow, wind and bitter cold, they battled for weeks to reach their destination, Haines Mission, on the Alaskan panhandle, not far from Skagway. It was only through Boyle's leadership and forceful determination that the party reached the coast safely. In gratitude, everyone chipped in to purchase a watch, which they presented to him once they reached Seattle.

Boyle was a force of nature. Stocky and barrel-chested, he had the chiselled features that would have made him a movie star in Hollywood. Contemptuous of bureaucrats and authority figures, Boyle was a take-charge man, attracted by adventure. He was a born storyteller who liked to be at the centre of things, but above all, he was a man who followed his own direction. He also had a vision of the future, and he could clearly see that mucking about in the frozen gravel was not for him. Instead, he saw massive machines chewing up the Klondike placers and collecting the gold trapped within. So he headed to Ottawa, where he was able to secure a concession for several kilometres of ground in the Klondike Valley upon which to build his dream. He was then able to secure financing from Rothschild interests in Detroit, and through a series of legal manoeuvres, took control of the Canadian Klondyke Mining Company.

Soon he had valuable waterfront property, a profitable sawmill business and a gold dredging company, which eventually built the three largest dredges in the Klondike. By 1912, he was a millionaire and had taken over the title of "King of the Klondike" from Big Alex McDonald, who had died a few years earlier (once the richest miner in the Klondike, he died penniless while chopping wood on his Clear Creek claim in January of 1909).

Boyle became a prominent benefactor in the community. He was one of the founders of the DAAA, the huge sporting complex that included a theatre, a hockey arena and an indoor swimming pool, which would host many a fundraiser during the war. He sponsored a hockey team, the Dawson Nuggets, which challenged the Ottawa Silver Seven for the Stanley Cup in 1905. They lost, but the epic journey to get to Ottawa for the matches has become part of Stanley Cup lore.[57]

When war was declared in August 1914, Boyle was ready for the challenge. Again, he foresaw the future and determined that he would sponsor a machine gun detachment of fifty men. He was not alone in his endeavour. At the same time, wealthy sponsors elsewhere in Canada were doing precisely the same thing, and his detachment would eventually join the ranks of the Bordon and Eaton Batteries in the fields of France.

He sent a telegram to Sam Hughes, the minister of militia and defence, who responded on September 2, accepting Boyle's offer.[58] Hughes had, at this time, a single purpose: to prepare Canada for war. Hughes also demanded that the Canadians sent overseas not be broken up and mixed with British units but remain as discrete Canadian units throughout the war. Boyle had a similar interest for his volunteers and also insisted that his unit was to be a specialist force, trained in the use of machine guns.

Within four days of Hughes's response, Andrew Hart, the Dawson City fire chief, acting as recruiting officer, started enrolling men in Boyle's Dawson brigade. At first, they were known as "the Boyle detachment."

Boyle was heaped with praise in an editorial in the *Dawson Daily News*:

Unbounded credit is due to Joseph Whiteside Boyle for his more than generous and patriotic contribution which makes it possible for Yukon to have a brigade in the great conflict. Mr. Boyle is a true Yukoner, a loyal Canadian and a sterling Britisher. His contribution proves him a man of action and a power for good in his country's service. If every wealthy Canadian did as much, Canada could place ten times as many men in the field as she has since the war has opened. The boys who are going in the Boyle Yukon contingent have not the wealth to give, but they are giving even more—their lives if need be.[59]

The *News* also suggested that a rally be held honouring the volunteers before they left Dawson: "The boys of Boyle's Yukon Brigade are the lions of the hour. Give them a grand sendoff. Give them a bully time. Give them the heart of Yukon. Sound the drums, strike up the pipes—send the boys to war with colours flying—buoyant with the fire of Britain, keen with the zeal of Canada, stirred with the spirit of Klondike, fast in the love of Yukon."[60]

Boyle received a telegram from Hughes stating that the men should be shipped Outside as soon as possible. He determined that his volunteers could depart upstream for Whitehorse on the steamer *Casca*, whose last voyage of the season was scheduled for October 7 or 8. Winter comes early to the Yukon, and any later in the month the river would be congested with ice floes. From Whitehorse, they would take the train to Skagway, thence travel by ship to Victoria, the capital of British Columbia. By the end of September, recruiter Hart could announce that thirty-eight Dawson men had passed the physical examination and would be joined by a dozen others in Whitehorse so that the contingent would be fifty strong upon leaving the territory.

Big plans were afoot for a community send-off for "Boyle's Boys." Commissioner Black called for a large get-together to offer them a proper celebration of their departure. School superintendent Thomas Bragg said that the schoolchildren were practising patriotic songs to be sung as the *Casca* sailed away, and the Boy Scouts would all turn out in full uniform. The Dawson brass band would join the event, and bagpiper Johnny

Joe Boyle sponsored the formation of a machine gun detachment from the Yukon, which later became the Yukon Machine Gun Battery. Here, they are assembled, without uniforms, behind the courthouse in Dawson City. YUKON ARCHIVES GEORGE BLACK FONDS 81/107 #148

MacFarlane sent a call to the gold-mining creeks for other pipers to join him for the farewell.[61]

A mascot was chosen to accompany the unit. It was a dog named Jack, which was purchased by territorial councillor George Williams from Bill Ferguson, the Glacier Creek mail carrier.[62] (Sadly, Jack, who had been raised in the wilds of the Fortymile goldfields, would be killed by a train when the Boyle unit was in England.) They also had a song—John Dines, "Dawson's troubadour," adapted the well-known song "It's a Long Way to Tipperary" for Boyle's Yukon Brigade with the following lyrics:

It's a long way to dear old Klondike,

It's a long way to go;

It's a long way to golden Yukon—

To the homeland of the sourdough.

You may sing of Tipperary,

Strand and Leicester Square

It's a longer mush to old Klondike,

But my heart's right there.[63]

The entire community became involved in this body of men and their imminent departure. Slides of "Joe Boyle's Yukon Contingent" were to be shown in the Family Theatre in the DAAA building on the evening of October 7. The new patriotic slides would honour the contingent, all of whom would be guests of the management.[64]

Fred Congdon, the former Liberal member of parliament, had dropped off one hundred dollars at the *Dawson News* to start a "pocket fund" for the men of the Boyle unit, intended to pay for things not covered by their wealthy benefactor. The *Dawson Daily News* of September 26 noted that this money would add to the comforts of these heroic volunteers, and the community was to be applauded, but went on to add:

> But the one great point which will send the men to the front most appreciative of their home will be the satisfaction of knowing that they left with every heart in Klondike accompanying them. They deserve it. And they deserve a genuine ovation as every fraternal society, every civic body, every man, woman and child of the Yukon should rise and cheer the men who go forth to battle for the preservation of all that means the life of Britain, the perpetuity of civilization and the continued prosperity and very existence of this happy realm.[65]

By October 12, the pocket fund had increased to more than $1,500, meaning that each Boyle volunteer would receive $31 from the fund. It didn't stop there. Fifty women met at Government House to make "housewives" for each of the men of the Boyle detachment. These small domestic kits sewn by the women contained needles, thread, buttons, pins, shoelaces and other things that the men might need once away from home. During the same meeting, the ladies formed the Women's Patriotic Service League, which would continue to meet periodically for the duration of the war for fundraising, or "as the necessity for concentration arises."[66]

The day of their embarkation was steadily approaching. The evening of Tuesday, October 6, the community turned out en masse to celebrate the pending departure of the volunteers. It was a gala affair: the gaily decorated Arctic Brotherhood Hall was filled to capacity. Schoolchildren occupied the first four rows of chairs in front of the stage, and many women were scattered in the crowd.

The volunteers were seated on the stage; a giant Union Jack hung above them. Flags for the allied nations were hung from the mezzanine that overlooked them. Commissioner Black spoke of the generous donations given by Yukoners, especially those of Joe Boyle. He then referred to the "unbounded contribution of the men who have offered their lives in Yukon for their country."[67] This remark was followed by an outburst of applause.

Black further stated that Britain might have retained peace had Germany not violated its treaty with Belgium, but Britain was unwavering, and when Belgium was invaded, she took up the sword, and volunteers were rallying from every corner of the empire. "Wherever the Yukon boys go in their campaign for the Empire," he said, "they may rest assured that they carry with them the hearts and hopes of Yukon."[68]

With reluctance, Joe Boyle then told the crowd it wasn't his place to make a speech, that he was satisfied to send "such a splendid and representative lot of Yukoners to the front." He added: "If I thought myself a better fighter than this bunch, I would leave them home and go myself, but I am sure they will be a credit to Yukon, and [that I will be] only too glad to do what I can to aid in the cause."

Fred Congdon then made a speech lauding the volunteers as heroes "of all time in Yukon," asserting that "their names ever should be preserved here as the most honored in all the history of the Northland."[69]

Mrs. Black got up and spoke on behalf of the IODE, thanking Boyle and the volunteers. In particular, she singled out gold miner Harry Lobley, the youngest member of the contingent, who had just turned twenty-two.[70] She then called forward the thirty-five men who attended and presented each, one at a time, with a souvenir button, and then shook their hands. The buttons were fashioned by Dawson jeweler Charles Jeanneret, and each had the word "Yukon" across the face. Buck Taylor of the contingent called out the names of each and every man as they stepped forward to receive their gift.

Several stirring songs followed, including "O Canada," sung by Mrs. Frank (Laura) Berton; "La Marseillaise," sung by Max Landreville; and "It's a Long Way to Tipperary," sung by Charlie MacPherson. The schoolchildren followed with "Rule, Britannia!" and other patriotic numbers, directed by Professor Gillespie and accompanied on the cornet by Constable Clifford. After the songs were completed, the crowd gave three cheers and a tiger for the volunteers—twice.[71] Then the ball began, and the dancing continued until one o'clock in the morning.[72]

The following day, during drill practice, the boys of Boyle's Yukon machine gun detachment presented Constable Stangroom, their drill instructor, with a handsome gold nugget watch chain. The gift was a token of appreciation of the services rendered in giving them instruction. The constable was more than pleased with the handsome gift and made a neat address appreciative of the remembrance, but more than anything, he wanted to be joining them overseas.[73]

A few months later, Stangroom and two other constables escorted a "lunatic" from Dawson to Whitehorse, en route to an asylum in New Westminster. Instead of remaining in Whitehorse as ordered, Stangroom boarded the train for Skagway, but the train was stopped at Carcross and he was arrested. Stangroom was an excellent police officer, but he was exceptionally anxious to enlist to fight for "king and country." He had repeatedly offered to buy his way out of the Mounted Police but was denied. Stangroom was later released from the Mounted Police to enlist and had some remarkable experiences on the Western Front. He would later be decorated for bravery.[74]

Three days later, a throng was assembled on the dock when the Boyle contingent departed for Whitehorse on the steamer *Lightning* at midnight. According to the *News*:

> At 9 o'clock in the evening... the troop assembled at the Royal North West Mounted Police barracks. The boys were attired in their natty new uniforms, comprising khaki trousers and woolen shirts to match, yellow mackinaws and stiff-brimmed sombreros. A finer looking body of men never before was assembled north of fifty-three... Not being formally enlisted, they carried no arms.

When the last whistle blew the boys in khaki were lined up on the forward deck with Andy Hart, their recruiting officer and chief, in the centre. The band played "God Save the King," and a more impressive rendition never fell on the ears of Klondike. The spirit of the occasion seemed to move all, and all stood and sang to the band accompaniment.

The boys proposed three cheers for the people of Dawson and yelled mightily. Then they gave three ringing cheers and a tiger for Joe Boyle and many more for Joe... With the exciting exhaust of steam, the kicking up of the foamy wake by the whirring wheel, the streaming of sparks and a column of smoke into the starry sky, the screaming of the steamer's whistle and the jostling of the dancing waves against the shore, the scene was one of superb climax to the departure of the pride of the Yukon.

Standing at the end of the coal barge, in the shadow of the bulk-head, with bared head during all the excitement as the steamer plowed past the shouting crowd was a silent man, who watched the ship and her brave boys until she was out of hailing distance. He stood trans-fixed, gazing until only the dancing lights were visible on the water. It was Joseph Whiteside Boyle... Quietly he turned from the place on the barge, and marched up the street with the people, and was soon happily relating in his characteristic style one of his tales of good cheer from the inexhaustible fund which is his.[75]

The lights of Dawson faded behind them as they headed for White-horse. The journey that Boyle's boys had embarked upon was not an easy one. Fog, shortened daylight hours and other obstacles slowed down their progress upstream so that it took them ninety-two hours to reach Fort Selkirk. At every camp they passed on their upstream voyage, they were greeted with cheers, and the recruits repeatedly sang, "It's a Long Way to Tipperary." Whether they used the original lyrics or those penned by John Dines is not known. When they reached Fort Selkirk, their singing was loud enough to scare the huskies into the woods. Finally, early in the morning on Friday, October 16, they arrived in Whitehorse, a week after leaving Dawson City. They had lunch on board, with Captain P. Martin, a Whitehorse

The Boyle battery in uniform in Vancouver. DAWSON CITY MUSEUM 1984.55.1

businessman, and E.J. White, the editor of the *Whitehorse Star*, as special guests. Jim MacKinnon, known as "Skotay" by his fellow volunteers, made a speech, and they presented Captain Cowley with a gold watch chain and fob in appreciation of the hospitality extended to them during their upriver voyage. As the *Lightning* vanished downriver later, they stood on the wharf, again singing "Tipperary."

Since the Canadian Pacific ship was not to arrive in Skagway for a few days, they remained in Whitehorse for a week; while they were there, they owned the town. A committee of Whitehorse citizens arranged some social activities for the Boyle boys. A dance was arranged for the Monday and a smoker for Tuesday. The five-piece orchestra donated their services for the dance. Across one end of the hall was hung a banner that read "Dawson to Berlin 7460 Miles." The Boyle men, all dressed in their uniforms, had earlier posed for a photograph with the banner supported on the build-ing behind them. A splendid supper was served after midnight, catered by Henry Kamayama, a local baker.[76] The dancing continued until two in the morning. The smokers outnumbered the dancers the following night in a program filled with movies, speeches, dancing, recitations, songs, banjo duets and boxing matches, which also lasted until two in the morning. The guests stated that they were well entertained during their stay in White-horse.[77] They then rode the train to Skagway and took passage on the *Princess May* to Victoria, where, after a three-day delay, they were transferred to Hastings Park camp in Vancouver, where hundreds of recruits were temporarily stationed.

Life took on some semblance of order at Hastings Park. Charles Jennings, a Whitehorse man, was appointed the colour sergeant, and James MacKinnon quartermaster. Harold Strong and Jesse Tolley became sergeants, and Robert Morton, Edward Fitzgerald, Frank McAlpine and William Black (Commissioner Black's brother, who joined them in Vancouver) became corporals. But if they thought that they would soon see action, they were sadly mistaken.

A NEW KIND OF WAR

THE MONTHS ROLLED by and the Boyle unit remained in Vancouver, and the men became restless with the delays. Finally, on May 19, 1915, an impatient Joe Boyle sent a telegram asking when the Boyle contingent was to be shipped overseas. Minister Hughes responded by issuing orders that they be shipped overseas immediately, without horses. Within a week, the men, and Jack the husky, were on their way to Montreal by train. They boarded the SS *Megantic* on June 11 and arrived in England a week later.

Six months after arriving in England, the Boyle detachment was still posted to Shorncliffe camp in Kent, still unequipped and yet to see action. The discontent of the Yukon men grew. For patriotic Canadians, there was nothing nobler than to serve and to see action "on the front." Many homesick enlistees wrote about their eagerness to go up on the line. "Yukoners are very much dissatisfied at being kept here so long," wrote Felix Boutin to his brother back in Dawson,

> In fact, a number of the boys have transferred and gone to the front with other units. There are only thirty three left and most of us would give

anything to get across to France, as we are ashamed to remain here. Last week a call came into this depot for twelve men to reinforce the Sifton battery and nearly all the Yukoners jumped at it. Twelve of them were picked out, including Forrest, Peppard, Black and Burgess. They got all ready to go, and at the last minute orders came from headquarters that Yukoners could not be taken on a draft as they were to remain as a unit. There seems to be no reason why we should be kept here so long as lots of men are being sent over that are less trained than we are.[78]

"As a matter of fact," wrote one of the volunteers, "we are all rather ashamed to be here so long in England, but there seems to be no way of getting machine guns with which to equip us."[79]

The year passed, and still the men had not seen action. Meanwhile, back home, the IODE and the civil servants of the Yukon each raised $1,000, and two cheques in that amount were sent to Ottawa for the purchase of two machine guns. Over the winter, the Boyle men remained at Shorncliffe and were formed into a battery that was later attached to the 4th Canadian Division.[80] In late February, they were moved from their comfortable billets into tents, which they found very disagreeable in the damp, cold winter.

The training for machine gun units was rigorous and physically demanding. Many volunteers found themselves transferred to other units if they didn't meet the standard. Leading commanders in the British forces did not grasp the tactical significance of the machine gun during the early years of the war. The generals did not see the need for them or to revise their tactical thinking. Machine guns were viewed as contrary to all accepted military practice. Tight formations by foot soldiers with bayonets fixed were the order of the day, and as a consequence, tens of thousands of soldiers, many of them Canadians, were sent to deaths that could have been avoided.[81] The machine gun took the nobility out of warfare. It was industrial-scale slaughter.

The hidebound structure of the British chain of command was not inclined toward subtlety and manoeuvre but rather believed that only the greatest display of moral fibre would win the day. By this structured thinking, soldiers who hesitated to advance under machine gun fire were not showing the stern qualities of a good soldier. A bold charge of infantry would cause the enemy lines to break and run, and the waiting cavalry would ride through the gap on their horses and take the line. As one observer noted:

In Britain, class was everything. The command and fabric of the British Army has been described by one critic as having "stiffened into a sort of Byzantine formalism." The other ranks, who belonged to the lower class, were expected to obey orders without question and without any real knowledge of the military situation, which was considered too deep and complicated for them to grasp. Such was the gap between officers and men that any private soldier who did try to ask a question of his seniors was considered by his own fellows a traitor to his own class.[82]

The combatants dug into opposing defensive lines zigzagging across northern France, for hundreds of kilometres from the North Sea coast to Switzerland. They were occupied by hundreds of thousands of soldiers—German and Austrian on one side, French, English, Australian, New Zealander and Canadian on the other. They called it the Western Front. The Allies' combat strategy quickly resulted in a stalemate in which the Germans had dug trenches and established defensive positions using machine guns with overlapping fields of fire, hidden behind rows of barbed wire. Such positions were virtually impregnable and could only be broken at terrible cost. "Three men with a machine gun can stop a battalion of heroes," noted one observer.[83] Then there were snipers hidden in nooks and crannies, their sharpshooting rifles trained upon the opposite line. If anyone dared to lift their head above the top of the trench, they risked getting it blown off. Between these lines lay No Man's Land. Varying in width from one hundred to several hundred metres, it was a zone in which nothing lived, and any man foolish enough to enter it quickly died. The men on the front lines figured this out almost immediately. The high command, securely positioned kilometres away from the action, and aloof from the enlisted men, denied this reality for far too long.

Between 1914 and 1918, the machine gun became the defining instrument of death for hundreds of thousands of soldiers on both sides of the conflict. By the time the Boyle detachment had made its way into the theatre of war, the Vickers machine gun was the weapon of choice. These guns had withering firepower, capable of firing up to five hundred rounds per minute. They required a team of five men to operate, because of their size and insatiable appetite for gunpowder and lead. They were heavy and awkward to carry from one position to another on the pitted landscape of No Man's Land. The gun itself weighed 13 kilograms, plus another 4.5 kilograms if the water jacket was full. The tripod weighed nearly 22 kilograms. Each ammunition box, which carried a cloth belt containing 250 rounds, weighed 9.5 kilograms. Given that they could run through two belts of ammunition every minute, it was a full-time job providing a constant supply of bullets. With the high volume of fire that machine guns were capable of, the spent casings would soon bury a gun emplacement; the support team was kept busy filling sandbags with spent cartridges, which were stockpiled and hauled to nearby dumps, where they would be removed by salvage companies for recycling.[84]

One soldier, Private George Coppard, described the procedure for setting up a Vickers machine gun to fire:

Number One dashed five yards with the tripod, released the ratchet held front legs so they swung forward, both pointing outwards, and secured them rigidly by tightening the ratchet handles. Sitting down, he removed two metal pins from the head of the tripod, whereupon Number Two placed the gun in position on the tripod. Number One whipped in the pins and then the gun was ready for loading. Number Three dashed forward with an ammunition box containing a canvas belt, pocketed to hold 250 rounds. Number Two inserted the tag-end of the belt into the feed block on the right side of the gun. Number One grabbed the tag-end and jerked it through, at the same time pulling back on the crank handle twice, which completed the loading operation.[85]

Once this was done, the Number One gunner flipped up the sights and was ready to fire. If properly placed along the battlefront, with well-designed overlap in their fields of fire, these machine guns could lay down an impenetrable and deadly curtain of lead. To attempt to enter into this field of fire would be disastrous for the enemy.

In order for each gun emplacement to operate smoothly, a constant stream of supplies had to be brought forward. Ammunition belts, water, lubricating oil and spare barrels, as well as replacement personnel in case of casualty, had to be kept in reserve. To work successfully, each machine gun team had to be well trained and ready to deal with all sorts of contingencies, from replacing another member of the team to repairing malfunctions quickly and efficiently. The training continued for months as the Boyle men waited for their orders to go to the front.

In June 1916, the Boyle unit was renamed the Yukon Motor Machine Gun Battery, but still they had seen no action.[86] Captain Harry F. Meurling, from the instructional staff of the Canadian Machine Gun School, was placed in charge, with Lieutenants Nicholson, Harkness and Strong under his command.[87] Captain Meurling, born in Sweden and later trained as a civil engineer, had seen service with the Swedish Royal Navy and in the Belgian Congo force before enlisting in Sherbrooke, Quebec, the previous year. Meurling would command the Yukon units for the remainder of the war.

Finally, on August 15, 1916, they shipped out for France aboard the SS *Nirvana*. This is what they had trained for, for so many months. Now fully equipped to go into combat, they were eager to get to the front. They did not know where that would be, and they had only a vague idea of what to expect when they got there. For the men of the Yukon Battery, the war was about to begin.

THE BATTLEFIELDS OF FRANCE

THE YUKON BATTERY arrived in Le Havre, France, the morning of August 16 and quickly made their way to Number 2 Rest Camp, at Sanvie, just outside Le Havre. From there, they moved steadily forward until they reached

Captain Harry Meurling commanded the Yukon (Boyle) battery, and later the 2nd Motor Machine Gun Brigade, which also included the George Black contingent. LIBRARY AND ARCHIVES CANADA 3219317

the camp of the 1st Canadian Motor Machine Gun Brigade at Abeele, Belgium. Now designated E Battery, they immediately took up position on gun emplacements.

The Yukon Battery was in the heart of the action. What followed was a constant cycle to the front, where they provided direct fire and barrage support along the Ypres (Belgium) Salient—a tiny piece of northwestern Belgium, including the town of Ypres, still held by the Allies, that protruded into the German line—then went back to the rear lines for rest and recovery. Over the next two months, they alternated between billets and the front line. Behind the lines they rested and trained, and cared for their equipment. Much time was spent at gun instruction, gun practice and filling machine gun belts. On September 16, they covered a raiding party that penetrated enemy lines in a night raid. On September 22, they opened fire on an enemy working party. "Enemy machine guns tried to locate our positions but failed," reported the entry in the battery war diary for that day.[88] On October 15, Privates McKinley and Bloor were wounded during routine duty installing splinter-proof shelters.

On October 21, the Yukon Battery, now attached to the 4th Canadian Division, became involved in the assault of Regina Trench (named Staufen Riegel by the Germans), a lengthy enemy trench system that was positioned behind the devastated French village of Courcelette on the Somme battlefield. According to historian Tim Cook: "The Somme battlefield was a wasteland of ruined farmers' fields; scummy, water-filled shell holes; and acres of unburied corpses... not a single metre of the war zone had escaped being chewed up by artillery fire... The mixture of blackened flesh and broken bones with thousands of tonnes of metal and shattered structures created a nightmare landscape."[89]

As for the village of Courcelette, like many others, Lieutenant A.B. Morkill, who had been a bank manager in Victoria before coming to the Somme, noted: "The battle-fields are indescribable. What villages there were, are as flat as ploughed fields, and most certainly the country is one of desolation. Not a tree, but occasionally the stump of one to accentuate the barrenness, and at night when it is lit up by the flames and flashes of the guns, it leaves the impression of a very modern hell."[90]

It was this shell-blasted wasteland that they sought to capture. The attack commenced at six minutes after noon with a heavy barrage. The Yukon Battery was positioned parallel to Sugar Trench and provided heavy barrage support. At first, it was an all-out burst of intense fire from each machine gun that lasted for twenty minutes, followed by a reduced rate of one hundred rounds per minute, and then slackened to fifty rounds per minute. The pace of firing varied but continued throughout the afternoon and overnight.

The Regina Trench was pounded into oblivion by the artillery barrage, which was supported by the planned machine gun barrage. Behind the carefully designed creeping barrage, Canadian infantry were able to advance and take the German positions. A curtain of lead from Canadian machine gun fire effectively prevented a successful counterattack by the

Germans. The machine gunners were not so much trying to hit specific targets as they were trying to drench the area with bullets, thus forcing the enemy to take cover while Canadian troops advanced. Those members of each gun crew not actively firing their weapon were kept busy bringing a steady supply of ammunition to the emplacements.

So intense was the rate of fire by the Yukon Battery that one soldier, Frank McAlpine, was sent to hospital, overcome by the noxious gasses emitted by the machine gun during the continuous firing.[91] The Yukoners were lucky, having come in at the very end of the Battle of the Somme, an offensive that started four months earlier and gained little at great expense of lives. A million combined casualties were inflicted upon the Germans and the Allies during this offensive; more than twenty-four thousand of them were Canadian.

Through the end of October and into November, the Yukon Battery followed its daily firing orders. Things became routine until, on November 15, Private Bob Ellis was hit in the head by a piece of shrapnel in the trenches near Courcelette. His fellow Yukoners carried him to a dressing station 3 kilometres distant. He was still breathing when they arrived but later died.[92]

Then, on November 18, the Yukon Battery was engaged in a major offensive action providing barrage support to the Canadian 10th Brigade over Grandcourt Trench. The barrage commenced at 10:00 a.m., and the machine guns spat lead continuously for the next six hours, and then provided continuing covering fire through the night until dawn of the following day. Captain Meurling, the commanding officer, reported: "It is impossible for me to lay too much stress on the enthusiasm, endurance and general good behaviour of both men and officers during the whole of these trying 36 hours, out of which 24 hours were spent under practically continuous firing."[93] These men, he noted, had already been on the line for five to six days before the offensive began. Heavy enemy shelling of their positions did not make their assignment any easier. Three of their guns were put out of action when two emplacements and a dugout were blown up. Miraculously, there were no casualties.

Captain Meurling praised his men for their ability to work the guns when under intense fire: "As long as any of them are left to teach the new ones our infantry will never lack the support that M/Guns, when properly handled, can give them, both before during and specially after a battle"[94] By November 19, they had expended 550,000 rounds of ammunition during this engagement.

Compared to the preceding months, which were filled with constant combat duty, the Yukon Motor Machine Gun Battery spent a quiet December, based at Divion, 25 kilometres from Vimy on the front. They did active duty laying down fire at La Folie Farm, perched near the top of Vimy Ridge, and adjacent roads, followed by time spent behind the line recovering and resting. Belt filling, machine gun instruction and drills occupied much of their time. On December 13, Captain Meurling and the Yukon men were decorated with the Military Medals they had earned in the battle at Grandcourt Trench the month before. Several men from the Yukon Battery were singled out for recognition: Privates David Roulston, Harry Walker and Ernest Peppard, as well as Corporal Anthony Blaikie and Sergeant Frank McAlpine. Sergeant McAlpine was not available to receive his medal, as he had returned to England to train for a commission.

Harry Walker was a good example of a Yukon volunteer. Raised in Victoria, British Columbia, he came north during the early days of the gold rush and was engaged in mining on Sulphur Creek. In the spring of 1915, he joined the 2nd Canadian Mounted Rifles, subsequently transferring to the armoured motor battalion. Walker was awarded the Military Medal for his "devotion to duty displayed when he assembled a machine gun under heavy fire" during the November 19 offensive:

In the midst of a heavy bombardment of the British Lines by enemy guns, Private Walker and two of his comrades, showing utter contempt for the existing danger, moved out into the open and assembled their machine gun at a point where the fire could be effectively directed against the German positions. Just as they got the gun properly mounted a German shell buried itself in the ground immediately in front and undid their work by disarranging and burying some of the parts. In the face of all hazards they managed to secure the parts, put them together again and were eventually able to operate the gun against the enemy with telling effect.[95]

Christmas came and went and the Boyle men were able to enjoy a belated Christmas feast on December 28. They had been initiated with a baptism of lead, gas and steel. They had proven themselves in battle; many had received decorations for their courageous actions. By war's end, nineteen had been decorated, but thirteen had paid the supreme sacrifice, and others were casualties unable to continue in combat. They didn't know it, but yet to come were some of the most brutal battles of the war: Vimy, Passchendaele, Amiens and the Hundred Days Offensive. Only a handful of the original fifty would remain in uniform by the armistice.

THE BLACK CONTINGENT

"MONTH BY MONTH I could see that George was growing more restless," wrote Martha Black about her husband, the commissioner of the Yukon. In her diary, she noted:

> George has just come in and told me he has to enlist—that he cannot stand it any longer, seeing our men go away, while he sits in his office and we have the comfort of this beautiful home.
>
> Of course, there's nothing for me to do but to act as though I like it. It will be a wrench—to leave this lovely place. There's the dreadful anxiety of our future, too. What will this horrible war bring forth? I dare not think of it. Yet why should I hesitate or try to keep him back? Thousands, yes, millions, already have suffered the horrors of this terrible war for over a year.[96]

But his decision was not as impulsive as his wife presented. The decision to raise a company of Yukon volunteers and act upon it took more than a year to bring to realization, and it was almost three years before he and his comrades saw action overseas.

In late September of 1915, Black sent a lettergram to Sam Hughes, the minister of militia and defence, offering to raise a company of volunteers— an offer that Hughes was quick to accept.[97] George Black came from United Empire Loyalist stock and it would have been difficult for him not to join the cause in support of Britain in the war effort. Black had left his home and his new law practice in Fredericton, New Brunswick, in 1898 and headed west and north for the Klondike with tens of thousands of others. He discovered gold on Livingstone Creek, north of Whitehorse, and after a couple of years of mining in that area, he went to Dawson and once again established a law practice.

George Black acquired a reputation as a good criminal lawyer, one who could take hopeless cases and deliver a verdict favourable to his clients. His opponents acknowledged his ability to pull off a victory in the courts in the face of seemingly insurmountable odds. A lifelong Conservative, George had campaigned for George Eulas Foster, one of Ottawa's most respected politicians, while he was a young man articling for Foster in Fredericton. He worked with others in the Yukon to organize the Conservative Party in the territory and campaigned fiercely to place Dr. Alfred Thompson in the Yukon seat in the House of Commons. Black was elected to the territorial council for three consecutive terms, and when he went to greener pastures in Vancouver, BC, around 1910, he became active in politics there. In 1911, he was campaign manager for H.H. Stevens's successful bid in Vancouver for election to the House of Commons. Because the Yukon held a deferred election, Black was able to return to the territory and campaign for Dr. Thompson as well. Both candidates were elected to a majority government and Black, now with numerous political credit notes in his pocket, was appointed the commissioner of the territory in February of 1912. Black was only the second man from the territory, not from Outside, appointed to this position.

A dozen years before, George had met and married Martha Munger Purdy, an American woman from a wealthy Chicago family. Martha embraced her new role without hesitation, adopting not only George's country but his religion and his politics as well. Together, they formed a formidable partnership that lasted more than fifty years. Martha Black was no shrinking violet, and together they tramped the mountains and valleys of the Yukon on hunting and camping trips. Martha was also schooled in the social graces and had once taken tea in the White House. Whatever George became involved in, Martha did too.

In October 1915, George and Martha travelled to the east on family business, but before he left Dawson, George spoke to the British Empire Club, where there was discussion of raising a Yukon corps for regular drills in preparation for enlistment in the expeditionary force, if necessary. Accompanied by Dr. Thompson, the Yukon MP, he met with an enthusiastic Sam Hughes in Ottawa about his intention to not only raise a company of volunteers but to join as well, and obtain his commission as captain. Robert Rogers, minister of the interior, welcomed Black's offer and would facilitate his desire to serve with his fellow Yukoners. George planned to take his officer's course either at Victoria or in the military college at Kingston, Ontario. He would decide once he had consulted with Colonel Ogilvie, the officer in command of the British Columbia military division.[98]

While in Ottawa, Commissioner and Mrs. Black were entertained by the Governor General of Canada and his wife, the Duke and Duchess of Connaught. The duchess and her daughter, Princess Patricia, were filled with questions about life in the North, while the duke expressed his regret at not having been able to visit the region. Before heading home, George visited the Montreal headquarters of the Canadian Patriotic Fund, after which he and Martha spent several days in Toronto in a whirlwind of activity, meeting and dining with various dignitaries, including the acting national president of the IODE, Mrs. E.F.B. Johnson.

In the following months, the Blacks spent time in California, visiting Martha's family and exploring the Panama-Pacific Exposition. While Martha remained with her family, George returned to British Columbia, where he completed his training in Victoria and qualified as captain in the 104th Regiment (New Westminster Fusiliers).[99]

Meanwhile, back in Dawson City, recruitment was moving ahead. The work of enrolling volunteers for a Yukon Company of the Canadian

Expeditionary Force started in Dawson at the Territorial Administration Building in January 1916. "The opening of the roll is in accordance with a telegram received by Administrator George Williams from Commissioner Black, who is now in Victoria," reported the *Dawson Daily News*.[100] The Arctic Brotherhood made its hall available for drilling. The government agreed to defray the cost of heat and light, and to protect the floor against damage. The company was to consist of 255 men, and volunteers from Whitehorse and the southern Yukon were welcomed. The men who signed the provisional roll had their first muster and drill the evening of February 11 in the south courtroom of the old courthouse. As the *News* described it: "The room has been cleared of all furniture and railings and the like and affords quite a comfortable room for a limited number of men. Thirty were present."[101]

Drill was to be held once a week, though later on, they planned to increase to twice a week. No rifles were being used yet; the initial drills were designed to harden the men for more strenuous drilling. The first volunteers included high school student Lyman Purdy, Commissioner Black's stepson. Other volunteers included another student, Norton Townsend; long-time barber Joseph Dubois; lawyer J.A.W. O'Neill; and former territorial councillor Andrew Smith, as well as Frank Thompson, a Canadian Bank of Commerce employee and son of local doctor W.E. Thompson. There was a former amateur boxing champion, a French teacher, a waiter, a piano tuner, a boilermaker, a gardener, a couple of "old-timers" and a veteran of the Balkan Wars.[102] Edward A. Dixon, territorial council member for Whitehorse, volunteered as well. Before the end of the summer, William Radford and Norman Watt followed his lead, leaving the council with barely enough sitting members to form a quorum.

Alaska wanted to be represented as well. A large number of Alaskans had left to join various armies of the Allies, and more were expected to go. As many as twenty-three volunteers at one time had left Juneau in the preceding months. Some mushed out over the trail from Fairbanks and other places. George N. Williams, acting as commissioner in George Black's absence, received a telegram from a man in Iditarod asking if he and others could join the Black contingent. Williams promptly replied by night letter that no doubt there would be opportunity to get on board and suggested that the Iditarod boys come to Dawson by "the first boats in the spring."[103] In the end, seventeen men of American birth would ship overseas with the Black contingent the following year.

The enlistment papers arrived from Victoria on April 8, and the formal process of signing up began. The North American Transportation and Trading Company (NAT&T Co.) offered the use of its former store as a temporary barracks, and those signed up would start receiving an allowance from the government of $1.25 per day. So far, fifty-two had done so, and Major Knight of the Royal Northwest Mounted Police was serving as drill instructor.

George Black's intended arrival in the Yukon was set back by surgery. Returning from Ottawa by rail to Vancouver, he became ill on the train and was taken off in Winnipeg, where he laid over for a week before proceeding. The diagnosis was appendicitis, and upon reaching the West Coast, he was sent to Royal Jubilee Hospital in Victoria, where he had surgery on May 4. Complications developed after the surgery, but despite being in critical condition, George was predicted by his doctor to recover. By May 17, he was recovering nicely and expected to be released within a week.[104]

By the end of May, more than ninety men had passed the physical examination for the Yukon Company, and more were joining up daily. It was expected that as many as one hundred would be ready to leave by sailing time in the middle of June. The recruits continued to drill, now outdoors in Minto Park, as the season had warmed up and the snow was gone. Over the summer, more groups of volunteers would leave Dawson aboard future sailings until the magic number of 250 was reached.

Immediately upon release from hospital, George Black headed north, now reunited with Martha, who had returned from her family visit in California. They arrived in Whitehorse, where the couple were entertained by W.D. Greenough, manager of the Pueblo copper mine. The following day, Black, still recuperating from surgery, visited all the government employees but otherwise took it easy, until he and Mrs. Black attended an informal dance at the North Star Athletic Association (NSAA) hall in the evening. On Monday, June 5, he delighted the schoolchildren of Whitehorse by giving

Commissioner Black addresses an exuberant crowd on Front Street upon his arrival in Dawson City, June 6, 1916. GATES COLLECTION

them a half holiday. At the dock, in the evening, dressed in full uniform, he was given a send-off by many of the new recruits before he and Martha boarded the steamer *Casca*, headed for Dawson City. The Whitehorse men would later join the Dawson party when it passed through town on its way south to Victoria.[105]

A large and enthusiastic crowd met the Blacks when they arrived in Dawson on June 8. Joe Boyle, who had often been George's adversary in the past, greeted them and escorted them ashore, while a brass band played patriotic songs. Black, still weak from the surgery, walked briskly in full uniform into the street, where he greeted a line of fresh recruits, one hundred strong. He walked along, shaking the hand of each man. Boyle then addressed the Blacks, acknowledging Martha, whom he described as "a faithful worker in the cause of the Empire."[106]

Young students from the Dawson Public School enlisted during the war. George Black (in uniform) and Martha Black were proud of their son Lyman (front row, third from left) for enlisting. YUKON ARCHIVES ROY MINTER FONDS 92/15 # 746

George responded by acknowledging the large number of Yukon men who had already volunteered and the amount of money that had been donated to the cause by Yukoners. He said that the time was past when only single men should enlist. "It is a thought that is not only for every lover of freedom and every lover of civilization; and it is the duty of every lover of freedom and civilization to make that thought his own."[107]

Black referred to the legions of Americans who had come north to cities like Toronto, Winnipeg and Vancouver to enlist: "American citizens who feel as you and I feel about this war—that they want to get in it and help the allies win, because if they don't—if the allies lose—it will not be long before the United States will come next, and that can only be prevented by fighting with us."[108] After the Yukon Company marched back down Front Street to the barracks, with hundreds of citizens following the parade, the Blacks were conveyed to Government House.[109]

The first contingent of volunteers was scheduled to leave Dawson the following day. Among them were a number of students from the Dawson City public school. Just before noon, they assembled on the front steps of the school with various dignitaries for a photograph. George and Martha Black were there, along with their son Lyman. It was a proud moment for George Black, Lyman's stepfather, and the only father Lyman ever knew. (Unlike his two older brothers, Warren and Donald, Lyman never met his biological father, who split up with his wife, Martha, before she departed for the Klondike.) A few months later, on November 15, Lyman Munger Purdy had his surname changed to Black, in recognition of George's parental role.[110] Among the other students were Alfred and Norton Townsend, Frank Thompson (son of Dr. W.E. Thompson), Toby Duclos, Joseph Harkin and little Jimmy Matthews. Matthews, the youngest of the lot, was also the smallest. A mere 157 centimetres tall, he had to stand one step higher than the other lads for the photo in order to be shoulder to shoulder with them. The only one absent was Charlie O'Brien, the son of the brewery king T.W. O'Brien. Other students had already gone off to war; included among them were Donald Chester Davis and Frank Gane, both of whom would die overseas.

School superintendent Bragg remarked: "You are now going forth to preserve and perpetuate those grand ideals of British freedom. Others from our school have preceded you and may now be on the field of battle."[111] They were all presented with a solid gold engraved disc, with the name of the recruit and a space for his regimental number on the reverse.

At eight that evening, the students were among the 129 men who lined up in front of the courthouse at the south end of Front Street for a photograph. There, the ladies of the IODE pinned a souvenir Klondike badge on every man's coat. The evening before, they had presented each recruit with a handsome monogrammed utility kit, containing buttons, needles, pins, shoelaces and such. They had also raised sufficient funds for all of them to be presented with a wristwatch when they reached Victoria. Lieutenant G.G. Hulme called off the roll, and the men responded, "Here, sir." Then Captain Black spoke to them. He "wished to congratulate the men on the manly part they have volunteered to do in the Empire's cause." Further, he said "the report has spread in certain places outside that men from the Yukon are much given to drinking." He hoped that "this company would prove to them such is not the case, and that the best of reports will be heard from them. Nothing is so disgusting... as to see one in uniform disgrace the uniform by being intoxicated."[112]

The men then fell into formation in front of the courthouse and marched down Front Street to the steamer berthed at the dock, followed by Mrs. Black and Mrs. Hulme, with her small son, Croft, in a carriage. George Brimston, who acted as parade marshal, led the home guard at the head of the procession. Then the Boy Scouts and the Girl Guides, all in uniform, followed. Next were members of the Yukon Order of Pioneers, two abreast. Pat Penny carried the banner of the order. Other members carried the flags of Britain, France and other allied nations. Then came the Dawson brass band playing stirring patriotic marches. One of the volunteers led the company mascot, a handsome grey malamute.

Finally came the volunteers, described in the *Dawson Daily News* as: "Stalwart, rugged, lithe, firm of step, resolute and ready for come what may. At the head walked Captain Black, presenting a splendid appearance in his khaki uniform... the men presented a stirring sight and as they marched past the large crowd of friends mingled emotions of sadness and pride struck every heart."[113]

At the wharf, the Yukon Rifle Association parted ranks and presented arms. The Guides, Scouts and Pioneers stepped aside on the wharf, and the men marched through and onto the deck of the steamer: "The brave boys destined for the front swarmed over the boat from the Texas deck to the lower deck and soon were bidding a fond adieu to old friends... Husbands were embracing wives and little children, sweethearts were tearfully expressing their last well-wishes, and old pards of the trail and camp were giving the firm hand and 'God Bless you Bill and good luck.'"[114]

As the summer passed, more recruits were signed up. On July 11, thirty-five "brave lads" were honoured by the community before leaving Dawson on the steamer *Selkirk*, bound for Victoria.[115] They assembled in front of the courthouse at the south end of Front Street, and after a group photo, they were greeted by the various chapters of the IODE, which were there

The first group of volunteers for the George Black contingent posed in front of the Administration Building for this photo, June 8, 1916, before leaving Dawson the following day. GATES COLLECTION

to hand out the usual sewing and repair kits ("housewives"), though the Klondike badges would have to be forwarded to them in Victoria. They then turned about-face and marched out of the Mounted Police parade square, where they joined up with the Dawson Guards, followed by the Boy Scouts, the flag-bearing ladies of the IODE and the brass band, playing a lively march. Behind them were citizens in automobiles and others on foot. They made their way past Government House, where Captain Black, still recovering from his surgery, watched them from the broad upper verandah and saluted as they passed. Mrs. Black watched them from the boardwalk along the side of the street until they passed and continued down Front Street to the wharf. The dock was thick with people who soon swarmed aboard the vessel, wishing the men farewell.

Just before their departure, Alexander Mahaffy, the former vice-principal of the school, and commanding officer of the party, was presented with a pair of binoculars of the type used by officers at the front, as well as a gold disc similar to those given to the departing students, and received a speech by one of his former pupils, who closed by wishing him a safe return. Once the well-wishers had gone ashore, the *Selkirk* cast off and headed upstream to Whitehorse as the band played gay and patriotic airs and the crowd cheered.[116] When this second party of volunteers arrived in Victoria, they were greeted by Lieutenant Hulme and some of the Yukon boys. Two days later, the Yukon Company was inspected by His Royal Highness, the Duke of Connaught, who stopped and talked to several men in the line of Yukoners before they formed up and marched by "like professionals."[117]

Among the new arrivals was Yukon territorial councillor Norman Watt, who came to Dawson in 1898 and worked first in the gold commissioner's office and then for the utility company. Back in 1905, he was a member of the Dawson Nuggets, the famed hockey team assembled by Joe Boyle that travelled east to Ottawa to challenge for the Stanley Cup. As Watt announced,

> I have enlisted as a simple matter of duty. I feel that the time has come when every loyal Canadian who can get away should go... I am going with Yukoners because I believe there are no more resourceful men in the world. I would select them above all others. I hope they are kept together. No part of the world can produce men more accustomed to all-round frontier experiences and the great experience of hustling for themselves in face of emergency. Any man can be trained for ordinary soldiering, but it requires years of frontier life to get the experience the Yukoners possess in regard to getting along in face of all kinds of difficulties which try every man's resourcefulness to the uttermost.[118]

The summer passed quickly, and the recruitment campaign continued. At the Discovery Day celebrations, Commissioner Black gave a speech praising the pioneers who settled Dawson City and wrenched $200 million in gold from the frozen earth. Black then turned his focus to the German conflict, accusing their enemies of barbarism. Germany has "therefore brought upon herself the odium, scorn and hatred of all decent people of whatever nation or race."[119] The Germans he painted as warmongers and fiends, whereas the British were peace loving. Black then praised the volunteers for stepping forward when duty called and stated that those physically fit men who had not yet volunteered were not doing their duty.

Although the number of available men had to be declining, the number of volunteers continued to rise. Toward the end of September, the IODE sponsored a dance at the Moose Hall in honour of the next batch of men from the Black contingent who were preparing to ship out to Victoria. George Black and many of the other volunteers attended the event; the hall was gaily festooned with flags, flowers and potted plants, and dancing to the strains of the John Dines Orchestra continued until two o'clock in the morning. The following day, Black aimed his sights at the Scandinavians, who were not stepping forward to volunteer: "Whether naturalized or not, they have the same opportunities as the native born in Canada and should have the same pride in the country... The company is not filled up and there is time enough yet for these descendants of the Vikings to show that red blood courses in their veins and that Canada may be proud of them as citizens."[120]

Although Martin Larson Hale, a Norwegian, and Pete Carlson Berg, a Swede, were the only Scandinavians to join the Black contingent, there were other Scandinavians who signed up. But they did not join in the numbers of other nationalities: twenty-two Balkan-born recruits and seventeen Americans could be found in the nominal roll of those who crossed the Atlantic with the Black contingent.

In October, as the remainder of the Black contingent prepared to leave Dawson, the *Dawson Daily News* singled out Mrs. Black for particular recognition: "For the loyal, capable and gifted helpmeet of Captain Black the Yukon ever will cherish the highest esteem and good wishes. The hospitality of Mr. and Mrs. Black at Government House and the devotion of Mrs. Black to the organization and promotion of patriotic societies in Dawson ever will be remembered in Dawson with pleasure and gratitude. Those societies and others will continue their work in Dawson mindful ever of the good that they can do for the Yukon boys at the front and the Empire in general."[121]

With only a few days to go before departure, the quota of volunteers had not yet been met, as some had failed to pass their medical examinations. Still short by twenty men, George Black announced publicly that some had no good reason for not enlisting. Looking around Dawson, he could see quite enough eligible men to fill two whole companies. On October 5, the Yukon Rifle Association gave a nice farewell at Lowe's Hall honouring their members who were headed for the front. At the function, George Black was loud in his praise for those who joined up, and, repeating a theme about Yukoners that would characterize his speeches and actions throughout the war, he said there were no men he would rather serve with than the Yukon's loyal volunteers.[122]

Also on the evening of October 5, the Yukon Order of Pioneers honoured the veterans of the gold rush and their sons who were going overseas. Taking a seat of honour along with George Black were Harold Butler, A.W.H. (sometimes known as "Alphabet") Smith, C.S.W. Barwell, C. McDonnell, Sam Miller and Pete Allan. The following night, it was the Girl Guides who entertained the volunteers as the Campfire Minstrels, after which a dance was held in the theatre in their honour. But the biggest event was the reception and banquet sponsored by the British Empire Club at the Moose Hall the evening of October 7. The volunteers marched into the packed hall and lined up in rows of twenty at the front, where the ladies presented each man with the Yukon crest in bronze, to be worn on their caps. Various people sang songs, but the real hit of the evening was when little Gordon McKeen sang his own composition, titled "The Yukon Boys Will Surely Win Where the English Channel Flows." Various speeches were given, including one by school superintendent Bragg, who acknowledged the deaths of four of the school lads who had already enlisted. The number would grow before the end of the war.

Speeches were given by several other dignitaries, including former commissioner and past member of parliament Frederick T. Congdon, and Judge Macaulay. After applause that lasted several minutes, George Black rose and thanked the IODE for the kindness they had shown his boys on the eve of departure, and, in particular, the purse of sixty dollars received from

Mr. Yamaguchi on behalf of the Japanese residents of Dawson, for the purchase of tobacco for the members of the company. He mentioned the Girl Guides, who put on entertainment the previous evening, and the George M. Dawson chapter of the IODE. He thanked the 10 percent of the male population of the territory who had enlisted so far. He said he expected 110 men to sail from Skagway. He had fully 80 men ready to go. More were joining them from Whitehorse, Atlin, the Fortymile district and the Stewart River region.

He referred to the Canadian Patriotic Fund not as a charity but as a fund to help the families of those serving overseas:

> I can truthfully say to you, in endeavoring to fill the office of commissioner, I have endeavored to give every man who had business to transact with me a square deal. I may have made some mistakes. I did make some, no doubt, as all do, but whatever mistakes I did make were of the head and not of the heart.
>
> I want to thank the people also for the kindnesses and the kind things they have said on many occasions to Mrs. Black. She has been more of a help to me in being commissioner of the Yukon than probably any of you can realize. She has tried to do her duty in this community and I am happy to say the people of Yukon give her credit therefore, and I want to thank them for it...
>
> I hope at any rate until the strife of this Great War is past, until this struggle for existence is finally over and the battle finally won, that the people of the Yukon Territory will lay aside their local and personal strifes and pull together for the good of the territory and for the good of the Empire.[123]

Members of the British Empire Club served the banquet, which continued until shortly after midnight.

Final preparations were made for the departure of the men. On October 8, Commissioner Black and other members of the infantry company attended a service at St. Paul's Anglican Church. The following day, the volunteers formed up in the rain and, in a ritual that was becoming all too familiar, marched from the courthouse with an honour guard of Pioneers and a brass band to the waiting crowd at the waterfront, where the men boarded the steamer *Casca*. With them was a solitary woman: Martha Black. Martha Munger Black was a force to be reckoned with, and she was determined to accompany her men overseas, at least to London, if not the battlefront. As the *Casca* pulled away from the dock only a few minutes behind schedule, the cheerful recruits lined the railing; at the centre of the happy crowd were George and Martha Black, wearing their greatcoats. All were waving farewell to those onshore.[124]

GOING OUTSIDE

EVERYBODY ABOARD THE *Casca* was subdued after the excitement of their departure from Dawson City. They settled in for the long journey up the Yukon to Whitehorse and beyond. Some played cards during the evening, and others crowded around the piano singing songs, while some wrote letters. A few just sat and stared out the windows, contemplating what was to come. Everybody slept soundly that night.

During the journey, Martha presented all of the men with the usual sewing and repair kits prepared by the ladies of the IODE. The men in turn presented her with a poke of gold nuggets, one from each member of the Martha Munger Black chapter of the IODE. Martha gave a little speech and everyone cheered; then "Sergeant Major" Thomas Greenaway presented several pairs of warm wool socks, also made by the ladies of the IODE, to George Black amid another bout of cheering.

As the *Casca* churned its way against the powerful Yukon current, Mrs. Black penned the following words, which she sent to her companions at the IODE:

> The men of the Yukon Infantry Company, irrespective of race, religion
> or party, will be very close to Captain Black and me. He can always be

with them to share in their work, their disappointments, their sorrows. But though the day will come when I see them all leaving to go where the stern reality of duty will face them from morning until night, yet I have dedicated my mind and my strength, God willing, to do all that I can to help our men, your men and my men until the day comes when the duty that calls will have become a thing of the past. In that work, I will need your help, the help of every man, woman and child in the great Yukon, and not only the help that your hands can give, but the help that your prayers and good wishes will always be to one who is your grateful and very sincere friend, Martha Munger Black.[125]

During the upstream journey, the men were kept active, performing drill twice a day on the flat deck of the barge being pushed by the *Casca*. All supplies delivered to Dawson came in by riverboat. Since much of the main deck of the boats was used to hold the wood that powered the boilers, barges were attached to the fronts of the riverboats to carry additional freight. Aside from people, the boats did not carry much freight on the return voyage to Whitehorse, so the empty barge served as an excellent space for the men to exercise. The drills were strenuous enough to keep the men quiet for a couple of hours after. They enjoyed excellent food and there were plenty of magazines to read. Martha Black served as the purser of the nicotine, dispensing cigars and cigarettes judiciously so that they would not be used up too soon.[126]

The journey passed quickly enough, and the ninety-two Dawson men, plus Captain and Mrs. Black, were joined by twenty-one more volunteers from Whitehorse and seven from Atlin.[127] The train ride to Skagway took just three hours, and then they departed Skagway on the *Prince Rupert* bound for Victoria, on October 14, arriving at their destination two days later. The same day that they arrived in Victoria, another group of eleven volunteers left Dawson City, including William Radford, who was in charge, and Hugh, Lawrence and Walter Chisholm. Less than two weeks later, a baker's dozen recruits aboard the steamer *Nasutlin* were joined in Whitehorse by Frank Berton, from the Dawson mining recorder's office, and

Officers and men of the George Black contingent (Yukon Company) pose proudly in Victoria before their departure for England, January 1917. YUKON ARCHIVES ROY MINTER FONDS 92/15 #146

Whitehorse men Louis Belney (a miner), Jack French (a carpenter), Billy Williams and Orris Church (a cook).[128]

By the middle of November, more than enough Yukon men had arrived in Victoria to form a company of 255 officers and other ranks. Some were billeted in the old drill hall on Menzies Street, and others in Sidney, but they would all soon unite in Victoria. They were a significant presence among the more than 1,000 soldiers temporarily billeted there before shipping out. At first, the men were accommodated in tents neatly arranged in a double row, with each named after a familiar Klondike feature, such as "Treadgold," or "Dominion Creek."[129] When the entire company had arrived in Victoria, the men took temporary possession of several buildings at the Willows Camp on the BC Agricultural Association's fairgrounds. One building was set aside for officers, and another for the men. The mess hall was nearby, though the officers were messing with the officers of the 50th Regiment (Gordon Highlanders), and the sergeants, the same.[130]

"We are all in one big building and this one big building is composed of one big room partitioned off by wire netting into twelve sections, each holding fourteen men," reported George Vail Raymond. "We are given a tick and are allowed 10 pounds of straw. The tick goes on the floor, on top of which we have three blankets, increased yesterday to four. This constitutes our bed and it is sufficient. I have not been cold yet."[131]

The week quickly passed with distributing the men's kits, getting settled into their new quarters and organizing into platoons. Only the men of the most unusual measurements were still waiting for their uniforms to arrive. They settled into a routine: reveille at 5:30 a.m., parade at 6:00 and breakfast at 6:15. Drill was scheduled morning and afternoon with a break for lunch.

The Yukon men retained a strong collective and egalitarian spirit, and although some were eventually rejected on medical grounds, and others, eager to get overseas, transferred to other units, the bulk of the men remained together. "The Yukon Infantry Company is more like a big party," wrote George Black. "Although the military requirements are observed in the performance of their work, the fact that a man having a commission is entitled to no more respect than the man in the ranks is never lost sight of and goes a long way to create and maintain a good feeling."[132]

The feeling seemed to be widely shared. "We will do our utmost to prove to Captain Black that we were all sincere in joining the army and had at heart the defense of our Empire," wrote Joseph Chabot. "I may tell you that the Yukon contingent is a model among the 1150 soldiers who are here. I hope that this will continue. We are very well thought of by everybody and they are pleased to have us tell them about the Yukon, which is still the country for us all."[133] Another member of the Yukon Company put it more directly: "Without being conceited," wrote C.S.W. Barwell, "we can say that we have a very good record in Victoria. Everybody says that we are the best behaved lot of soldiers that have been here since the war started."[134]

That may have been in part because of Mrs. Black, who had remained with her husband and the men in Victoria, where they were reunited with her youngest son, Lyman. Then Lyman was dispatched to training as a non-commissioned officer. George and Martha settled into accommodations at the Angela Hotel, and they were immediately involved in the social circles of Victoria. On October 26, they met Sir Herbert Ames, prominent eastern businessman and member of parliament, at Government House. Ames was on a fundraising campaign for the provincial patriotic fund, and they attended his speech at the old Victoria Theatre. Martha soon began taking lessons in first aid and home nursing at Royal Jubilee Hospital. She was fully prepared to accompany her husband and his men overseas, and with that in mind, she took whatever courses and other preparation she could to be of service while in England. She almost required the services of the hospital herself, coming down with appendicitis, but her doctor was able to treat her without having to perform surgery. She also carried with her letters of introduction to ease her entry into patriotic activities in London.

Martha took advantage of opportunities to speak about the Yukon at social events. She spoke in particular about the patriotic activities of the Yukon. She said that more than $2,000 was donated every month to the patriotic fund, and in total, more than $165,000 had been raised since the beginning of the war, and five hundred men had been sent to the front.[135] She slipped away to California to visit her parents, and returned in time for Christmas. Christmas morning, she visited several men who were in St. George's Hospital for surgery. To each she gave a pack of cigarettes and a deck of cards. Later, at the Christmas gathering, greetings were read out from the *Dawson Daily News*, Acting Commissioner George N. Williams, the British Empire Club, the George M. Dawson chapter of the IODE, and Captain and Mrs. Barrington.

The meal consisted of turkey, plum pudding and a plentiful supply (but not too much) of the "cup that cheers."[136] The money to cover the meal came from the British Empire Club and the Dawson chapter of the IODE, and was supplemented by the Yukon Comfort Fund. After the meal, the entire company attended a film at the Pantages Theatre, where slides were shown of views between Skagway and Dawson City.[137]

While waiting impatiently to be shipped overseas, the men continued to train in bayonet work, musketry, bombing, physical training and other drills. By the New Year, they were in top physical form and eager to transfer overseas and get to the front. Their experience on the frontier paid off for them in one way. In target shooting at 300, 500 and 700 yards, the Yukoners scored far above the average compared with any other unit in camp.[138] Morale was good. The solicitous attitude that both Captain and Mrs. Black showed for the Yukon men had a positive influence on their behaviour. And they went out of their way to help the other men. Little Jimmy Matthews, the company bugler, feared that he would be rejected because of his poor eyesight, but Captain Black intervened. He took Matthews to the best eye specialists, until he found a surgeon who was able to correct the condition with an operation. Jimmy could see as well as anyone in the company afterward, and was able to ship out with his comrades as he had hoped.[139]

John MacDonald dispelled any notion of partisanship in the actions of Captain Black:

> The discipline of the company was splendid and I cannot say too much in praise of the officers from Captain Black to the corporals. I never heard the word "Politics" mentioned once while with the company and I was there for weeks. The only time I heard that distasteful word "Politics" was on my return North. Captain Black and I were on opposite sides of politics here. I always was opposed to him strenuously, as I was a Liberal and he Conservative. But in the Yukon Infantry Company all that kind of business was forgotten. The Captain showed himself broad on these lines, and appointed his officers irrespective of any previous political persuasion. Norman Watt, who was recommended by the captain for lieutenant, and went through and made good and now occupies that position in the company, as well known here, was an ardent Liberal and recent president of the Liberal Association of the Yukon. The selections of the other men who received commissions and the non-commissioned men always were conducted with the utmost care and based on merit.[140]

The men spent the first weeks of the new year waiting impatiently for the order to ship out for England; it wouldn't be long in coming.

RHYMES OF A RED CROSS MAN

ROBERT SERVICE IS the most unlikely of heroes. His writing career was a product of accident and his fame came suddenly and unexpectedly. After living the life of a vagabond, wandering the West, he finally settled into a job as a clerk for the Canadian Bank of Commerce. He was transferred to Whitehorse in 1904, and it was there that he penned his first book of verse. He sent it off to a publisher to have a small number of copies printed to give to friends. They returned his payment and offered him a contract with royalties of 10 percent. This first book of verse contained "The Cremation of Sam McGee" and "The Shooting of Dan McGrew," poems that made him world famous.

After spending three years in Whitehorse and a brief furlough in Vancouver, he was posted to Dawson City, where he continued to work as a bank clerk until his term of commitment was fulfilled in November of 1909. By then, he was making more from his book royalties than from his meagre salary as a bank clerk. In fact, he was making more than the bank manager, so he quit the bank, left the company barracks and moved into a tiny two-room log cabin up on the hillside overlooking the gold rush town.

In this tiny cabin, he continued to write poetry and novels, until he left in 1912. He never returned to the Yukon, but by then, his writing had become the defining literary work of the gold rush and the Yukon for generations to come. He accepted an assignment from the *Toronto Daily Star*, as a war correspondent, covering the Balkan conflict, after which he wandered through Europe, and then settled in Paris, where he met and married Germaine Bourgoin in June 1913. His second novel was completed then and published in 1914. That summer, war broke out and Service attempted to enlist. He was rejected because of his age and varicose veins, so he once again turned his hand to journalism, getting accreditation with the *Toronto Daily Star*.

The German advance into Belgium and France seemed to progress at an unstoppable rate. Within weeks, it appeared as though they would soon be marching into Paris, but in early September, the French rallied and stopped the German advance on the Marne. The two opposing armies then tried unsuccessfully to outflank each other as they moved toward the North Sea. The line solidified with most of Belgium in German hands, except for a tiny segment in the northwest, including Ypres that remained in Allied possession. British reinforcements poured in through the French port of Calais and moved into position on the rapidly developing defensive line.

The military high command did not want journalists in the trenches or at the battlefront, so in the fall of 1914, Service joined other correspondents as close to the front as he could get at Calais. "At the Station Hotel of Calais were a brilliant band of journalists," he wrote, "but they depended on leave men and Blighty victims for their stories. I was not very successful. The regular newspaper men got tips that left me an outsider. I did not get much help from them; but one and all said: 'If you value your skin don't go near Dunkirk.'"[141]

So that is exactly what he did. He clambered onto a train headed for Dunkirk, a coastal town located between Calais in France and Ostend in Belgium. Because it was so close to the advancing German line, access was restricted to civilians. Knowing this, Service got off one station before and walked into Dunkirk. He certainly got an eyeful:

> I saw Indian troops looking strangely out of place in the mud and rain. I spoke to the weary *poilus* [French soldiers] fresh from the front. I could hear the cannonading and it gave me a thrill of delight. I beheld my first string of German prisoners in grey-green coats, marching methodically. Troops were being landed in the Port and supply columns congested the narrow streets. All day I dodged from one vantage point to another, seeing a hundred things I was not supposed to see. And I was innocently happy thinking how I was getting ahead of the boys back in Calais.[142]

He was arrested that evening by a local gendarme who suspected him of spying. He was interrogated by a major, whose suspicions were heightened by the stamps in his passport from various countries, including Germany. He was taken before a general and then locked up. Eventually, he was turned over to the port captain, who, after questioning him extensively, pointed out his suspicious activities during the day. He told Service: "But are you aware you have no right to be here, and the faster you get out the better. As for the spy business, let me tell you that you've had a narrow escape. There's a big scare on and they seem to have lost their heads. Only this morning they shot a half a dozen poor devils off hand. I am sure that some of them were innocent. If I had not been there to intervene you might have become one of them. Now take your papers and GET OUT!"[143]

Service retreated from front line reporting for the time being, but a year later, in September 1915, having read an advertisement in a Paris newspaper,

Too old for active duty, Robert Service volunteered as an ambulance driver until he was forced to quit for health reasons. GATES COLLECTION

he joined a volunteer group called the American Ambulance Unit.[144] This volunteer unit was one among several formed during the war that consisted of an international array of volunteers, including such illustrious figures as Walt Disney, Somerset Maugham, Ernest Hemingway and E.E. Cummings. That winter, Service spent time near the front lines driving an ambulance. In their off-hours, the volunteers, who consisted of well-educated men, many of them academics, returned to their headquarters. There, they may have had to sleep on the floor, but they relaxed with food and wine that supplemented their French Army rations. They may have enjoyed good cheer during such respite, but the concussions from shells landing nearby were a constant reminder of the immediacy of the war.

Service wanted to get closer to the action, so he volunteered for outpost duty, where they slept rough, under constant shellfire. He had named his ambulance Dorothea, and it was while driving her back and forth that he saw his first mud-splattered German prisoners up close: "Their faces are pasty, pale, smeared with sweat and dirt, and their lips quiver as if they had gone through a terrible ordeal... Callow boys, most of them with crop heads and loose-swinging limbs. On seeing my English uniform they are taken aback. Their lips freeze to a hymn of hate. If looks could kill I am sure I would perish on the spot."[145]

In a letter he wrote to the *Dawson Daily News*, he said that on one particular day, he had been driving since three o'clock in the morning, and had made thirteen trips back and forth to the front without relief. At one point, during a shelling, he took refuge beneath Dorothea. On another trip, he picked up two wounded men near the front—"shattered masses of blood and bone."[146] One was near death, and a priest stopped the ambulance to tend to the soldier. Glancing through the flap, he saw the priest kneeling over the dying man. The priest held a crucifix to the bloody lips, and the bearded soldier kissed it. They then moved on. When he passed through a village en route to the field hospital, three more wounded soldiers climbed into the ambulance. But when they reached the hospital, they were turned away, as it was already filled with wounded and dying men. Before they reached another hospital, one of his passengers was dead.

When they finally got to that hospital, it was set up in the village town hall, under a rough tent that took up half the courtyard, where lay "the wounded, row after row of them, blood-glued to their stretchers and awaiting their turn."[147] More than one hundred were waiting for treatment, and ambulances continually arrived with more casualties. Inside, he could see surgeons "slicing and cutting, crimson to the elbows." An orderly came out carrying a bucket holding a severed limb.[148]

On one trip to the front, Dorothea sputtered to a halt, and a passing soldier examined her and cleaned the spark plugs. In fifteen minutes, she was on the road again. Service returned with his crimson cargo, every bump torture for the injured soldiers, who pleaded with him to slow down. Slowly he crept forward, but the hospital was already full to capacity, so he returned to the crater-pitted road and drove to the next hospital. Sputtering and backfiring along the road, Dorothea finally expired, and a passing truck towed her the last kilometre and a half. Service had transported twenty-three injured that day. He did not have the heart to ask if number twenty-three lived or died.[149]

"So, I end the day by rolling home on the tail of a motor lorry," reported Service. "It is one of the hardest days of my life. Actual results cannot measure the travail of it, and yet it is just a representative day. For a week the attack rages. Night and day we bring in the red harvest."[150]

Service continued to drive ambulances until he was forced to leave the front by a bad case of boils. Over the next eight months, he was plagued by them. Sometimes they came in multiples; other times, they became enormous. Nothing he did cured him of this plague until they finally cleared up on their own. In the meantime, he and Germaine relaxed at Dream Haven, his refuge on the coast of Brittany at the small village of Lancieux. The ambulance corps got in contact, asking him to return to the front, but he had other ideas. He started writing poetry:

Ideas for story poems came surging at me—the man with no legs, the man with no arms, the blind man, the faceless man—all seemed capable of treatment in verse. I made a list of themes, adding to them from time to time. I was so eager to begin, I could not sleep that night, and next morning with a heart of joy I began to write. I took the first item from my list and stared at the blank sheet in my typewriter. Inspiration was not long in coming. By night I had written the first poem… On an average I wrote three poems a week and in five months I had over sixty.[151]

He submitted his collection of verse to his publisher, and it was published in 1916 under the title *Rhymes of a Red Cross Man*. The book was an instant success and remained at the top of the best-seller list in the British magazine *The Bookman* for the better part of a year. For a while, Service said, he felt as if he were sitting on top of the world. *Rhymes of a Red Cross Man* would become the best-selling book of poetry of the twentieth century, and it made Robert Service a lot of money. It was heralded as the work of a legitimate poet, who got into "the trenches, the hospital and the camp."[152]

Service's wartime poems did not address the big issues of the war or dwell on jingoistic sentimentality. Nor did he write about the officer class. Instead, he focussed on the ordinary soldiers in the trenches on both sides of the conflict.

"The Man from Athabaska" is about a soldier drawn away from the wilderness of northern Canada that he loves so much, and to which he dreams of returning after the war.[153]

"Jean Desprez" tells of a barefoot boy who offers water to a dying French soldier nailed to a church door by his German captors. For his kind act the little boy is forced by the German major to shoot the suffering French soldier. The poem concludes when the little boy, who even at his young age sees the glory of France, turns the gun on the Prussian major and shoots him instead.[154]

Robert Service was not a social activist by any stretch of the imagination, yet his poetry connected with a mass audience at the human level the way no other wartime author did.

Service did not think immediately of returning to the war. Among other things, Germaine became pregnant shortly after he returned from his ambulance service and gave birth to twins on January 28, 1917. Robert and Germaine retired to the Riviera, but a month later, one of the twins contracted scarlet fever and died. A short time later, he wrote to the ambulance corps, but by then, America had entered the war and the volunteer corps had been disbanded. During 1918, back in Paris, the Service family endured the bombardment of the city by the long-range German siege gun known as "Big Bertha." Mounted on a railcar, Big Bertha had a barrel 34 metres long and was capable of lobbing 100-kilogram shells 130 kilometres from behind German lines, into Paris. On March 29, 1918, one of these shells scored a direct hit on the Church of St. Gervais, which was packed on that Good

Friday, and killed or wounded 156 people. Service and his family once again retreated from Paris to Dream Haven on the Brittany coast.

Overcome by guilt, Robert volunteered his services to the Canadian government, and in due course was posted as an intelligence officer to the Canadian Expeditionary Force during the last months of the war, touring France and reporting on the activities of Canadian troops. He was assigned a Cadillac, a chauffeur and an officer guide, and the freedom to plan his own itinerary. He visited lumber camps all over France:

These were hectic times for the war was drawing to a climax and the scene was one vast battle ground. Every day I poked around, appalled at the plentitude of rich, gory copy. I ceased to take notes and my diary was unwritten. I have no record of this period but my memories are too many to put on paper... Le Cateau, with its reek of mustard gas and its streets strewn with civilian corpses. One stepped over them, taking little notice. One peered through the open doors of houses, empty but for the dead. In a dim room I saw five wax-like women lying on their beds as if sleeping peacefully. In a kitchen were a Tommy and a German who had fought it out with bayonets. The Tommy had spitted the Hun and was poised over his still defiant foe. Again, in an open space a Belgian machine gunner lay sprawled over his mitrailleuse while round him were seven dead Germans. Everywhere macabre scenes like the chambers of horrors of some super Madame Tussaud...

Heaps of bodies littered the ground. Some were headless, others mere torsos, like butcher-meat fresh from the slaughter house. Dead, dead everywhere—so many of them. One hoped they would be buried before they had time to putrefy. But the burial parties were working night and day. It was so terribly tragic, this last of the battle-fields. In one village street every door was open and the interior a scene of wanton destruction. The floor was usually a mass of feathers from ripped bed-covers. Stuffed chairs and sofas were slashed open, inlaid cabinets smashed to matchwood, pictures scored by knives—everything of beauty destroyed by a beaten and bitter Hun. Except one. Under a heap of debris I found an ivory figure of Christ on the Cross. Even the vandals had held that inviolate.[155]

One day, Service and his officer ventured so far forward that they were ahead of the advance. Germans were retreating in the distance. His guide, a Canadian major, was uncertain of whether to go any farther. As the Germans retreated, the Belgian civilians emerged from their cottages—women, children and old men, who "wept and cheered at the same time. Miserably thin and ill nourished, at that moment they seemed the happiest people on earth. They kept telling us that the Boches were running away, that we could go forward, for we would meet no Germans of the rear-guard ... So we marched merrily on the road to Lille."[156] Service and the major were the first Allies to enter Lille by the Cambrai gate. And what a welcome they received:

> I never saw people more mad with joy. They pressed bottles of wine and cigarettes on us and it was difficult to refuse. In front of the gate was a gigantic crater, down which we had to climb, but on the other side the women of Lille awaited us in a serried mass ... They clutched us hysterically and swept us through the massive portals of the city.
>
> Now we were in a maelstrom of mad women, all of them making desperate efforts to get at us. Hundreds there were, fighting to embrace us. They flung their arms around us and pressed their lips to our cheeks ... And so we were tossed in a tempest of osculatory enthusiasm, in which the major with his superior sex appeal was the chief victim. I could see him struggling in that welter of womanhood, for now they were begging for souvenirs and tearing away his buttons. I feared he would be reduced to a state of near nudity, so I shouted: "We'd better beat a retreat!" He agreed and after he had sawn off a few more chunks of osculation, gallantly defending his few remaining buttons, he fought his way back to the edge of the crater.[157]

When the formal military party arrived at Lille (Lille was liberated by the British on October 17, 1918, when General Sir William Birdwood and his troops were welcomed by joyous crowds), Service and the major removed themselves discreetly from the town. When they reported on the event at supper later that evening, the other men scoffed at the notion, until they received official word that Lille had been taken.

After that experience, anything else would have been anticlimactic, so Service returned to Paris and worked day and night, turning out article after article:

> I described saw-mills, hospitals, bakeries, ordinance camps—all the organization that makes fighting possible. I gave the names of hundreds of those who also serve and said something interesting about each. As I went on I saw a book in the making. *War Winners* I would call it, and it would deal with the efforts of those who worked without glory to win glory for others. I never wrote better. Graphically I covered all France with its pictorial background. I became more and more enthusiastic, then...

> The bells started ringing on Armistice Day at 11:00. All Paris was celebrating in joyous release that lasted for two days...

> For a while I remained in the midst of it, carried away by the extravagances of a mirth-mad mob; then I tired of it all. I thought of those who had given their lives for this, and for whom no one in all that cheering multitude had a single tear. So back to the Rabbit Hutch I crawled with sorrow in my heart. There on my desk were the articles I had written with such enthusiasm—excellent work, a month of effort. With sudden loathing I looked at them. I need not go on. Taking up my manuscript I tore it in tatters. "That ends it," I said. "No more war. Not in my lifetime. Curse the memory of it. Now I will rest and forget. Now I will enjoy the peace and sweetness of Dream Haven."[158]

1917

BOUND FOR BLIGHTY

FINALLY, ON JANUARY 16, 1917, the Yukon Infantry Company made their departure for Europe in a businesslike manner. The men shouldered their packs, lined up in a column four abreast and marched from Willows Camp through the streets of Victoria to the waterfront. When they reached the intersection of Fort and Cook Streets, they were met by the marching band of the 143rd Battalion, which led the advancing column down the avenue. Along the way, thousands of people lined the streets, cheering them on. When they turned onto Belleville Street in the final approach to the Canadian Pacific Railway (CPR) dock, a company of two hundred men from the 143rd Battalion lined both sides of the avenue, and behind them was a crowd of onlookers. The Yukon men marched proudly down the street, and quickly and efficiently boarded the *Princess Victoria* for Vancouver. They swarmed the decks and crowded the handrails, and climbed the ratlines to view the crowd as the vessel pulled out into the harbour and turned away. The crowd on the dock cheered them on, and, as the steamer passed out of the harbour, the guns at Work Point fired a salute, and factory and boat whistles blew a chorus.[159]

In Vancouver, George Black's Yukon Infantry Company transferred to a waiting train, which, over the course of several days, clattered across the country to Halifax. They were joined at North Bay by Yukon member of parliament Dr. Thompson, who accompanied them for the next twelve hours, but they did not stop over in Ottawa.[160]

A large crowd and an honour guard were on hand to watch the Yukon Company march down Belleville Street to the CPR dock in Victoria, January 16, 1917. YUKON ARCHIVES GEORGE BLACK FONDS 81/107 #8

While the Yukon boys were making their way across the country, the people back in Dawson City were getting their own glimpse of their boys in khaki. Jack Suttles, a Kentuckian and former member of the Georgia Minstrels, sent to Dawson City copies of films taken of the Yukon Company in training at Sidney a few months earlier. Dawsonites filled the DAAA theatre to view the films, which depicted the men doing physical drill, reveille, dinner parade, bayonet drill and route march, and included a panoramic view of the entire company. The films brought cheers and applause from the appreciative audience. While the films were projected on the screen, the front of the theatre was filled with children from the public school, who sang patriotic songs like "O Canada," "Rule, Britannia!" and "Soldiers of the King." Next, the children danced in Russian and then Irish costumes. Max Landreville played "La Marseillaise" on the piano, which was followed by vocal arrangements by William Ward, accompanied by Messrs. Templeton and Chamberlain on the piano.[161]

The Yukon men board the *Princess Victoria* and leave Victoria amid cheers, steam whistles and gunfire. YUKON ARCHIVES GEORGE BLACK FONDS 81/107 #13

Mrs. Black was also travelling east by rail, but by a different route. She stopped over in Ottawa and petitioned every authority she could meet to be allowed to accompany the men overseas. Prime Minister Borden and John Hazen, the minister of marine, were both supportive, and Mrs. Hazen placed calls to key people on Mrs. Black's behalf. But in the end, it was up to General Biggar, the officer commanding of transportation in Halifax. As journalist Anne Merrill tells it, he asked her, "in a slightly horrified voice, if she would have the necessary courage and would be willing to be the only woman among several thousand men, to which she bafflingly replied, 'But General, I walked into the Yukon with thirty thousand men!' His only and final comment as the lady gained her point was 'Well Mrs. Black,' he said, 'you certainly are incorrigible!'"[162]

Biggar withheld his approval until he talked to Captain Black, who had been appointed officer commanding for the fifteen hundred men aboard the SS *Canada*. After a lengthy discussion with Black, the general granted approval: "Your wife tells me you want her to go to England with you. I have held back permission until I found out from you personally if you really want her. Some husbands prefer their wives to stay at home."[163]

A month after Mrs. Black was granted permission to travel to England, an Order-in-Council would be passed by Ottawa that prohibited women and children from visiting Britain and France. Mrs. Black, however, beat that legislation and was ferried to the SS *Canada* in a launch, and it sailed from Halifax Harbour on January 24.

The crossing was a stormy one, and Mrs. Black soldiered on despite being seasick much of the time. An adjacent cabin was set up as an infirmary, and using the training she received in Victoria, she tended to the sick during the crossing and assisted the doctors on board. As to how the men felt about having a woman in their midst:

> Their feelings were best expressed in a rollicking impromptu shanty, sung lustily on deck every day between dashes of salt-sea spray, which showed that the one and only lady voyager was far from being an unwelcome mess mate or any damper on soldier's merriment. This is the jingle:

> > We have stolen Mrs. Black and we will not bring her back,
> > Till the Germans quit and when the Allies win
> > Till we nail the Union Jack to the Kaiser's chimney stack,
> > And we toast the Yukon Daughters in Berlin.[164]

Despite the inclement weather, the troops were able to put together an evening of entertainment on February 2. The troops were entertained by eighteen performers, including Mrs. Black, who gave a recital of "Red Cross," and six other Yukoners, including Kentucky minstrel Jack Suttles. The *Canada* slipped quietly into its mooring in Liverpool on February 7, and the Yukon men were transported to their new encampment. The next phase in their journey had begun.

They were soon stationed at Witley Camp in Surrey, as part of a new brigade. There were thirty thousand men, broken into various units: engineers,

Mrs. Black with her husband (to her right) and other officers of the Yukon Company aboard the SS *Canada* en route to England. LIBRARY AND ARCHIVES CANADA C-6118

flying corps, army service corps, ambulance, infantry and machine gun batteries. "We are known as the Seventeenth Canadian Machine Company, attached to the 128th battalion," reported William F. Mills in a letter.[165] The Yukon Company men spoke with some pride about their new assignment because the machine gun brigades were considered the elite units of the Canadian Expeditionary Force. Captain Black got the credit for engineering this posting, thus keeping the bulk of the Yukon men together. "We have been turned into a Vickers' machine gun company," wrote Frank Cooper. "Of course a machine gun company consists of 187 men all told. They put us through a severe medical examination here and they culled out a lot of good men, too. A machine gunner has to be supple, young and have a mechanical turn of mind."[166] The older men were transferred to other units, such as the Pioneers. "About thirty-eight of our fellows have been rejected for the machine gun company, they are awfully sore," reported Eric Marshall.[167] Those who survived the cull received intensive training in machine gun operation. "We have this machine gun work down to a gnat's hair," continued Frank Cooper. "We could put one of them together blindfolded. We have no more route marches, physical jerks or bayonet fighting. We don't use rifles at all, but revolvers are our defensive weapons."[168]

The training was intensive and focussed, and would delay their shipping out to France considerably. It was a badge of honour for the men to be sent to the front. The men were eager for it; they sought it, and they prized it. They wouldn't be considered blooded soldiers if they didn't see action on the front. Yet they remained stationed in England, like the Boyle unit before them, waiting impatiently for the order to proceed to France.

In the meantime, they were subjected to barracks living, food shortages and cold, damp weather. To add misery to insult, communicable diseases spread quickly in the close quarters of the military camps. Measles, mumps and influenza were three of the most common afflictions. In mid-March, twenty-one men were placed in quarantine because of an outbreak of measles. Being isolated from the rest of the camp because of one of these outbreaks only added to their discomfort. Eric Marshall cited his own personal experience:

Our hut, No. 60 here at Witley was inspected on Friday [April 6] and one of the boys, named Whitehouse, was found to be pretty bad with the measles. You can guess how pleased I am seeing that it is Easter week and I had already made arrangements to go to Edinburgh and spend the week with my wife. The last two days I was just as sore as a bear. I would not have minded so much if I had got the measles myself, but to be shut up in a hut for a month and not allowed to go out is the limit, and the beggars put sentries on the door and barbed wire all around the place so there is no chance to sneak out at night.[169]

The Black contingent lost their first comrade before they shipped out. Lieutenant Frederick Russell Chute was killed in a freak accident. The Yukoners were out on a route march on the Portsmouth Road when a motorized Red Cross ambulance, which was going far too fast for the sodden conditions, came careening around a bend and lost control when the brakes were applied. The vehicle skidded sideways toward the advancing column of men, then suddenly swung to the right, crashing into Lieutenant Chute and his horse. They were both knocked down and Chute was killed instantly. Chute, who was a tall, dreamy, pipe-smoking Englishman born in Norfolk, had been a Yukon miner before enlisting. He had a title back in England but tried to keep the fact quiet.[170]

The Yukon men shared the sorrow of this tragic loss, but it would be nothing like the pain they would feel as their comrades fell on the battle-fields of France and Belgium.

TRENCH WARFARE

THE MEN OF Joe Boyle's Yukon Battery, meanwhile, had become veterans in the field, having experienced battle and the extreme conditions along the Western Front. Both the Germans and the Allies had become firmly dug into heavily fortified positions facing each other along a line that stretched from the Belgian coast across France for hundreds of kilometres. Often separated by only 100 metres, both sides had protective barbed wire barriers and machine gun nests to counter any advance from their enemies. So firmly fixed were these positions that for most of the war, the adversaries remained in a terrible stalemate that could only be changed at great expense and loss of life. The gaining of a few hundred metres was treated as a major victory, but the real war was one of attrition in which both sides invested massive resources and sacrificed hundreds of thousands of lives. The world had gone mad with war.

The landscape between the opposing armies was known as No Man's Land for good reason. As the war progressed, it was blasted and battered beyond recognition; no life existed there. It was a terrible place, pock-marked with craters, which became sodden cesspools during the rainy season. All life had ceased to exist in this zone; not a blade of grass, a flower or a tree grew there. The forested land had been converted into a grotesque and barren zone filled with broken stumps. The bodies of the dead often remained out of reach of recovery parties, slowly rotting, filling the air with a nauseating stench. Tens of thousands of hapless souls were blown into eternity and their remains were never found for burial.

On each side of No Man's Land were the trenches—vast networks of them—which afforded some protection against enemy gunfire. When it rained, they turned into quagmires. Men's feet rotted away from trench foot, the result of being immersed in cold water for days on end. With the constant rain, the trenches turned into a slurry and the walls were perpetually collapsing.

Volunteers who were eager to get to the front quickly lost their enthusiasm when they saw, smelled and felt the austere horror of the trenches, which were populated with countless rats. Infested with lice, the men quickly learned to take off their garments daily, reverse them, and use their cigarette lighters to burn off the hundreds of vermin populating the woolen folds. Men became numb to the conditions. A human shinbone protruding from a trench wall made a grotesque coat hook. Men kept below the lip of the trench; to peer over might earn the curious a sniper's bullet or a machine gun round in the head. They shivered to keep warm in the rat warrens, cubbyholes and dugouts. A constant barrage of shellfire and shrapnel filled the air, and tension reigned where trench raids, poison gas attacks or frontal assaults could happen at any time. Sleep was impossible and nerves were shattered under the ceaseless deafening bombardment from heavy artillery, machine guns, howitzers and mortars.

The war turned Canada's young soldiers into old men. And men contrived devious ways to be relieved of duty, purposely cultivating infections, or shooting themselves so that they could be removed to a casualty station. The only thing the soldiers universally looked forward to was their daily rum ration. The burning sensation as it went down the throat and the numbing it imparted made the otherwise unbearable conditions almost tolerable. The memories of the endless months in the trenches of the Western Front would be etched in their souls and the horrors burned into their subconscious for the rest of their lives.

Many Yukon volunteers would have experienced these conditions, but thankfully, the month of January 1917 was a continuation of quiet along the Canadian sector. Sergeant Major William Black, brother of Captain

George Black, and a member of the Yukon Battery, was appointed to a temporary rank of lieutenant on January 1. Two weeks later, he returned to England on leave, thus missing the only major action the Yukon Battery was engaged in that month. The battery was moved to Bully-Grenay, closer to the front. On January 18, after the mission had been postponed three times, the Yukon Battery supplied barrage support for a trench raid in which one hundred Germans were captured. Sergeant Peppard was the only casualty, being slightly wounded in a narrow escape during the raid. After this, they returned to Divion.

Canadians had turned the trench raid into a fine art. To relieve the monotony of trench life, a year earlier, the 7th Battalion (1st British Columbia) conceived a raid on the German line using nearly two hundred men. The raid was highly successful, and Canadians began making regular raids into No Man's Land and attacking the German line. Another such raid, in January 1917, involved an assault on a German observation post at Birkin Crater by the Princess Patricia's Canadian Light Infantry (PPCLI). When they were within 10 metres of the post, they rushed it and took three sentries prisoner, but not before one of them dislodged a bomb. Both Lieutenant Mortimer and Yukoner corporal Bertie Stangroom were seriously wounded and had to be carried back to the Canadian line by other members of the party. Stangroom was the former Mountie who so desperately wanted to serve overseas that he attempted to desert his Yukon post in 1915. He was eventually able to volunteer in July 1916 and was assigned to the PPCLI. An early report in the newspaper stated that he had received twenty-five machine gun bullets to the legs, but a later article revealed that he was in a raiding party when a bomb landed in the German trench they were raiding. "With quick presence of mind, he threw a big German on top of it, at the same time holding him down. The German was blown to hell and killed. Stangroom was blown some himself, but the worst he got was a leg full of bomb shrapnel."[171] This may have been the action for which he was later awarded the Military Medal.[172]

No one envied the men seriously wounded or disfigured in battle, but sometimes soldiers wished they could get hurt just enough to get them away from the trenches. A wound, or "blighty," was an opportunity to leave the battle line and return to England. Sometimes that was a wish regretfully fulfilled. One morning, Felix Boutin, Kenneth Currie, Sergeant Larry Peppard and Private Morris Anthony were standing together in their trench. A sniper's bullet struck Anthony in the mouth, knocking out two teeth and exiting the back of his neck. Anthony was sent back to England, recovered from this awful wound and was eventually invalided back to Canada.

The Canadians set the standard for trench raid technique among all the Allied forces. These raids boosted morale and honed them into an elite fighting corps that became feared by the Germans. The Canadian troops could take some pride in the assertion that they owned No Man's Land. If they were the masters, then one of the best among them was "Grizzly Bear" Jim Christie, despite his having been so badly mangled in the grizzly attack five years before the war. Even though he was old when he enlisted, at forty-seven, he rose through the ranks, earning a field commission and leading a reconnaissance unit on raids in No Man's Land.

According to Lieutenant Colonel H.W. Niven,

His long life alone in the mountains made him the most observant man I have ever known. He saw everything and said nothing. He could put his hand on the ground in No Man's land and tell whether a man had walked there one hour ago, two hours ago, three hours ago. It was uncanny, and he was never wrong. He would lie out in the open behind our trenches, day after day... and get his sight on some part of the enemy trench and wait for someone to put his head up. If he did not put it up today, he would be there tomorrow, and sure enough some German would come to that spot, and Christie would get him. This happened year after year. I have never known anyone outside an Indian who had the patience of Christie. He would concentrate hour after hour on one spot. No white man that I know of can concentrate for more than, say, three hours on one spot. Christie could do it for two days. Everything told him a story—a bent blade of grass told him something.

Christie wandered over No Man's land all night long, and he came back one morning saying that he thought a German patrol went past our front about 2 am. He wanted four men to go out next night to scupper the lot. I rode into Headquarters and spoke to Gen Sir George Milne . . . who said he would come along about midnight.

About 2 am a hell of a row started away to our left front in No Man's land. We could not fire and neither could the Germans as we both had patrols out. About 3:30 am Christie and his men came in and Uncle George [General Sir George Milne] questioned them.

Christie and his men had lain out in the open ground each with four grenades and his rifle. The German patrol, one officer and sixteen men came across where Christie thought they would. First he shot the officer, each of his men threw two Mills bombs and finished them off with their rifles. Then Christie cut off their shoulder straps for identification and put them in a sand bag, and put all the officer's papers, etc., in. But Christie was in a state of consternation. He found that his patrol had pinched the German rifles and two of his men had left their own. Christie asked Sir George for permission to go out and get the rifles as he was responsible. The General's face was a study, but he gave permission and he awarded Christie an immediate Distinguished Conduct Medal (DCM).[173]

Christie is just one example—a well-documented one—of the men who came to war from the Yukon. The skills they developed from trapping, hunting, prospecting and mining in the Yukon served them well in wartime conditions. They could handle a rifle and endure harsh and challenging conditions, but life in the trenches and the horrors of No Man's Land were something that nobody could prepare for.

HOME FIRES

WHILE SO MANY of their husbands and sons were fighting on the front lines, the women of the Yukon were not satisfied just to be fundraising; they became socially active on a broader scale. They became a force behind the push to institute prohibition in the territory. Prohibition, or the ban of alcohol, was the objective of an international movement of the late-nineteenth and early-twentieth centuries that believed that alcohol was the root of many social problems. The onset of war provided the opportunity to make prohibition a patriotic movement as well. How ironic that, while the people back home were trying to ban the consumption of alcohol, on the front lines, it was the daily shots of rum that kept the men sane amid the dreary trench life.

Through 1915 and 1916, a ban on alcohol was imposed upon all provinces across Canada, except for Quebec. By 1917, the Yukon was the only other jurisdiction in Canada that had not banned the sale of booze. The Yukon still bore the legacy of the gold rush two decades earlier, when, for a few years, everything was wide open. Gambling, drinking and prostitution were woven into the fabric of the territory.

During that time Dawson City, more than Whitehorse, had a reputation as a place of wild excesses and dissipation, all under the watchful eye of the Mounted Police. At its peak, there were eighty saloons in Dawson City selling liquor day and night. As the wave of stampeders receded and the population declined, Dawson City took on an air of Victorian respectability, yet it remained a demographic oddity, with a high proportion of highly mobile single men. After the turn of the century, a series of ordinances began to restrict the freedom of alcohol use. Gambling was closed down, dance halls could no longer sell alcohol and the number of licences for saloons was reduced until the last two saloons closed in 1916.

During the war, the British Empire Club in Dawson advocated prohibition as a patriotic act. Then there was the People's Prohibition Movement, or PPM, which was formed in May 1916.[174] Among the 120 Dawson members, some of them the most prominent citizens in the community, were fifteen women. Henry Dook, the manager of the Pacific Cold Storage Company, was elected president; Joe Boyle and all the Dawson clergy were strong supporters of the cause. Members of the PPM voted almost unanimously in favour of banning alcohol. They petitioned the territorial council to ban the production, distribution and sale of alcohol by January 1, 1917. The petition contained the names of two thousand people, twelve hundred of whom were eligible to vote.

In a special session of the territorial council, which was full to standing, Cornelia Hatcher, president of the Women's Christian Temperance Union

(WCTU) of Alaska, was allowed to speak. Then another session was allowed in response to a petition of 550 names representing the "wets." When commenting upon the prohibition petition, spokesman Charles Tabor said, "There are very few men who can refuse ladies when they come around with a petition. They were a great factor in getting the petition signed."[175]

The opponents of the PPM, the Licensed Victualers' Association (LVA), stood to lose a lot of money if the prohibition campaign succeeded. The hotel business was a major part of the local economy. But it was broader than that, so another organization was formed to combat the anti-booze league. It was called the Association of Business Men, or ABM. The ABM launched their own campaign to counteract the prohibition movement. One business that did well out of this debate was the *Dawson Daily News*, which was filled with pages of paid advertising, both for and against the issue.

The ABM argued that prohibition would ruin the economy of the territory. Fettered by federal control, the territory had few options for revenue generation. Some years, liquor revenues represented almost 25 percent of the income for the territory. To lose that revenue would be disastrous, they said. Besides, they pointed out, if a man wants liquor, legal or not, he will find ways to get it. Further, they characterized the prohibitionists as being socialists. Women were behind the movement, they suggested, and they didn't contribute to the economy like men did. In addition to ruining the economy of the territory, banning booze would take away man's right to drink. Real men, they argued, face temptation and battle it; take away the choice and you take away their manhood, their free will. Only a vocal minority, they argued, wanted prohibition.

For every argument put forth against booze, the ABM had their own arguments, supported by their own statistics, to contest them. Pressured by both the PPM and the ABM, the territorial council resolved to put it to a plebiscite on August 30, 1916, and let the citizens of the territory have the final say. "Banish the Bar on August 30" became one of the slogans for the "drys." In the end, the vote was hardly decisive; the "wets" won the day by a mere three votes: 874 to 871. Ninety percent of eligible electors had turned out to cast their ballot on the matter.[176]

Because they didn't have the right to vote, the ladies who had battled long and hard in the cause of prohibition had been denied the final choice at the ballot box. As a consequence, they gathered on September 1 and formed the Yukon Women's Protective League. Although born in the ashes of defeat, the league had the franchise as its aim. And it didn't take long for the league to take action. A week after the vote, Marie Fotheringham, the secretary of the organization, wrote to Commissioner Black, who had not yet departed with his contingent of volunteers, requesting a meeting with the executive of the league, as well as the presence of Mrs. Black, and Mr. and Mrs. Congdon.

Mrs. Fotheringham was one of the most vocal advocates for social rights in the community. Fotheringham can be labelled in many ways. She was a labour activist, an author, a journalist and poet, a suffragette, a public pest, a troublemaker and an ex-con. Regardless of which you apply, she was an enigmatic and little-known character from Yukon's early-twentieth-century history.

And she was the polar opposite of Martha Black. She was born Marie Josey in Belleville, Ontario, in 1864. Her labourer father, Michael, died when she was young, and her working life started when she was just eleven years old. At age seventeen, she was a servant in the household of a widowed Belleville lawyer with two young children.

Self-educated, she was never afraid to express herself; some recipients of her correspondence included the prime minister of Canada, the commissioner of the Yukon and even the future king of England. She was competent in verse, and she did not appear to be ashamed of being a working girl who earned her way from a young age. The first woman labour poet in Canada, she began to publish her poems in newspapers and labour journals as early as 1886, when she was just twenty-two years old.

By 1893, she was well known in Toronto for organizing domestic servants into the Working Women's Protective Association. She championed Sunday streetcars, for those who had to work on the Lord's Day. She started travelling west in 1895, ending up in Vancouver in 1901, and then moving to Dawson City in 1902. A year later, she married David Hetherington Fotheringham, a young Mountie from South Africa, who was assigned to show her around the district when she first arrived in Dawson City.

Their lives together led over some rocky trails. A year after their wedding, Marie was sentenced to two months of hard labour over questionable dealings related to mining properties and the misuse of another woman's diamonds. She was involved in a number of legal tussles in the ensuing years, including a long-simmering dispute with a mining developer named Margaret Mitchell. She also vociferously protested the corruption of the Liberal administration of the period.

Unpaid debts related to a failed venture to revive a Dawson hotel landed both her and her husband in the slammer for a month in the fall of 1912. When David enlisted during George Black's recruitment campaign in 1916, Marie remained in Dawson, but again became a visible social activist and a driving force behind the Yukon Women's Protective League.

The ladies of the league met Commissioner Black on September 6, bringing with them a petition. "There are some who contend that a woman's proper place is at home," they wrote. "But when those same critics go farther and insist that woman's interests, energies and activities should be confined within the four walls of her home, and must not extend to the community at large, we wave such assertions aside with all the contempt they deserve."[177]

The women of the Yukon had risen above their household duties and made major contributions to the war effort through their fundraising. They were not about to be pushed back into the kitchen, so they had come to the commissioner to seek advice about how to go about getting the vote. The petition was signed by eight women, including Dora Dook, wife of the president of the People's Prohibition Movement, and Marie Fotheringham.

George Black replied to their request by referring to the voters' qualifications specified in the Elections Act, pointing out that the elimination of the word "male" would automatically include women as voters. He further noted that the same result could be achieved at the territorial level with a similar change of wording in the elections chapter of the Yukon Act.[178] A few weeks later, the league had established themselves in their new headquarters in the White Lunch Building on Second Avenue. Within a couple of weeks, they were circulating a petition destined for Ottawa. It was quite specific as to why the women of the Yukon wanted the vote: too many "foreign born" men were living in the Yukon, and the illiterate alien vote was having too much of an influence on the elections. Not being fluent in English, they did not have a clear understanding of the issues upon which they were voting. In other words, the vote of the large number of patriotic, educated, English-speaking men who were out of the country was further diluted by the remaining voters, many of whom were illiterate foreigners. However, the petition noted, the nine hundred Canadian and American women who were fluent in English would "offset and overcome the deteriorating effect of an illiterate foreign vote."[179]

They further noted that from Manitoba in the east, California in the south and Siberia to the west, these nine hundred women were the only ones who were disenfranchised. A simple change in the wording of the Dominion Elections Act and the Yukon Elections Act would "lift from the mothers, wives and daughters of men the shame and degradation of being legally classed with idiots and criminals."[180]

With far too much misunderstanding among Dawsonites as to the aims of the league, it was decided to have a public meeting where the facts could be set forth accurately. One thing was clear, said an article in the *Dawson Daily News*, which was that the working men of the Yukon were clearly behind the league, heart and soul.

The Arctic Brotherhood Hall was filled almost to capacity on the evening of November 25, with a large representation of women and many of the most prominent citizens in the territory in attendance. A small orchestra was assembled to play a number of patriotic songs and a campaign song written specifically for the Protective League. Frederick Congdon then traced the progress of women in Britain and attributed much success in industry to women. A few months later, with a territorial election in the offing, the league, in conjunction with another newly formed organization, the Yukon Progressive League, posted a manifesto in the *Dawson Daily News*, proclaiming, "Equal Rights to All, Especial Privileges to None," and presenting fourteen points for the candidates to respond to. They included fair administration of the Canadian Patriotic Fund, endorsement of the Women's Protective League petition for the franchise, an eight-hour workday, a Workers' Compensation Act, establishment of an old people's home and support for the territory's bona fide prospectors.

As a result of the war, the women of the Yukon were called upon to perform patriotic duties that gave them, in a territory quickly being depleted of men, a voice that they never had before, and they proved equal to the challenge. At the same time, they bridled at the restrictions that muted their voices at election time. As the war progressed, the forceful petitioning of the women in the community was finally gaining attention, and in conjunction with the efforts of women across the nation, they would achieve their objective before the end of the global conflict. On May 24, 1918, An Act to confer the Electoral Franchise upon Women was passed, which stated, "Women who are British subjects, 21 years of age, and otherwise meet the qualifications entitling a man to vote, are entitled to vote in a Dominion election."[181] It came into effect on January 1, 1919.

MRS. BLACK GOES TO WAR

AS SOON AS she arrived in London, Mrs. Black, carrying her letters of introduction, established a hectic round of activities. Many years later, she remembered this period:

> After three months of arduous steady service in the Prisoners-of-War Department, the routine became disorganized by loss of Canadian mails, delays of prisoners-of-war letters, governmental regulations cutting the amount of food parcels in half, an epidemic of measles (which meant double shift), and two personal attacks of appendicitis. I filled in the odd hours by doing Y.M.C.A. canteen work, attending meetings and investigations of the Women's Battersea Pension Board, sewing for the Red Cross, administering the Yukon Comfort Fund, visiting wounded Yukoners in hospital, giving lectures on "The Romance of the Klondyke Gold Fields," writing letters to family and friends, and to two Yukon papers, as I was "our own correspondent" for the *Dawson News* and the *Whitehorse Star*. I tried magazine writing, but when I came to the actual recording, my pen scratched, my typewriter needed cleaning, and when this was done, inspiration

was ever jeering at me from outside my window, and I set to work darning socks.[182]

In the first weeks of their arrival in London, Martha and George visited as many attractions as was possible. George seemed to have boundless energy for such occasions. They attended lectures and visited museums and art galleries, theatres, music halls and the zoo. They visited the House of Commons, where George, being in uniform, was whisked away to preferential seating, whereas Martha was escorted to a small "cell," where, from behind an iron grating, she was able to witness the proceedings of parliament. "It's rather curious," she said, "how in Dawson you have to protect the women from the men; while over here they seem to find it necessary to protect the men from the women!"[183]

Londoners were not spared direct confrontation with the war. There was food rationing: two meatless days per week, five potatoless days, and limitations upon the amount of bread, sugar or flour to which they were entitled. Mrs. Black also remembered her first aerial bombing experience as an "altogether horrible affair for those in the damaged zone."[184] Further, she noted: "The air raids more than anything else brought personal realization of the horrors of war, and I went through twelve. It was a fearful and nerve-wracking sensation to know that sudden death is lurking in the heavens above you."[185]

A few diary notes she made on one of the worst air raids are telling: "Guns have been going hours, and they do make a devilish noise. What must it be like for our men in France, where they never cease? Fire engines are tearing up and down. Sirens are screaming. The London searchlights, huge phantom fingers, not unlike northern lights without colour, are sweeping the sky, making it light as day."[186]

Her heavy work schedule wore her down such that within a couple of months of her arrival, she was downed by a bout of rheumatic fever that knocked her out of action for two weeks. Then she developed another case of appendicitis, and the doctor told her to slow down. But she never did, so she alternated between frenzied activity and periods when she was confined to bed.

Captain George Black, 2nd Motor Machine Gun Brigade. LIBRARY AND ARCHIVES
CANADA 1961-005NPC 4947

Martha embarked on an ambitious schedule of public speaking,
criss-crossing the country giving talks about the Yukon to every stratum of
society. As she later noted: "I particularly enjoyed talking about the Yukon,
on which I gave almost four hundred lectures—the majority illustrated.
I averaged a daily talk for months, to audiences which numbered fifty to
seven hundred. One day I gave three, but this was too much."[187]

These speaking tours were physically demanding as well, Black
recounted:

My most strenuous lecture trip was one lasting three weeks under the auspices of the Y.M.C.A., in South Wales, where the barren rugged Cambrians reminded me of the hills of home which flank the Yukon and Klondyke Rivers. It meant catching trains at all hours to all places, carrying heavy "boxes" of slides and clothes, blocks on end in all kinds of weather, and all kinds of accommodation, from the humblest to the highest, as my "hospitality" was provided.[188]

Wherever she went to speak in Wales, she was hosted by local mining families, who treated her royally from their own rationed food supplies. "Everywhere I was shown a courtesy and kindness that could not be exceeded," she said. "My taste and wishes were always considered, and when the time came for me to return to London I was sorry to leave so many, many new acquaintances."[189]

Being from northern Canada, she was something of a novelty, and was frequently interviewed for newspapers and magazine articles. She was proud to tell them of how 10 percent of the population had volunteered to fight for king and empire (it was more than that), and how Yukoners had given so much more money per person to the patriotic fund than those anywhere else in Canada. She also spoke proudly of those brave Yukoners who were decorated for their deeds.

Her lectures followed a standard format. Accompanied by glass plate slides taken by George and herself to illustrate her words, she set about to educate Britain about Canada and the Yukon. Mrs. Black described the lakes and rivers teeming with fish, the fields alive with game and magnificent fur-bearing creatures. Game in the Yukon was varied and plentiful; huge herds of caribou could be found within 100 kilometres of Dawson, she said. And she mentioned the wealth of agricultural land and abundant mineral resources. Dawson City had a thoroughly modern electrical plant, operated by a British company. Mining had evolved from primitive hand methods to sophisticated dredges, she noted. Then she recounted her adventure of hiking the Chilkoot Trail during the Klondike gold rush. She described the trip by boat to Dawson City and the various obstacles along the way. She described permafrost, the Mounties (many of whom were

British) and the Lost Patrol (a party of Mounted Police who perished during their annual patrol from Fort McPherson to Dawson City in 1911).

In conclusion, she stated: "Let not the traveler remain away to scoff because we are in the Arctic region, but let him come to be conquered alike by the magnificence of our scenery, the vastness of our golden territory, the charm of her floral offerings, the paradise she offers to sportsmen, and the rest from the conventionalities of the world."[190]

"My lecture work resulted in a distinctive honour," she later noted in her autobiography. "On July 18, 1917, I was elected a fellow of the Royal Geographical Society. My name was proposed by Miss Pullen-Bury, F.R.G.S., F.R.A.I., author of *From Halifax to Vancouver*, and seconded by Sir Thomas Mackenzie, High Commissioner for New Zealand."[191] On two points, she got it wrong. The honour was bestowed upon on her June 18, 1917 (not in July), shortly after she arrived in England, long before she had completed her arduous and lengthy lecture circuit.[192]

On one lecture trip to Southampton, she was asked to go to a big English hospital to see a terribly wounded American soldier. His only audible word was "Hun." It turned out that he was a third cousin from Chicago named Fred Hunn whom she had not seen for many years![193] Her visits to hospitals required a strong constitution and the ability to absorb the most heartbreaking scenes. One such case was an English lad she visited who had lost both legs, one arm above the elbow and the sight in both eyes. He had been a prisoner of war, and all the operations while he was imprisoned were performed without the benefit of anaesthetic. "I will take him some fruit, tell him about the Yukon and try to learn something of life and patience from him," she said, ever mindful of her three sons, who were in service, and her husband, who would later be wounded in action.[194]

Martha was once asked to give a talk at Church House in London, and was introduced in a very offhand manner. She was never one to let a slight of that nature go by without responding, as she reported in her memoirs:

"My Lord Chairman, my lords and ladies and gentlemen, if this is the way you usually treat women who are invited to address you I do not wonder suffragettes go around with axes over here."

The Bishop half rose to speak, but I continued, "My Lord, several times in London I have had to listen to you without interrupting when I should have very much liked to do so. Now please listen to me without interruption." The audience of some five hundred applauded. I then expounded the theory of my basis of married life (harmony in religion, politics and country), and continued: "And so because I married an Anglican, I am one. But had I married a Fiji Islander I would probably be eating missionary now instead of talking missionary."[195]

Despite her sometimes gruelling schedule, she also took time to visit the Yukon Company at Witley Camp. She came to visit on July 10, 1917, while the men were on the practice range at Aldershot. Captain Black let her try her hand at firing a machine gun. Mrs. Black did not shrink from the opportunity; she had many years of experience hunting in the Yukon wilderness with her husband and was not afraid to fire a weapon. According to one eye witness,

> Well, she sat down to the gun, laid it on the target, tapped it into correct position, and first burst down goes all the ranging plates; second, taps the gun onto the target and blazes away 75 times and puts 64 on the bull. I never saw anything like it for a beginner. She seemed to be right at home. One of the new men said "Gee, she can shoot some," and I said, "Well, why shouldn't she; she is a Yankee-Canuck." You should have seen him look at me. He is an Englishman.[196]

She returned again at Christmas to Witley Camp to join in the festivities with 150 of the men, some of whom were joined by their English wives for the affair.

Martha became a mother figure to the Yukon men who were serving in Europe. When one soldier asked her if he could call her "Mother," she consented gladly and later considered that to be a greater honour than being addressed as "The Honourable Member for Yukon," as she was years later as a member of parliament. In a similar way, when these soldiers on leave visited her in her London flat, it helped her forget that she had three sons of her own serving their countries.

If they didn't visit her, they often wrote, but how could they describe the horror of their days at the front? They lived for the moment, for death could come at any time, and rarely did they complain about cold, dirt or discomfort. It could not have been easy for her. Her husband and her sons were away who knows where, doing who knows what. At any time, she could receive notice that one of them had been killed. Still, on the occasions when she and George were together, they would entertain, take in the sights or go to the theatre. On one such occasion, at a performance, they encountered Marie Thompson, daughter of Dr. W.E. Thompson of Dawson City, a few seats away from them. She was in London on sick leave, away from her hospital posting in France, and expected to be sent back soon.

Because of George's position as the commissioner of the Yukon, they were invited to many important social functions. They witnessed the lord mayor's procession from the balcony of Mansion House, the home and office of the mayor of London, at the invitation of Sir Charles Hanson, the incoming mayor, a former Canadian businessman. They were among the party that attended the service at St. Paul's Cathedral celebrating the entry of the United States into the war. They were once invited by Sir George Perley, the High Commissioner to Canada, to attend a function in honour of Queen Marie of Romania. During their two and a half years in England, George and Martha Black were invited to many weekend country house parties. Martha was in her element, having gone to private school when she was young. On one occasion, thanks to the influence of Joe Boyle, she was given a personal guided tour of Buckingham Palace. By the time she was ready to return to Canada, she had formed the opinion that the British people were the most durable on the planet. She saw the Royal Family as "a shining example of courage, duty and devotion to the Empire. No sacrifice was too great. They rejoiced and suffered with their people. They were always in and among and of them."[197]

For the task of administering the Yukon Comfort Fund, she had to keep meticulous records to avoid criticism or attack from political enemies.

Christmas dinner at the barracks in Witley Camp, 1917. Mrs. Black, second from the right; George Black, fourth from the right; Jimmy "Spot Cash" Breaden, extreme left. YUKON ARCHIVES GEORGE BLACK FONDS 81/107 #42

Martha retained all bills of sale and receipts from the men to whom she dispensed aid. She corresponded with George Jeckell, the chairman of the Canadian Patriotic Fund back in Dawson, which contributed to the Yukon Comfort Fund. Send more socks—and tobacco—she wrote to him.

Shopping for the comfort fund meant hours spent in crowded stores for such varied things as machine gun buttons, razor blades, food, soap, green grapes or fresh eggs. On one occasion, she heard of a Yukon soldier in a hospital at Willesden who wanted her to visit. She picked up a bouquet of flowers and caught a Number 8 bus after a long wait. The bus was full and she had to stand for the longest time. Eventually, she found a seat behind two nurses, who ridiculed hospital visitors who brought flowers instead of something useful. At Willesden, she walked through a heavy downpour down one street and up another and across a field to get to the hospital. By the time she arrived, she was thoroughly drenched. The soldier was delighted to receive the flowers but asked if he could give them to one of the nurses, who was celebrating her birthday. It was one of the nurses she had sat behind on the bus trip to Willesden![198]

July 10, 1917; Mrs. Black visits Witley Camp and tries her hand on a machine gun. She scored 64 hits out of 75 rounds. YUKON ARCHIVES GEORGE BLACK FONDS 81/107 #53

But Martha Black would have many trying times before her wartime ordeal came to an end. In August 1918, she received news that her husband was wounded, and rushed off to the hospital to determine how serious the injury was (he would recover). Once, for a week, she was beside herself with worry because her son Lyman had been reported missing. "I would go in rags the rest of my life if we all could be in our Yukon home again," she later wrote.[199] On another occasion, she had the pleasure of seeing Lyman awarded the Military Cross at Buckingham Palace, by King George V himself. To keep her worries at bay, she kept busy. "I never worked so hard in my life," she said, "as I did those overseas years."[200]

THE BATTLE FOR VIMY RIDGE

BY FEBRUARY 1917, the Yukon Battery was part of a bigger initiative being planned—a major offensive along the Western Front. The task given to the Canadians: take Vimy Ridge. The Canadian Corps was assigned the goal of taking control of the German-held high ground along a ridge at the north-ernmost end of a major Allied offensive. This would ensure that the Allied southern flank could advance without suffering German cross fire. The British did not hold out much hope that the Canadians would achieve the objective. After all, the ridge was impregnable: the French had tried to take it and lost fifty thousand soldiers in the attempt. How could the Canadians do any better? In the period leading up to the opening of the offensive, the Canadians launched fifty-five raids against the German positions surrounding Vimy Ridge. The raid by the Yukon Company on January 18 was one of these.

The death toll of Yukoners began to mount with the preparations for the Vimy assault. Lieutenant Howard Grestock had been one of the first Yukon men to sign up, and had sent a continuous stream of letters back to Dawson, which were invariably published in the *Dawson Daily News*. Shortly after enlisting, he wrote warning that they were in for a bad war, and that they would be extremely lucky if they ever came back. A few weeks later, in England with Lord Strathcona's Horse, he complained about the constant rain on the Salisbury Plain. "I did not come out to do barrack room work," he said. "If we don't go to the front before Christmas I shall apply for a transfer to [a] British regular... regiment."[201]

By June 1915, Grestock was in France. "When I left Dawson," he wrote prophetically, "we thought that the war soon would be over, but now I think it has just started and is good for years."[202] Grestock already had a taste of action on the front and considered himself lucky. He had been spared from artillery fire, shrapnel, sniper attacks and poison gas.

In April 1916, he was again on the front, waiting for a big offensive to begin. Later in the year, he saw heavy action with the 73rd Battalion (Royal Highlanders of Canada) but came out of it unscathed. Several times he reported on his good luck at not being shot, blown up or gassed.

Since his arrival in France, he had seen action in all of the major battles: Hooge, Festubert, Givenchy, St. Eloi and the Somme, and he had served for many months as head of the grenade section of Lord Strathcona's Horse. At one point, he received a slight shrapnel wound to the leg, during an assault in which the Canadians captured the Regina Trench. On another occasion, he was instrumental in beating off a bombing attack by the enemy on one of their posts. The night following that occurrence, he again showed his keenness by going out into No Man's Land and bringing in the body of one of the Germans he had killed the night before. The body was badly needed in order to identify the German unit opposed to them. Grestock seemed to be leading a charmed life.

On February 4, 1917, his luck ran out. As a lieutenant in the 73rd Battalion, he was in charge of a raiding party on the Vimy front, and did not return after completion of operations. At first reported killed in action, he was in fact wounded and captured by the Germans. He died a short time later while a prisoner of war in a Bavarian field hospital at Hénin-Liétard. In the few weeks before he was killed, Grestock had been planning to join the Yukon Battery.

Four days later, Private William Hayhurst, an Englishman who had been mining in the Dawson vicinity before the war, and was serving in the 47th Battalion, was wounded and died of his injuries at the Number 11 Canadian Field Ambulance. Today he lies buried in a cemetery 5 kilometres west of Souchez. Five weeks after that, Fred Polley, an American volunteer originally from Massachusetts, in the 50th Battalion, was killed by a single bullet during a raid at Souchez.[203] The Yukon Battery then laid down supporting fire for a raid that took place on March 1 without casualties.

Activity increased and preparations presaged the coming major offensive on Vimy Ridge, which would involve all four Canadian divisions—more than 100,000 men. On April 7, the Yukon Battery was moved into position to the left of the Neuville-Saint-Vaast–Thélus road. Men and supplies were carefully and systematically placed in position for the surprise attack on Vimy Ridge. The plan was not to take the ridge in weeks or days, but in hours. The French allies who would advance on their right flank must have scoffed at the idea of capturing their primary targets in just eight hours, but the attack had been carefully planned, coordinated and rehearsed. Nothing was left to chance. The two divisions to the left of the assault were to be dug in on the far side of the ridge in less than two hours.

At 5:30 a.m. on April 9, the Canadians unleashed the greatest military bombardment of the war to that date. As the carefully planned and timed barrage moved forward, infantry moved closely behind, giving the Germans, who hunkered down in concrete bunkers during the bombardment, no time to set up to repel the coming attack. The Yukon Battery began its machine gun barrage seventy-nine minutes after zero hour. By 10:00 a.m., hostile counter fire was minimal. The men had shown exemplary performance as the tanks moved by them at close quarters. The positions were taken according to plan, and the bulk of the targets were captured within hours.

In the afternoon, the Yukon Battery moved into a new position to provide barrage support through the night on roads leading into Givenchy. The following day, the Yukoners provided heavy fire into areas where the enemy was expected to mass troops for a counterattack. Then, at 3:15 p.m., they provided support fire for the successful capture of Hill 145. Following night fire on predetermined targets, they focussed upon targets in the vicinity of Givenchy. On April 11, under heavy enemy counter fire, Felix Boutin was wounded, and Private Herbert Lawless, who later received the Military Medal, was killed by shrapnel from a high-explosive shell.[204]

On April 12, they turned their attention to their final target, a low hilltop known as "the Pimple." Zero hour was 5:00 a.m., and the Pimple was successfully taken without any more casualties to the Yukon Battery. The Yukon Battery provided night covering fire on the evening of April 12; then a ceasefire was called at 10:00 a.m. on April 13, as the enemy had retreated out of range of Canadian fire. The Yukon men were called back to their camp behind the line at Verdrel, 15 kilometres from Vimy. The success of the Canadian Corps in capturing the ridge resulted from a combination of technical and tactical innovation, careful planning, powerful artillery support and extensive training. This was the first occasion when all four divisions of the Canadian Expeditionary Force went into battle together, and the battle has become a national symbol of Canadian identity.

The battle of Vimy Ridge was a great military victory for Canada, but it came at a price. The four days of this battle were the costliest of the war for the country. There were more than 10,500 casualties, nearly 8,000 of these falling on the first day of the assault, April 9. The Yukoners engaged in this battle survived relatively unscathed, with Herbert Lawless, a former Mountie who had patrolled the creeks of the Klondike a decade earlier, being the only mortality of the campaign.

The highly mobile Yukon Battery continued follow-up actions as ordered, for the next two weeks, until they were withdrawn from combat and replaced by the Eaton Battery on April 26.

The contribution of the Yukon Battery during this highly successful campaign was to provide supporting barrage fire behind the line; the few casualties were the result of enemy artillery fire. This was not the battle line combat portrayed in film and literature; this was the integrated support fire that pinned down the enemy and saved the lives of their comrades at the sharp end.

The Yukon Battery was called into action again during the successful assault on the village of Fresnoy on May 3. On May 2, the battery was in position, with its carefully calculated barrage tables and operational orders in hand. These orders dictated the inclination of the machine guns, as well as the duration and the rate of fire. Their barrage would drench the area in front of the advancing Canadian infantry with protective cover, forcing the Germans to remain under shelter and allowing the Canucks to close in on the enemy without enduring deadly defensive fire.

At 3:45 the following morning, the attack began, with the Yukon Battery laying down a curtain of heavy protective fire ahead of the advancing infantry. Private Reginald Gilbert was killed early in the battle, when a piece of shrapnel struck him in the back of the neck. He was given first aid immediately, and taken to a dressing station, but succumbed almost at once without regaining consciousness.[205] William Black witnessed the injury: "He died a hero's death," reported Black, "actually firing when hit."[206] Black related that he, personally, was lucky: a piece of a shell splinter tore a hole in the shoulder of his coat and his gas mask, but he came out of it without a scratch.

The battery was not so fortunate a few days later. In an operation on May 8, nine members, including Private Russell McCollom, were wounded. McCollom survived the war, only to die, while still in service, of pneumonia in early January 1919. The battery then fell into a dreary routine that continued for months: drill, route marches, instruction, and practice, practice, practice. The men could disassemble a machine gun blindfolded—and then put it back together again. June rolled into July.

On July 16, the battery took a position on the line and for the next two weeks provided supporting night fire near Cite St. Pierre.[207] Several men were wounded by shellfire, shrapnel and gas, but no one was killed, while they laid down nearly half a million rounds of covering fire. Their role was defined by numbers, and each day the deadly toll of bullets mounted.

Their fire support continued into August, culminating in barrage support for a raid by the 4th Canadian Division on the afternoon of August 9, and withdrawal from the line two days later. In summing up this operation, Captain Meurling reported that more than a million rounds of machine gun fire had been thrown at the enemy. For the next week, the Yukon Battery was assigned anti-aircraft and brigade duty before being sent back into the line near Loos, Belgium. Similar duty continued through September and into October, when the Boyle unit was moved to Flanders. Their objective: to help capture the now decimated village of Passchendaele.

DEATH AND GLORY AT PASSCHENDAELE

THE LOSS OF life in the sodden wasteland that Flanders, in northwestern Belgium, had become was too great an investment to simply abandon it. Over the course of the war, this region, surrounding Ypres, was hotly and repeatedly contested. By the middle of October, the third battle of Ypres had dragged on for three and a half months at great loss on both sides. The Allies had suffered 160,000 casualties and another 40,000 missing. Neither the Australians nor the New Zealand regiments had been able to dislodge the enemy from Passchendaele Ridge. When British commander General Sir Douglas Haig asked Canadian general Sir Arthur Currie to take the village of Passchendaele, atop that ridge, Currie predicted that it would cost 16,000 men.

Around the city of Ypres lay a zone 10 kilometres wide of water-filled craters and bloated, rotting corpses. "Passchendaele Ridge dominated the Allied Front," writes historian Tim Cook,

with spurs and heights that channelled attacking soldiers into killing grounds and provided the enemy with sweeping fields of fire . . .

A fit man could probably have run up the ridge in ten minutes; through the glutinous mud, barbed wire, and enemy fire, it would take the Canadian Corps nearly three weeks and every step cost a few lives... The eviscerated dead and desiccated horse corpses jutting from shell craters or pushed off the few dry roads provided clear evidence of the terrible battles that had been fought over this godforsaken land.[208]

Passchendaele was the bloodiest engagement for the Yukon during the entire war. In a period of three weeks, eleven brave souls were taken, nine in one day, seven of whom were from the same unit. But great acts of bravery were also performed by Yukon volunteers.[209]

The strategy to taking Passchendaele was to approach the village site along the two flanking ridges, the Third (left) and Fourth (right) divisions would advance on four successive dates in set-piece assaults. The first advance on October 26 was successful in reaching higher, drier ground, but at the loss of nearly 2,800 men. One of these was Yukoner Fred Wyatt, with the Seaforth Highlanders.

The second assault began at 5:50 a.m. on October 30, when 420 guns opened fire at the same time. The Seaforth Highlanders were part of the assault on the right flank. They were covered by a near-perfect barrage, making their task much easier. Their rapid advance caught the Germans by surprise. General Haig later described this as "a feat of arms which would go down in the annals of British History as one of the great achievements of a single unit."[210]

The Highlanders suffered 270 casualties in their attack, 50 of them killed in action. Among the dead were Frank Desales and George Cassidy. Desales was an Irishman who had been mining in the area of Atlin, British Columbia, before signing up in Victoria in June the previous year. Cassidy was a miner who had enlisted in Victoria three days after Desales.

Meanwhile, on the other flank, three battalions, the 5th Canadian Mounted Rifles, the 49th Battalion and the Princess Patricia's Canadian Light Infantry (PPCLI), advanced toward the German positions. Seven Yukoners with the PPCLI died that day. Among them was Peter Allan, a forty-five-year-old Klondike miner from Dawson, who was last seen around six o'clock in the morning, just as his company jumped off in the attack. George Otis, a Dawson volunteer, was, like Allan, originally from Quebec, and also a miner. Short and stocky, with dark hair and hazel eyes, Francois "Frank" Pregent was a miner at Granville on Dominion Creek. Joseph Tilton's remains were never found after the battle. Before the war, he had been a teamster living at Moosehide. All four men, in their mid-forties, enlisted with the Black contingent but found themselves transferred to another infantry unit. As a result, they reached the Western Front in time to die for their country at Passchendaele.

More fortunate than his comrades was "Grizzly Bear" Jim Christie. Despite being wounded in April 1916, and again in July the following year, Christie had had a remarkable rise through the ranks. As a corporal at the second battle of Ypres in May 1915, he received the Distinguished Conduct Medal.[211] A few weeks before the advance on Passchendaele, Christie, now a sergeant, led a small raiding party into No Man's Land, where they encountered a large German patrol. Quick thinking and action on his part caught the enemy off guard, and allowed time for him and his small party to withdraw. Again remaining behind to provide covering fire, he enabled the entire patrol to return to the Canadian line without casualty.[212]

In the October 30 battle, their objective lay along the north side of a bog, protected by several pillboxes—fortified concrete guard posts from which heavy machine gun fire could be laid down with immunity from Allied rifle and artillery fire. With communication lines broken, and under heavy fire, Lieutenant Christie passed through the enemy barrage several times to deliver vital information to the command. His party took brutally heavy losses, until they reached a seemingly unassailable pillbox, with machine guns firing in every direction.

Most of the officers had been wounded or killed. So Christie and two other Patricias—twenty-six-year-old American-born sergeant George Henry Mullin, and Lieutenant Hugh McKenzie, of the 7th Canadian Machine Gun Company—took the initiative. As historian Jeffrey Williams described it:

There was little time to take the pill-box. At the rate casualties were occurring, there would soon be no one left to assault it. Christie ran and crawled forward on the left to a position where he could bring his deadly fire to bear on the pill-box and the sniper posts around it. McKenzie turned over the command of his machine guns to an NCO and took over the command of his old Regiment. After a quick reconnaissance, he dashed from shell hole to shell hole to organize the assault. As his small party rushed up the slope, machine guns in the pill-box concentrated their fire upon them and McKenzie was killed. Meanwhile, Sgt. Mullin crawled up the slope and took the pill-box single-handed. He rushed a sniper's post in front and destroyed the garrison with bombs. Then, crawling onto the top of the pill-box, he shot the two machine gunners with his revolver. Mullin then rushed to another entrance and compelled the garrison of ten to surrender. His clothes had been riddled by bullets, but miraculously he was not wounded.[213]

Both McKenzie (posthumously) and Mullin received the Victoria Cross for their valour. For his bravery under intense conditions, Christie received the Military Cross. The citation read: "For conspicuous gallantry and devotion to duty during an attack. He made three separate journeys through an intense artillery and machine gun barrage, bringing back valuable information. He also took part in hard fighting round the enemy strong points, and by his initiative and resources accounted for several of the enemy. His courageous conduct was an inspiration to all, and assisted materially in the success of the operation."[214]

While Christie, Mullin and McKenzie were taking out the pillbox, another Yukoner, farther to their left flank, with the 5th Canadian Mounted Rifles, was finding himself and his men in serious trouble. George Randolph Pearkes, who was born in Watford, England, came to Canada in 1906. He had joined the Royal Northwest Mounted Police before the war and had been stationed in Whitehorse and Carcross. The summer that war was declared, Pearkes was posted to the summit of the White Pass, the rail access to the Yukon from the Alaskan coast (and the only means of getting to the Yukon at that time), where he assisted the immigration officer stationed there. Pearkes was able to enlist in Victoria in March 1915 as a private, and quickly rose through the ranks.

On the morning of the attack, Major Pearkes, already wounded twice before in previous actions, led his men along the extreme left perimeter of the Canadian attack. Ahead of them lay a number of heavily armed strongpoints known as Source Farm, Vapour Farm, Vanity House and Vine Cottages. These points held a commanding view of the Canadian operation and had to be taken if the Canadians were to succeed. Early on, Pearkes received a shrapnel wound to his thigh but continued his advance. As they approached their objectives, he took some men and pushed toward Vapour Farm, which they took at bayonet point. By 7:45, he was able to report that they had successfully taken Source Farm, Vapour Farm and Vanity House, with fifty men from "C" and "D" Companies.

Within an hour, a plea was received to send reinforcements to help Pearkes's position, and a platoon from the 2nd Canadian Mounted Rifles "B" Company was dispatched. They encountered heavy enemy fire while exposed on low swampy ground that was continually swept by machine gun fire. Only a handful of men from the reinforcements made it through. By 11:00 a.m., the situation had worsened for the trapped infantrymen. They still held Vapour and Source Farms, but the enemy had taken back Vanity House. They were able to beat back a strong German counterattack and had dug in to defend their positions. Sixty men from the 2nd Canadian Mounted Rifles joined them by 1:00 p.m., but they were exposed to enemy fire on both flanks. They were now running low on small arms ammunition.

As 3:00 approached, Pearkes's situation was getting worse. The Germans were in force at the top of the ridge only 200 metres away, and he had only twenty-seven men remaining. Source Farm was being held by six men. They were so low on ammunition that they were exposing themselves to hostile fire to retrieve the ammunition, grenades and Lewis (machine) gun pans from their dead comrades. With daylight fading, Pearkes and his few men were holding on with the thinnest of lines. They had formed a defensive flank to the left of Source Farm, spread across to their right to a small copse of trees named Woodland Plantation. They had fended off another German counterattack, and suffered more casualties, but ten more men from "A" Company of the 2nd Canadian Mounted Rifles were able to get through to bolster their thin defensive position. Pearkes was hoping for reinforcements after dark and was desperately short of ammunition, though a supply of ammunition was sent forward at dusk. "Men of 5th CMR Bn all in," he reported. "Do not think I can hold out until morning."[215]

Shortly after midnight, the wounded Pearkes and the exhausted survivors of his company were relieved by a company from the 1st Canadian Mounted Rifles, and they returned to headquarters to the rear of their front line. In summarizing their effort in his report on the offensive, Lieutenant Colonel Draper, the commanding officer of the 5th Canadian Mounted Rifles, stated: "The boldness, initiative and skill displayed by Major G.R. Pearkes cannot be too highly commended. It was entirely due to his leadership that the operation of this Battalion was so successful. For a considerable time he held Vapour and Source Farms with a mere handful of men, beating off the first German counter attack without any other assistance. His appreciation of the situation was most accurate and his reports at all times were clear, concise and invaluable."[216]

If they had not taken and held this position during the bloody battle, it is likely that the entire Canadian attack would have failed. For his leadership in this battle, Pearkes was decorated with the Victoria Cross. During the war, Pearkes was wounded five times. He seemed invincible. One soldier later remarked, "I would have followed him through Hell if I had to."[217]

The Yukon Battery was not left out of the action entirely. They were involved in an operation the morning of November 9. Their guns were set and laid on barrage targets; at zero hour, and over the next hour, they fired twenty-four thousand rounds into the enemy position, which responded with a continuing artillery barrage for several hours. A little after 11:00 a.m., Lieutenant William Black and five other men were buried alive in their trench by the backlash of a shell landing nearby. All of these men were eventually dug out of their temporary graves and whisked off to a dressing

George Randolph Pearkes was a Mounted Policeman in the Whitehorse division before he enlisted. Pearkes was awarded the Victoria Cross at the Battle of Passchendaele.

CANADA. DEPT. OF NATIONAL DEFENCE/LIBRARY AND ARCHIVES CANADA PA-002364

station for treatment. Lieutenant Black was sent to England for treatment and never returned to front line action during the remainder of the war. The operation continued for two days, until the Yukon Battery was withdrawn from their position and returned to camp.

On November 26, Lieutenant Black's replacement arrived at the Yukon Battery. His name: Lieutenant Lyman Black. Lyman Black was the nephew of William Black; he was only eighteen years old.

By the end of the Passchendaele campaign, the Canadians had successfully taken the rubble that was once the small Belgian village. During the operation of November 9 and 10, the Germans laid down a heavy artillery barrage, causing one thousand Canadian casualties. But they were overwhelmed by the Canadian barrage. During the Passchendaele campaign, Canadian forces unleashed nearly a million and a half shells on their enemy. Ultimately, careful planning and flexible tactics won the day. Working in conjunction with British, Australian and New Zealand units, the Allied forces dealt the Germans a heavy blow.

The final tally of Canadian casualties was almost exactly the number predicted by General Currie: 16,404 for the Canadian Corps, most of which were sustained during the heavy fighting between October 26 and November 10. The ratio of dead to wounded was much higher during this battle because so many wounded men had drowned in the water-filled craters of No Man's Land.[218] The German and Allied forces suffered nearly a half million casualties between them, and for what? A few kilometres of devastated moonscape on which no living thing dared venture. The campaign was to become symbolic of the callous waste of human life, in the face of some of the worst battlefield conditions ever encountered.

THE ADVENTURES OF JOE BOYLE

BACK IN DAWSON City during the summer of 1916, while the flames of patriotism were being fanned by George Black's enlistment campaign, Joe Boyle was growing increasingly restless. In Dawson City he was known as a mover and shaker. He was the master of the grand gesture, who sponsored an annual picnic for the children of Dawson, while troubleshooting the operations of a big dredging company. When war was declared, he became the most enthusiastic of patriots. When asked for money, he gave large amounts, and he could be an inspirational speaker at wartime rallies, not to mention having financed the fifty volunteers who went to France and became the Yukon Battery.

Yet none of this seemed to be enough for Boyle, who was always looking for the next grand adventure. The Klondike Valley could no longer contain his ambitions; there were bigger events stirring, and he wanted to be part of them. On July 6, 1916, he sponsored his annual children's picnic at Swede Creek, a few kilometres upriver from Dawson. Then he made arrangements to travel to London on business. Leaving his wife behind in Dawson City, and his son Joe Jr. in charge of his company, he left for Whitehorse on July 17 on the steamer *Dawson*. "I am going to London on business in connection with the Canadian Klondyke and on several other matters," he told the *Dawson Daily News* prior to his departure. "I will consult in connection with a large dredge of the seventeen-foot bucket type, similar to our largest, for the Lenisky Company of London, for use on the Lena River."[219] Boyle never saw his wife again, and wrote only one letter to her after leaving the Klondike.

It is surprising that Boyle left his son in charge of the company in his absence. Joe Jr., who had been born in the United States, took a neutral position over the war raging around the globe. This did not sit well with his patriotic father, and their relationship was forever strained by their differing views of the war. But it may not have mattered to Boyle. The company he had established and run successfully for more than a decade had lost its lustre for him. Costs were escalating because of the war, but the price of gold remained constant. The daily operations of a dredge company in the Klondike were old hat for a man used to challenge and adventure. A persistent urge was stirring in his blood as the *Dawson* steamed out of sight around a bend in the Yukon River. As he stood at the railing, staring at the familiar scar on the hill behind Dawson City, he may have already known that after two decades in the Klondike, it was the last time that he would ever see the gold rush town that had meant so much to him. Joe Boyle was turning over a new leaf.

Within a few weeks, Boyle was in London, meeting with Canadian minister of militia Sam Hughes, who appointed him to the honorary rank of lieutenant colonel in the militia. The announcement was posted in the *Canada Gazette* in September 1916.[220] Because of his age, Boyle was excluded from active military service. From his experiences in London grew a "withering contempt for military officialdom and the average brass hat."[221] During the next ten months, Boyle attended to business and extended his circle of social acquaintances. Despite befriending Walter Long, secretary of state, he could not exert enough influence to secure an appointment to a field placement. He took advantage of his honorary commission to have uniforms tailor-made in the pattern worn by Canadian officers. With an added flair, he used Klondike gold to fashion general service badges and had the name Yukon embroidered into the flashes at his sleeve-tops. He rented quarters in London's prestigious Savoy Hotel and established a reputation as a man whose energy and action got things done. Among his efforts, he successfully lobbied Canadian authorities to have the Yukon Infantry Company converted into a machine gun unit.

Circumstances developed rapidly for Joe Boyle after the American Congress voted to enter the war on April 6, 1917. He attached himself to the American Committee of Engineers (ACE), a group of seventy scientists and engineers (including future American president Herbert Hoover), and was sent to Russia on the recommendation of US ambassador to Britain, Walter Hines Page. His assignment: assist the Russian railways immediately behind the front lines (inefficient supply of food and materiel were hampering the Russian war effort). Travelling through neutral Sweden and Norway, he arrived in Russia in July 1917 and immediately began introducing himself to Russian Army officials.

Boyle arrived in Russia at a pivotal moment in history. The nation was in turmoil. Torn apart by three years of war with Germany and the Austro-Hungarian Empire, the Russian Army was in a state of mutiny. Czar Nicholas II abdicated, and his autocratic government was replaced in March 1917 by a shaky provisional government that consisted of a loose coalition between the Russian parliament and a network of socialist Soviets. Conflict, strife and civil war would continue for a period of five years before the Bolsheviks would finally gain control and create the Union of Soviet Socialist Republics in 1922.

By July, Boyle was inspecting the rail system in southwest Russia. His assessment of the situation was grim. The Russian Army's chief transport officer was "singularly uninformative and downright stupid."[222] His role, the officer said, was to give orders, not worry about how well they were carried out. Things got worse. None of the officers in the railway battalions showed any spark of initiative. They followed orders but went no further. The leaders were dispirited and the soldiers lazy and insolent—and on the verge of revolt, with things made worse by Bolshevik and German agitators who were stirring the pot of discontent behind the scenes.

The infrastructure was dysfunctional, lacking adequate equipment and leadership. Everywhere he stopped, Boyle saw "long-standing shortage of tools, track, supply wagons and almost everything required to make a train system function."[223] Communication was inadequate, and of nine hundred railcars in one unit's inventory, only seventy could be counted on for service. The average locomotive was only covering 85 kilometres of track per day.

His presence caused some consternation to British and Canadian diplomatic officials, who could not fully explain what Boyle's mission was in this country. Boyle was direct and action-oriented, and paid little heed to the delicate diplomatic manoeuvrings of nations; things were happening too fast for diplomatic processes to have any effect.

One thing was clear: Boyle was loyal to the British (thus Canadian) cause. He acted to keep Russia in the war, thereby dividing the German and Austro-Hungarian forces between two fronts. He was also eager to represent British interests in Russia, where he saw them being undermined by American capitalists. American interests were "endeavouring to procure control of the entire railway systems of the country for private American interests; at the same time getting concessions and privileges in this country."[224] He identified US Steel, J.P. Morgan and the Guggenheims, among others, as trying to corner certain markets in Russia. Through the National City Bank of Petrograd, they were buying up Russian wheat crops with advance payments to peasants. US Steel was negotiating post-war contracts to sell steel to Russia. Despite this, Boyle eventually came to the conclusion that Bolshevism posed an even greater threat than the Germans and campaigned against that movement.

Boyle could not speak Russian. During his frenzied activity moving back and forth through Russia, haggling with Russian officials, then with

Colonel Joe Boyle, Canadian Militia. YUKON ARCHIVES GEORGE BLACK FONDS 81/107 PT.1
FOLDER 1 #05

Bolshevik commissars, he relied on a small platoon of faithful interpreters
to help him communicate. He had no official status in either Canadian or
British circles and was regularly vilified by them one moment, and tolerated
grudgingly the next because he had gained the confidence of the Russians
and got things done. He was impatient with bureaucracy, and on many
occasions, his intolerance of incompetence created enemies.

Boyle went to Mogilev, the Russian Army headquarters on the central
front, where he gathered information on the confusion and disorder of the
Russian train system. Things became even more difficult for him when

he arrived in the Galician city of Tarnapol at the wrong time. In late June 1917, the Russian Army embarked on an offensive on the Eastern Front that quickly bogged down. The Germans counterattacked and were moving against the city of Tarnapol. Under the withering artillery fire of the German bombardment, the Russians fell back in a retreat that bordered on panic. In the confusion and disarray as the Russians retreated before the German push, Russian headquarters staff fled, leaving no one in charge. Boyle seconded two Russian lieutenants into his command, and, in the absence of official authority, he was able to establish a semblance of order and set up a Russian defensive line around Tarnapol for four days, allowing seven Russian divisions to pass through and establish a new defensive line farther to the east. Boyle and his entourage left Tarnapol on July 23, the day before the city fell to the Germans. Two weeks later, on August 8, Boyle was awarded the Order of Saint Stanislaus. His actions at Tarnapol, and the report he prepared regarding the Russian train system, impressed civil and military authorities, who were reaching for any lifeboat amid rampant civil unrest and a collapsing military. British authorities, perplexed by the behaviour and actions of this Canadian interloper, took a noncommittal wait-and-see attitude.

Boyle had had some time to digest what he had learned and prepare a report. "With Russia... entirely disorganized," he wrote, "with all known rules of procedure abolished, it is difficult to suggest a remedy, and impossible to predict the results of any attempt at restoring order."[225] Nevertheless, he reported later, his transportation changes were accepted by the Russians and would free 300,000 horses from the front, provide more heavy locomotives and railcars, improve repair services and make available 300,000 men for more important work.

On July 28, he was a delegate at a major transportation conference at Stavka (the term given to the location of the field headquarters of the Russian Army). The following day, he met General Tickminev. His obligations to Russia were to end with the completion of his report. Would he, asked General Tickminev, consider staying in Russia beyond this commitment? Boyle accepted and was assigned to investigate the transportation system at the border with Romania, where more than 1 million troops were bottled up. Under the authorization of ways and communications minister Nikolai Nekrasov, Boyle was outfitted with his own railway car, interpreter and servants. Travelling via Kiev and Odessa, he arrived at Jassy, Romania, where he met British engineer and officer General Raymond de Candolle. De Candolle oversaw a chaotic rail system that wasn't moving. Train schedules were ignored, repair shops were inefficient and trains with vital wartime supplies and cars containing wounded soldiers stood idle for days. In short, there was a lack of coordination.

Boyle accused de Candolle of incompetence; de Candolle, in response, reported back to his old-boy network about this troublesome newcomer. Nevertheless, Boyle imposed a new set of traffic priorities, with food as the first priority, the movement of the wounded as second and the movement of military stores and equipment, third. He gave orders, and the Russians and Romanians, grateful for some direction and overawed by Boyle's presence, sprang into action. De Candolle never forgave him for this intrusion into his area of authority.

Boyle was working directly with the Russian ministry of ways and communications without the benefit of Foreign Office intervention. He was now in virtual control of the military railways from Petrograd to Odessa. The British War Office, alarmed by Boyle's intrusion into what they saw as their jurisdiction, considered placing Boyle under the command of General de Candolle, but Canada fended off this proposal by referring them to Sam Hughes, the minister of militia. Preferring not to deal with Hughes, who was becoming more of a loose cannon as the war progressed, the War Office chose not to follow this avenue of communication.

Boyle was taken by the perilous situation in Romania. He made pleas for food, clothing and other humanitarian supplies. The million Russian soldiers stationed in Romania were keeping the Germans in check, but the pressing need for food was causing unrest among the troops. Boyle tried desperately to obtain important supplies, writing letters and filing reports, but diplomatic rivalry, and the ineptitude of the Russian provisional government, slowed the flow of essential supplies from Russia's allies.

One night in October, in the dreary approach of winter, Boyle met George A. Hill, a British army officer and agent working for the British

Secret Service. Hill had been born in Russia, the son of a British business-man, and was fluent in Russian. Both were staying at the Bristol Hotel in Mogilev, a small provincial town on the Dnieper River. Hill had just fought off two German agents in the darkened streets using a blade hidden within his cane and was examining the bloodstained blade on the stairs as he climbed toward his room. He bumped into Boyle, a man whose demeanour immediately captured Hill's attention:

> He was a born fighter, a great talker and blessed with an exceptional amount of common sense. He was independent to a revolutionary extent. Etiquette and procedure meant nothing to him, especially if a job had to be done. He was in Russia to get on with the war, to harry the Germans and to help the Allies, and in so doing he cared not over whom he rode roughshod.
>
> Such was Colonel Boyle, a man whose equal I have encountered nei-ther before nor since, and to have enjoyed his friendship and to have worked under and with him will always remain one of the proudest memories of my life.[226]

As the end of October approached, turmoil in Russia was reaching its peak. The situation was made even worse by interference from German agent provocateurs, who were agitating among the soldiers, sailors and peasants' councils to have the Allied representatives either thrown out, or murdered. Hill and Boyle learned of a special meeting that was being held to determine their fate, so they decided to attend. Their arrival was unwel-come, and it did not appear as though they would be given the opportunity to speak before the vote was taken, but, said Hill:

> In the middle of all that turmoil of wrath and hatred, and without waiting for anyone's leave, Boyle stepped on to the stage. I followed. He gazed for a moment at the audience, and then spoke. His voice was clear and musical, his sentences short and crisp. It was a terrible moment. At first the crowd was taken by surprise. Then there was a move to rush

the stage. But it was too late. Boyle had got hold of his audience, while I translated sentence for sentence, though I do not mind confessing that I did not find it at all easy to keep my voice level, and my manner calm and undisturbed.

Boyle knew crowd psychology. He gripped the attention of his hearers. He began with stories about Canada. Then he switched into Russian history. The speech did not last more than fifteen minutes, and concluded with a stirring peroration in which he reminded his listeners that Russians never surrendered. They might retreat into Russia, as they did during Napoleon's invasion, but it was only to return to the attack with renewed ardour. "You are men," he concluded, "not sheep. I order you to act as men."

Thunders of applause followed. A soldier jumped up on the stage and shouted "Long live the Allies. Down with the Germans!" The ovation continued for some minutes.[227]

Boyle and Hill decided to join forces. By that time, the provisional government of Alexander Kerensky had been replaced by the Bolshevik regime. Although not sympathetic to the Bolshevik cause, the two men decided that throwing in their lot with the Bolsheviks was the best way to harry the Germans and the Austrians. They decided to go to Petrograd, the capital, to see what they could do at Bolshevik headquarters to further that cause. Perhaps they could do something to clear up the dreadful congestion in the railway centre known as the "Moscow Knot."

In Petrograd, they made their way through the chaos and confusion to the office of Comrade Joffe, the president of the Petrograd Military Revolutionary Committee. Boyle's reputation preceded him, and they obtained papers from Joffe that gave them the authority to move freely. Their goal would be to get food and supplies moving freely to the southwestern army, as well as to Petrograd.

When they arrived in Moscow some days later, armed with a fistful of permits and passes, they met in the offices of the Central Railway Board with Nikolay Muralov, a man who would later become the commander of the entire district. With his backing, Boyle rolled up his sleeves and exhorted the workers to throw their might into their efforts to untie the "Moscow Knot." Empty cars were pushed off the tracks, and although railway officials were aghast and railway owners appalled, Boyle got the job done in a mere forty-eight hours. Supplies were again moving in and out of Moscow, to Petrograd, and to armies along the Eastern Front. Boyle and Hill left Moscow on November 15 and returned to Stavka, where they were provided a new luxury bulletproof railcar, the first one having been destroyed on their way to Petrograd some days earlier.

Boyle was once again in demand by the Romanians. Because of his previous success in resolving rail supply problems, and because he had contacts among high Russian officials, he was commissioned by Romania to purchase supplies on behalf of the Romanian people. Despite the hijacking of seven carloads of foodstuffs, which were sent to the Russian Army on the Northern Front by a Bolshevik official, Boyle was able to arrange for the delivery of 155 boxcars of supplies for Romanian soldiers. This success was tempered by the fact that the Bolsheviks negotiated a temporary truce with the Germans in early December. With the withdrawal of Russia from the war, Romania, who had fought the German and Austro-Hungarian forces in conjunction with Russia, now found herself alone. On December 9, 1917, Romania signed the Armistice of Focșani, ending hostilities with Germany, Austria-Hungary, Bulgaria and the Ottoman Empire.

After several months of negotiation, the Bolsheviks signed a treaty with the Germans at Brest-Litovsk on March 3 the following spring that would end Russia's involvement in the war. This freed up resources for the internal civil war that was expected as a result of their takeover. It would also allow the Germans to transfer much-needed troops to the Western Front.

With the change of government in Russia, Romania now had concerns about its national treasury, which had earlier in the war been relocated to Moscow in the face of the imminent German advance. Now, it was possible that the Bolsheviks might not feel inclined to return the treasury to its rightful owners. The Romanians wanted these items brought back as quickly as possible. Could Boyle achieve this for them? He was the right man for the job, being held in high esteem in Moscow by the Bolsheviks for his success in untying the Moscow Knot. The treasures in question consisted of the crown jewels, currency, the national archives and £25 million in gold. Following the Central Powers' occupation of Bucharest in December 1916, the city of Jassy, in the principality of Moldavia, became the capital of a severely reduced Romania for the duration of the war. The route to Jassy was a formidable journey—1,300 kilometres through a nation in turmoil.[228] With civil war breaking out, it would be hard to tell through whose territory the train was passing.

Once the decision was made to move, the treasury was quickly removed from the Kremlin in thirty-one small and five large packages. The archives filled two boxcars and Red Cross supplies filled two more. The crown jewels were placed in covered wicker hampers to make them less conspicuous and placed aboard the special luxury car that had been assigned to Boyle weeks before.[229] Only the gold was left behind, and presumably rests in Russian vaults to this very day. The cars were then attached to an outbound train, and after overcoming bureaucratic obstacles, they steamed out of Moscow on December 17, 1917.[230] The journey would be long and dangerous.

Hill and Boyle had been warned at the last minute that an attempt would be made to ambush them 80 kilometres from Moscow, and sure enough, the train was halted at a small station and a shadowy figure attempted to disconnect Boyle's cars from the train. Boyle, who was lying in wait, personally knocked out the robber and reconnected the cars.[231]

Fearing that more attempts would be made to take the treasury, Boyle assigned the six able-bodied men among his party to an around-the-clock watch. When they reach Briansk, they found themselves caught in a firefight between two opposing factions. The bulletproof frame of Boyle's special car proved its value, and the engineer sped the train through the station—and the gunfire—without stopping. Forty passengers in other cars on the train were wounded in this exchange of gunfire.[232] The second night, the train stopped near a burning distillery while passengers and crew pilfered liquor from the conflagration before continuing.

The following afternoon, they were stopped by a detachment of Bolshevik cavalry. As the Bolsheviks began searching the train from the front to the rear, Boyle locked up the two Romanian bankers accompanying the

Colonel Joe Boyle, wearing medals he was awarded by Russia and Romania. YUKON
ARCHIVES OXFORD HISTORICAL SOCIETY 82/243#7

treasury and the cabins containing the crown jewels. When the search party
reached Boyle's special car, he explained through interpreters that it had
the extraterritorial rights of a diplomatic party but invited the commissar
in for food and drinks. After this distraction, they were able to continue

toward their destination. At a mere 15 kilometres an hour, the train clicked and clacked, swayed and lurched its way across the dark, stormy, snow-blanketed landscape.

Headed for Kiev, the train again stopped, this time for minor repairs. It was also desperately short of fuel. While the repairs were being made, Boyle's party mustered the other passengers on the train into a human chain through nearly 2 metres of snow. Firewood, which they found nearby neatly cut in appropriate lengths, was loaded onto the train. The train rumbled on and came under fire in one station from a unit of Ukrainian nationalists. When the Ukrainians learned that the train was not loaded with Bolsheviks, they stopped their assault and the train was allowed to continue.

When they reached Kiev, arrangements were made to transfer the special car to the next train to leave. This afforded Hill and Boyle the time to go to the Continental Hotel for a bath. Boyle was delayed during his return to the station when a bomb exploded near him, blowing him through a store window and knocking him out. When he came to, he purchased from the shopkeeper a fine turkey dressed and ready for cooking and took it with him, to the delight of the others in his party when he arrived back at the train. Hill was able to delay the train's departure until Boyle returned by appealing to the railway regulations that required a safety cord to run the entire length of the train.[233]

The procession slowly made its way toward Bessarabia, which was at that time in Romanian hands. Sixty-five kilometres short of the border, the train inexplicably came to a halt in Zhmerinka station in the dark, in a raging snowstorm, but no one appeared to meet them. The locomotive got under way again but soon stopped at another small station, where Boyle's cars were shunted into a siding and unhooked from the train. Bolshevik soldiers placed the entire Boyle party under arrest, but Boyle devised a plan to escape their custody. He brewed up a large samovar of tea and spiked it with vodka looted from the distillery. He then offered it to the soldiers, and they sang and drank together (Boyle was a teetotaller) until all were snoring in a drunken sleep. Meanwhile, the wind roared outside and whipped the snow crystals into a frenzy.[234]

According to a long-standing imperial order, a locomotive was kept fired up and manned around the clock at this station for no purpose known to the Boyle party. It was fortunate for them. With revolvers in hand, they convinced the trainmen on board to back the locomotive into position and hook it up to Boyle's special cargo, after which they quickly powered up and puffed out of the siding, expecting at any time to be fired upon by the Bolshevik artillery. But the Bolshevik soldiers slept through their escape, and the Boyle party continued on its way. Boyle and Hill should have cut the telegraph lines sooner than they did, however, because a few kilometres farther down the track, they saw a barricade across the rails. Fearing that the train might derail, the trainmen refused to speed up; at gunpoint, they were ordered to stoke the boiler while Boyle took over the controls and pushed up the speed of the tiny convoy careening wildly toward the barrier across the tracks. They hit it at full speed, shattering the barricade into splinters and barrelling through.[235]

From there to the Romanian border, they had no more difficulties, until they reached the boundary line, stopping where an outpost of Romanian soldiers had placed a huge earthen mound on the tracks. This was one barrier that the little convoy would not be able to knock aside. After identifying their mission to the trigger-happy troops, they commenced excavating the barrier together while Boyle notified Jassy of their arrival. So it was that on Christmas Day, 1917, Boyle signed over possession of the priceless shipment to two more Romanian treasury officials. In a few short days, Boyle, Hill and the small party of Russians and Romanians who accompanied them had lived through an adventure worthy of a Hollywood blockbuster. Boyle became an instant Romanian hero. A few days later, Hill was presented with the Order of the Star of Romania, and Boyle received the Grand Cross of the Crown of Romania.

1917–1918

CHANGES AT HOME

WHILE WAR WAS being waged in a conflict that spanned the globe, there was a different type of war taking place back in Canada. The stream of new volunteers was not keeping up with the senseless, enormous losses that the Allies were suffering in the trenches of France and Belgium. By April 1917, 424,526 Canadians had volunteered to serve in the Canadian Expeditionary Force, but the death toll was mounting and the numbers of wounded soldiers unsustainable. In April alone, 3,500 Canadians lost their lives and another 7,000 were wounded.[236]

If Canada was going to sustain its commitment to Britain to supply a steady stream of replacements, then drastic measures would have to be taken at home. Prime Minister Robert Borden's solution was highly controversial and led to one of the most bitterly fought elections in Canadian history. The issue was conscription, and it nearly tore the country apart. Conscription, or the arbitrary enlistment of new recruits, was highly unpopular, especially among the citizens of Quebec. Of course, many of those who would have supported conscription had already enlisted and were serving overseas.

The Military Service Act was passed on August 29, 1917. It made men between the ages of twenty and forty-five eligible for call-up for service until the end of the war. Call-ups began in January 1918. Of the roughly 400,000 men who registered, about 100,000 were actually drafted. Of those, only 24,132 served on the front lines in Europe. Although the number of conscript soldiers was small, had the war continued, they would have become an increasingly important part of Canada's war effort.

Before ending parliament and calling an election, Prime Minister Borden's government passed several other important pieces of legislation that were strategically designed to favour the conscription issue. One was the Military Voters Act, which conferred upon any British subject, male or female, who was actively serving in the armed forces, the right to vote. This included some two thousand military nurses, with several from the Yukon. These voters could assign their ballot to any riding in Canada in which they had previously resided. In addition, the act conferred upon the party that they voted for the right to allocate the votes as they saw fit.

The second law, the Wartime Elections Act, gave the vote to spouses, widows, mothers, sisters and daughters of any person alive or dead who was serving—or had served—in the Canadian forces. The act also disenfranchised conscientious objectors and individuals born in enemy countries who became naturalized British subjects after March 31, 1902.[237] Finally, the act assigned the responsibility of drawing up federal voters lists to federally appointed officials.

Together, all of these acts were intended to tip the scales in favour of the Borden government. The changes would have been well received by women in the Yukon, and the Yukon Women's Protective League in particular, who at that time were in the midst of petitioning the territorial and federal governments for the right to vote.

The election of December 17, 1917, tore traditional political alliances apart along conscription lines. Members of the Liberal Party not from Quebec crossed the floor to join the Conservatives, forming a coalition named the Unionist Party. The election was held just as George Hill and Joe Boyle were beginning their fateful journey by train across Russia with the crown jewels of Romania. When the dust settled, the outcome favoured Borden's Unionist Party by a substantial landslide, but the Yukon could not yet be counted, as a deferred election wasn't held until January 28, 1918. (Ever since the Yukon came into existence as a political entity in 1898, election of the Yukon's member of parliament had always been held after the rest of the country had voted.) Frederick Congdon, the Liberal, was facing off against

Dr. Alfred Thompson, the Conservative incumbent, with conscription as a central issue.

The campaign became nasty when Congdon attacked George Black for seeking promotion while still in England, and for continuing to receive his commissioner's salary while serving overseas.[238] Other enlisted men were receiving only their $1.10 per day. He further criticized Black for remaining in England while other brave Canadians were risking their lives on the front line. George's wife, Martha, came under attack for abusing the Yukon Patriotic Fund, which she administered, and for dispensing the funds along partisan lines.

Neither George nor Martha Black was in a position to put up a defence against such accusations because they were thousands of kilometres away. Dr. Alfred Thompson leapt into the debate, defending George Black by pointing out that although he was on salary while overseas, it was reduced by half to $3,000, and he no longer received the generous living allowance that came with the job. Furthermore, he added that George's brother, his nephew and his three stepsons (two with the United States) were seeing war-related duty. He further pointed out that it was not George Black but imperial command that determined when he would be sent into active duty on the Western Front.[239]

The Dawson newspaper also stepped in to defend the absent commissioner in an editorial, attacking those in the community who would malign the volunteers who were in England awaiting assignment to battle:

There are some people in Yukon today... that ... dare drag the names of some of these brave and self-sacrificing heroes into the depths of political mire and ... cast reflections on the character and intentions of these men with the colours. Subtle and insidious whisperings, about some of the loyal Yukon sons and intimations that they never enlisted to go to the front and do not intend to fight...

[E]ven the name of Commissioner-Captain George Black has been referred to by some adversely, and his good intentions and his ability impugned. To think that anyone would stoop so low as to make reference of this kind in political campaigns is almost unbelievable...

He gave up the highest and most lucrative position in Yukon, struggling against ill health to prepare himself as a soldier; succeeded in enlisting several hundred men; took them to England and with them has been trained until they comprise what experts now declare one of the most efficient bodies of machine-gun men in England...

Further let it be said to the credit of Captain Black that he has been a hard-working, clear-headed and energetic citizen aside from his war record. No commissioner measured up to him in point of experience and knowledge of detail of Yukon affairs, and, without question, the most able and generally satisfactory man who has occupied the chair... But whether he return or not, he and his loyal boys deserve and should be spoken of now by those who enjoy the luxury of home in no way but that which will inspire them with the conviction they have the love, admiration and esteem of those at home.[240]

The *News* also published letters from Yukoners overseas defending the reputation of and acknowledging the work of the Blacks. Andrew Hart, just recently returned from battle, wrote in support of Black, pointing out that he was popular with his men, and that he was not the one who would make the decision as to when they would ship out to France.[241] His letter, unlike countless others from Yukoners serving overseas, was placed on the editorial page.

Another letter in the *Dawson Daily News* not long after the election accused Martha Black of only providing aid to those men in the Yukon Company, George Black's contingent, but this was rebutted by a response from Joe Newman, who served with Black. "It is not easy to locate all Yukoners because they are scattered all over, unless you are notified about them," he stated. "Since Mrs. Black came to England she has done very good work in lecturing on behalf of the Red Cross and has raised hundreds of pounds, and Mrs. Black has found time to visit us often."[242] Mrs. Black herself responded in the *Dawson Daily News* to accusations that she discriminated against John McFarlane and Felix Boutin, to which she responded that she had helped Boutin on a number of occasions, and admitted that she had not sent a parcel to John McFarlane, but only because she had no address for him. She further responded to accusations of misuse of the Yukon Comfort Fund by providing a meticulous accounting of how the money was spent, and having the bank manager co-sign on all expenditures. This was supported by a number of letters of thanks sent to the *Dawson Daily News* by various Yukon men serving overseas.[243]

When the final ballots from the Yukon riding were tallied, Frederick Congdon received more votes in the territory, but when the overseas votes were factored in, Dr. Thompson won by a margin of 157 votes.[244] Congdon quickly complained about the election outcome, particularly regarding the handling of the overseas votes, which were decisive in his defeat. Among his accusations were that only literature favourable to Dr. Thompson, his opponent, was distributed to the men, and that they were not informed of his own position regarding the Unionist Party. He further stated that the soldiers were allowed to vote before the nomination period had expired, and that they could only vote for "government" or "opposition," without a named candidate. He threatened to have the vote thrown out as illegal.[245]

Dr. Thompson jumped into the fray in his own defence by accusing Congdon of attempting to deny the men overseas the right to vote. As for dodgy election practices, Congdon only had to look in the mirror on that point. (In 1902, Congdon had been elected member of parliament in a highly partisan campaign that included ballot box stuffing and use of ineligible voters![246]) The protest raised by Congdon went to the clerk of the crown in chancery, who ruled that the only redress would be through the election courts.[247] The protest of the vote was taken into consideration. On May 13, at the opening of the day's sitting in parliament, Hugh Guthrie, the Solicitor General, submitted a report on privileges and election, recommending that "the Yukon election case be referred either to the supreme court, or to a court consisting of two judges of the Ontario Supreme Court."[248] After much sparring between Sir Wilfrid Laurier and Prime Minister Borden, the report was left without a recommendation, which implied a lengthy debate with the possibility of the report being sent back to committee. After debate and three votes, the report from the committee was adopted on May 22. It authorized the chief returning officer to count the soldiers' votes and to declare a winner. Motions by the opposition to declare the seat vacant, or to refer the case to the Supreme Court of Canada, were voted down. A few hours later, the returning officer declared Dr. Thompson the winner of the election.

Meanwhile, the ladies of Dawson City continued their determined efforts to raise money for the patriotic funds. One of the most noteworthy of these was a large quilt to be raffled off, assembled by the ladies of the Martha Munger Black chapter of the IODE. Each square on it had the autographs in needlework of men from the volunteer contingents, mostly from George Black's Yukon Company. The quilt squares were assembled with the autographs of Captain and Mrs. Black, as well as those of the women in Red Cross or nursing work overseas, placed in the centre, surrounded by the squares autographed by the men. At a patriotic fundraising bonspiel, the winner was drawn from the thousand tickets sold. The lucky number, drawn at the DAAA building by little Mary Ross, daughter of Reverend and Mrs. Arthur Ross, was number 173, which was purchased, fittingly, by Mrs. Black. Arrangements were made to have it shipped to her immediately.[249] That quilt survives today and is in the care of the MacBride Museum in Whitehorse. At the end of the year, the cumulative total of funds raised in the Yukon for patriotic purposes was determined to be well in excess of $150,000.[250]

While the local community groups were active in raising money for patriotic causes, the government of Canada had the more onerous task of raising money to feed the war machinery. A Victory Bond drive in 1917 was successful in raising $420 million, and a second drive was aiming to raise another $300 million in 1918. Large full-page advertisements encouraged citizens to purchase these bonds, which would yield 5.5 percent over five or fifteen years, depending upon the series of bond purchased.[251] Similar drives for Liberty Bonds, it should be noted, were being well promoted and advertised in newspapers in neighbouring Alaska. Alaskans, like the people of the Yukon, contributed far more per person than the US national average for the patriotic cause.[252] By the end of the war, Yukoners had donated money, knitted socks, written letters and given of themselves until it hurt. As the war continued, how long would it be before they were also in tatters?

The federal government was feeling the financial pinch as the war continued, and the costs rose at an alarming rate. Other measures were taken to reduce government spending, and decisions regarding the Yukon would have repercussions that would last long after the sound of canon fire had died away. At the urgings of former comptroller John T. Lithgow, Prime Minister Borden, and more specifically Arthur Meighan, minister of the interior, examined the expenditures in the territory. The decision was made to cut the federal payroll from twenty-two positions to nine. The total budget to the territory was to be reduced from $286,436 to $185,000.

Figures tabled in the House of Commons showed that the total revenues for the Yukon were $505,643, while the federal expenditures amounted to nearly double that: $956,664.[253] More alarming was the decline in gold production, by nearly half since 1912. Clearly, the Yukon was a costly fixture during wartime austerity. Included among the positions eliminated by the federal cuts was that of commissioner. George Black received a telegram from Yukon's member of parliament, Dr. Thompson, advising him that although his job was abolished, he would retain his salary of $3,000 per year, for the time being.[254]

More alarming perhaps than the cuts was an amendment to the Yukon Act on May 24, 1918, that gave the Governor-in-Council the authority to abolish the elected territorial council and to substitute an appointed council of two or more members. Although that authority was never exercised, the council was reduced from ten members to three, and the indemnity for councillors reduced from $500 to $400.[255]

The community responded quickly. A group of one hundred Dawson people met and sent a telegram to the prime minister. Mining was their mainstay, they asserted, and roads were essential to mining. The acting manager of the Yukon Gold Company stated that the big companies might pull out of the Yukon if the roads weren't maintained. They had more schoolchildren than ever before, and more aging miners to care for. Production of minerals had declined as a result of men being siphoned off for the war. Yet their loyalty could not be questioned, and they expressed shock that the government would hold back the support vital to the very existence of the territory. Despite the protests, Ottawa stood firm, and the Yukon was decimated. For the men returning after the war, the Yukon would be a far different place from the one that they had left.

The first selective Yukon draft in Skagway en route to Victoria, summer of 1918. YUKON
ARCHIVES WADDINGTON FONDS 82/331#25

By the middle of May 1918, the first batch of military conscripts was
ready to leave for the front. Between 100 and 150 were selected to be part of
the first Yukon draft contingent to head for Victoria. They were the youngest contingent that had thus far signed up, and many of them, having been
born or educated in Dawson, had never been Outside before. According to
the *Dawson Daily News*:

> With the men who are to go within the next month or so, Yukon will be
> stripped practically of her young men. No part of the Empire has given
> up more completely of her splendid men than Yukon. With the hundreds
> now over there and the many more going, the prospecting and other
> industries of this region will feel it materially. But Yukon is not com-
> plaining. She is standing staunchly by the Allied cause through thick
> and thin . . . Yukon's percentage of population in the war exceeds that of
> many other localities. Such being the case, the Dominion should not be
> forgetful of this region—the Empire's farthest North, and take pride in
> the encouragement of the spirit that dominates the people of the Land
> of the Midnight Sun.[256]

The *News* reminded those who remained behind that the need to supply socks and other comforts would be even greater. While the conscripts remained in the Yukon, said the *News*, make their time as pleasant as possible so that they will be inspired for the job that lies before them in Europe.

On the evening of June 20, the first contingent of ninety-one draftees left Dawson City aboard the steamer *Selkirk*. Aged twenty-one to thirty-five years, these men were a significant cross-section of Dawson society. The majority were listed as miners and dredgemen, but there were teamsters, blacksmiths, cooks, clerks and trappers. There were two electrical linemen, a steam engineer, a farmer, a farrier and a jeweller. One of them, Joseph Dupont, would die of influenza before ever leaving Canada. Many conscripts had reached England by the beginning of September, and were part of the twenty-five thousand or more who saw active duty on the front before war's end. Among them were five Japanese conscripts: Kazue Matsumoto, Frank Morishige, Frank Murata, Yoshitada Murata and Daiken Nagao. Morishige later sent a letter back to Dawson while he was in hospital in England. "I think Mrs. Black is doing great work among our Yukon men who are suffering in the trenches or sick in the hospitals," he reported.[257]

Now that America was in the war, they too were conscripting men into service. Americans in the Yukon were alerted to the necessity of registering for the draft. As the summer turned to autumn, the river steamers continued to come and go, forcing hasty goodbyes at dockside and busy work in warehouses along the river. In the midst of it all, a US government vessel, the *General Jeff C. Davis*, arrived in Whitehorse from Fort Gibbon, Alaska, with eighty American recruits drawn from the lower reaches of the Yukon River valley and destined for the battlefields of Europe. They were draftees, fine husky young lads, from the Tanana Valley and other points from Eagle to St. Michael. Because of imminent freeze-up, they were the last contingent Uncle Sam was sending out through the Yukon that year.

Unfamiliar with the upper Yukon River, the crew of the *Davis* took nineteen days to complete the eleven-day trip to Whitehorse. There, the *General Jeff C. Davis* was pulled up on the ways for the winter.[258] Upon their arrival and short stay in Dawson, the draftees were treated royally. Local citizens with automobiles took the recruits, who had been stuck aboard the *Davis* for days, on sight-seeing trips through town.[259] From Whitehorse, the American draftees travelled to Skagway by train, and then by coastal ferry to Seattle.

LETTERS HOME

TO REMEMBER THE boys serving overseas, the *Dawson Daily News* began a pictorial display in the front window of the *News* office on Third Avenue. The photos, sent back from Europe, depicted the men in uniform. As the number of pictures grew, new ones were added to the display, while others were removed, thus keeping the array in the wartime gallery fresh. Included were photos of groups of men, like one of Joe Boyle's Yukon Machine Gun Battery before shipping out for France, and individuals like Harry McLennan, the son of the former mayor of Dawson; Major L.G. Bennet, a former Dawson lawyer; Bob Gourlay, of the Princess Pats; and Tommy McSmart, a gunner in the 68th Battery. Among those in the display were some who lay in cemeteries far and wide: Jack Watt and Harold Butler of Whitehorse, and Charley Phillips, who had been killed in the East African campaign.[260] The *News* also served the community as a conduit for information about what was happening overseas. Amid the official dispatches printed on its pages were letters sent back from the men and women in England, France and Belgium.

For the men thousands of kilometres away in a bizarre landscape more foreign than any of them could have ever imagined, communications from home and family were extremely important for both peace of mind and sanity. Letters were a lifeboat to which men posted to the chaos of the front lines could cling.

Although the letters home from the war provided a glimpse into the lives of Yukoners overseas, there were restrictions and limitations on what they could say without falling victim to the censor's scissors. Anything of a strategic nature, such as where they were posted or to which unit, or descriptions of the conditions at the front, were likely to be excised from letters home for security reasons. Such information was considered bad for morale. Some letters were even delivered in regulation military envelopes with the stern warning: "I certify on my honour that the contents of this envelope refer to nothing but private and family matters..." followed by a space for the sender's signature.[261]

Once the volunteers left the Yukon, their letters provided the details of their initial training in military camps like those in Vancouver (Hastings Park), Victoria (Willows Camp) and Valcartier, Quebec. They described the conditions of the camps and the newly established routine of drills and training, of the movements of their friends and neighbours. When he was shipped to the East Coast, Frank Douglas recounted leaning out the window of his train passenger car to talk to a girl in North Battleford, Saskatchewan. She knew a friend of his from Dawson City, but that was his only remarkable encounter on his travels across the country. Some of the others took pains to get acquainted with the young ladies who would meet the troop trains as they passed through their towns. As reported by Douglas in the *Dawson Daily News*:

> At each station when the train would stop, everyone aboard would get out their little books that the M.M.B. chapter, I.O.D.E. had given them, and, with pencil in hand, would solicit the names of the various girls that invariably turned up at each stop to shake hands with the boys and give them a word of cheer. John MacKenzie was one of the worst, and his book gave out about the third day out and he had to use another. Harry McDonald was not much better, and when he reached Portage La Prairie, his home town, he had to borrow another book from his folks, who were there to see him pass through. He saw them for only about ten minutes.[262]

Douglas, who arrived in Victoria with a shipment of conscripts from the Yukon on July 2, 1918, described in detail his trip across Canada by train and to England by ship. When he reached Truro, Nova Scotia, where he had lived when he was a child, it had changed so much since 1903 that he hardly recognized the place. The ocean voyage was filled with reports of seasickness and the ever-constant fear of being torpedoed by a German submarine.

Influenza swept through the thousand troops on his ship. "Many of our Yukon boys in my platoon, and all who slept in deck No. 5, were taken sick and the last two days things on board have been rather bad," he reported, and added that one of the Canadian Military Engineers was buried at sea after having died of pneumonia, which often followed influenza attacks.[263]

On September 1, Douglas wrote from Aldershot, England, where he had been stationed and was serving as a stenographer and clerk for the catering inspector. The food servings he described seemed to be low in quantity, by Yukon standards.[264]

And it wasn't just the food that the letter writers found lacking in England. Despite having lived through the harsh Yukon winters, many of the Yukoners stationed there complained about the weather. Norman Watt, a regular correspondent wrote:

> I think that I would sooner be in any part of Canada—even Yukon with its 50 and 60 below zero weather. Not a single day since our arrival have we had a stretch of ten consecutive hours free of fog. Hardly a day passes without a fall of rain, and, to make matters still worse, the ground is of a putty-like formation and does not absorb the water as at home. The atmosphere is very damp and cold and penetrating. Some of the boys find the cold worse here than in Yukon. Most of them have had severe colds. Fortunately it has not affected me in the least as yet.[265]

Norton Townsend lamented about the snow and cold in camp, and in one letter acknowledged receipt of packages from home, some containing edible treats. When it wasn't snowing, it was raining. "Froze half the time and up to your knees [in mud] the rest," he wrote on December 12, 1917.

William Douglas, who was placed with the Canadian Engineers, described camp life with a footnote about the weather:

> We are given two route marches a week. We were out yesterday for eight hours on one, in the rain, and we were in full marching order—kits, rifles and so on. We were a hungry lot when we got home. We don't get as much to eat as we do at home, but we make out. The boys in the huts,

when they get any candy or cake from home, divide up. There are sixty in our huts. We get up at 6 o'clock, breakfast at 6:45, parade from 7:45 till 9; physical drill from 1:15 to 2:30; squad drill from 2:30 til 3:00; from 3:30 til 4:30 bayonet drill; supper at 5 o'clock; bed at 9:30. It keeps us busy cleaning brass and rifles. I am feeling fine now.

I will be glad when the mud dries up. We have about three inches of it. Our feet and clothes are wet all the time.[266]

Douglas was quick to thank Mrs. Osborn in Dawson for the socks she sent: "It is one thing that we all need badly, for it is very wet and cold over here."

"Tell the IODE that we have received their socks," wrote William Black from France, "and that they are very much appreciated. The only way to escape trench feet, which, by the way, is a crime to have, is to change socks very often, at least every twenty-four hours, so you see the demand is a big one. That chewing tobacco has not turned up yet."[267]

"I received two handkerchiefs and a card from the Patriotic Service League of Dawson," scribed Joe Harkin, "and it made a lump come up in my throat to think that someone remembered me outside my home."[268] Harkin may have been a little too candid about the conditions overseas, as farther on in his letter, a segment was clipped out by the censors.

Through the letters of Norton Townsend, we can trace his progress and experiences overseas. The first letter appeared in the *News* in the spring of 1917, describing his sailing with the Black contingent across the Atlantic. He thereafter wrote regular letters to his mother and grandmother.[269] The correspondence contained few details of war.

His first letters were sent from Witley Camp, near the south coast of England, where the recruits took extensive training while waiting for deployment to France. Christmas of 1917 was celebrated with a large dinner for 150 men, attended by Mrs. Black. Turkey, goose, mashed potatoes and peas, soup, pudding, candy, cake and beer were on the menu that day.

In January 1918, he complained about not having received any letters from home in a long time, speculating that it was because of the "Halifax affair." A month earlier, on December 6, 1917, the *Mont-Blanc*, a French cargo ship filled with munitions, exploded in Halifax Harbour, destroying much of the city in the biggest explosion in history.

Norton spent several periods in hospital during his time overseas, once for a case of mumps, which he wrote home about in April 1918. Communicable diseases such as mumps, influenza and measles were commonplace among the large concentrations of soldiers in the training camps. He commented on the young nurses attending to him and complained that there was nothing to do while recovering except eat and sleep.

In June, he referred to the recent federal election in which Alfred Thompson, the Conservative candidate, won the Yukon seat, and the soldiers' votes had been the deciding factor. "Who ever thought we would swing the election," wrote Townsend.

On August 15, 1918, he wrote another letter home. The Black contingent, now part of the 2nd Canadian Motor Machine Gun Brigade, had just participated in a major offensive at Amiens, France.

The Canadians were in the lead formations of this assault, which was the beginning of the end for the enemy. It was also the bloodiest offensive of the war and casualties were very high. Norton blandly summed it up this way: "Well Mother, things have quieted down a bit, but for two or 3 days our boys sure gave Fritz everything he was looking for. The weather has been great and very much in our favour."[270]

Marie Thompson also wrote home about her experiences as a front line nurse. Before enlisting in the Canadian Expeditionary Force in July of 1916, she had been a volunteer nurse in the American Ambulance Corps, in charge of a hospital ward in France for eight months. After serving at the IODE hospital in London, she found herself in a clearing station, a field hospital most closely positioned behind the battle line.

"We are under shell fire and frequently have a taste of it," she wrote. "This morning just at sunrise, two German planes flew over and a shell from our anti-air craft guns dropped just in front of where I was standing... Many casualties in that way are caused by our own shells, but that cannot be helped." They had been bombed by German aircraft flying over, and the guns roared as close as eight kilometres distant, and the black sky would light up from flares and artillery flashes. Streams of military transports rumbled by and the marching footsteps of advancing battalions were heard occasionally, all of which were constant reminders of the horrid battle taking place only a short distance away. Marie thanked the ladies of the Martha Munger Black chapter of the IODE for the money order they had sent her. She thought the best use would be to purchase a gramophone and records to entertain the wounded soldiers, or tobacco and other luxuries that they might need. "I always have wanted a little fund just to be able to draw upon it," she wrote, "and here is the beginning of it."[271]

One of the most consistent letter writers was Mrs. Black, who, after a brief stint in rooms at the Savoy, had settled into a small three-room suite in London at 113 Clarence Gate Gardens on Upper Baker Street. Despite having braved the frigid Yukon winters for two decades, she found London perpetually cold. "I have never suffered with cold there as I have here," she would tell the curious:

And it was true—the misery of trying to keep warm over grate fires which barely took the chill off the rooms! It was a criminal waste of fuel, too, as most of the heat went up the chimney. Our little Klondyke stoves could have warmed the rooms with half the fuel. Preparing for the night was a real ceremony. First I took a "red hot" bath, then put on my long-sleeved, high-necked flannel nightgown and bed-socks, and crawled into a bed warmed by two hot-water bottles. To think I had to go to London to get chilblains![272]

Meanwhile, George was at Witley, and Lyman, after receiving officer training, was dispatched to France to replace his uncle in the Yukon Machine Gun Battery. George was able to make periodic visits to Martha, whereas Lyman only returned to London on occasional periods of leave. "He's grown like a weed," she noted during one visit, "loves his work and never forgets he's a soldier. He's the picture of health, but shows the strain of the war—looks twenty-nine instead of nineteen."[273]

Like everyone else, she was subject to food shortages and rationing. "This is the first time I have had to do all the buying for my own table," wrote

Martha in another letter published in the *Dawson Daily News*. "For the first time since living in England to buy for my own rationing, and for my husband's dinner only is more or less of an amusing experience. This week, by using my entire week's ration tickets, I was able to buy one fairly large chicken. The first evening the chicken was baked with stuffing and gravy; the second evening the chicken was served cold; the third evening the same bird, or what was left of it, was served "picked up" on toast."[274]

Once, while dining at the Savoy, she saw a guest ask for more sugar for her strawberries. The waiter brought some out, but when she asked for more for her coffee, he reached into his pocket and took out three lumps! Another time, she used a week's ration (one half kilogram) to bake Lyman's favourite cake. Nor was it fine white sugar, but dark brown and sandy.

Food rationing was a small sacrifice for the people in England to make while their men put their lives on the line across the channel, and things were about to get a lot worse for them on the battlefields.

NOT QUIET ON THE WESTERN FRONT

THE YEAR 1918 began quietly. The Boyle men in the Yukon Battery remained stationed near Vimy, where January and February were divided between time at the front, where they wrapped themselves in blankets for protection from the cold, and time in camp behind the line. While in the rear, they served brigade duty and spent time drilling, practising and doing route marches. They practised assembling and disassembling their machine guns, with gas masks on, and loaded bullets into machine gun belts. They waited. During these quiet months, nobody in the Yukon Battery was wounded or killed, though George Byron Currie, serving in the 10th Battalion, was killed near Lens on March 18.

Everyone was waiting for the hammer to fall, and it did—but it still caught the Allies by surprise. After the Russians and the Germans signed the Treaty of Brest-Litovsk on March 3, 1918, the German armies along the Eastern Front were quickly transferred to the west. General Ludendorff fooled the Allies into thinking that they would be attacking much farther to the south, where the French Third Army was massed to defend the line. The British reinforced the lines closer to the English Channel to protect their coastal ports. The British Fifth Army, protecting the zone in the middle, was desperately understrength. Its divisions had half the men that they should have, because of the chronic shortage of men that they had suffered through most of the war.

The German plan was to attack the British and drive them from the Somme and the French from the Aisne before the Americans could fully enter the war. Although the United States had declared war on Germany the year before, it had taken them a considerable amount of time to mobilize and transport a fighting force to France, so in March of 1918, they were not fully prepared to enter the field of battle. The Germans launched their attack early in the morning of March 21, starting with a massive artillery attack from six thousand German heavy guns, supplemented by three thousand mortars. The impact of the attack was made harsher by the firing of gas shells at the British lines; more than 3.2 million high-explosive, shrapnel and gas shells would be launched during the next two weeks, to add to the chaos.

Two and a half hours after the artillery barrage began, the German infantry attacked, catching the British off balance. In the first day of their attack, they advanced more than 7 kilometres and captured twenty-one thousand British prisoners. Winston Churchill, who had been visiting the front lines at the time, came close to being captured as well. By March 23, the British had retreated to the Somme River, and the Kaiser, returning to Berlin, announced that the battle was won and the English were utterly defeated. That same day, the Germans started long-distance shelling of Paris with three large siege cannons.

Day by day, the Germans advanced, taking more prisoners—as many as forty-five thousand by March 25—and appeared ready to take the city of Amiens. Amiens was of great strategic importance because it was a major railroad transportation hub; if the Germans took it, the Allies would lose a great logistic advantage. The Canadians were not, broadly speaking, drawn into the heaviest of battle during this offensive, which does not mean that their role was not critical.

At Vimy Ridge, the Canadians now controlled the high ground, and it would have been foolhardy and costly for the Germans to attempt to retake this strongpoint. At the end of March, the Canadians held 15 kilometres of the line, and within two weeks were holding one fifth of the total frontage of the British Expeditionary Force. The Canadians were, in other words, a formidable presence on the Western Front.

It was at this time that the motorized machine gun units came into the fore as a potent force against the advancing Germans. For the first time since the beginning of the war, the Canadians found a combat situation for which these units were created. The 1st Motor Machine Gun Brigade was equipped with a number of armoured machine gun carriers that had a combination of mobility, defensive strength and firepower not well suited for the fixed positional battle of trench warfare, but in the open-field advance of the Germans, these machine gun carriers became vitally important. Moving into the line wherever they were most needed, they slowed down and stopped the German advance at critical moments in the battle.

According to one participant: "We would take the four or eight guns of a battery and open fire as the enemy would be advancing and bring them to a halt. Then the enemy would be ready to shell us out and the thing to do was to move your guns back to a rear position—maybe a thousand yards, maybe five hundred—and as the enemy started to move forward again, then you'd give it to them again. Day after day it was the same sort of thing."[275]

In one instance, an aerial observer witnessed two armoured cars holding up the advance of six hundred Germans. It was like this all over the battlefront.[276]

On March 22, the Yukon Battery received orders to stand ready for battle. They received orders to move from their well-fortified position near Vimy south to Amiens, toward which the Germans were making significant advances. For the next three weeks, the Yukon Battery was subjected to some of the bloodiest combat of their war.

At 5:00 a.m. on March 23, the 1st Canadian Motor Machine Gun Brigade, including the Eaton, Borden and Yukon batteries, moved south toward Amiens and forward to Villers-Bretonneux, from where they were dispatched 25 kilometres to the southwest to join the British 18th Corps at Roye, arriving there at 9:30 p.m. From Roye, they were sent 10 kilometres farther to Nesle, arriving at 2:00 a.m. Not having slept for two days, they took the opportunity there to catch a nap, but at 8:00, they were roused and ordered to move into the defensive line. Lieutenant Richard Babb of the Yukon Battery was ordered to take four machine guns to support the British 60th Brigade at Bacquencourt, while Lieutenant Lyman Black was sent to protect an artillery brigade northwest of Nesle.

When he arrived at Bacquencourt, Lieutenant Babb immediately went into action and his crew succeeded for a short time in checking the German advance. Then a report came back that he was missing and probably killed in action. They had lost one gun, and five other ranks were missing. Letters would be sent back to Dawson reporting that Babb had been killed, but it later came out that he had been captured by the Germans and was now a prisoner of war. Meanwhile, Captain Meurling, the officer in command, dispatched his two reserve guns under the command of Sergeant Major Aubrey E. (Bob) Forrest to stop an enemy advance on a road north of the village of Rethonvillers.

About midnight on March 24, Captain Meurling decided to send rations forward to resupply his men. In his war diary, he notes that he

sent a car loaded with rations up the main road to Nesle with orders to go as far as the Boche would let them, but at all costs to find the crews and deliver the rations. This car, which was driven by Pte. [E.B.] Mowat, went at full speed along the road, passed the gun line, and turned around in No Man's Land, where Mowat called to the boys to come and unload it. At once our men clustered round it and soon had it unloaded. This was done in full sight of the enemy in No Man's Land, with machine gun bullets flying thick. The [British] Infantry looked on in astonishment, and one officer asked Lieut. Black what the devil the car was doing there.

"Bringing up rations to the machine gunners," said Lieut. Black.

"We have had no rations for six days," said the Officer, "Do you always bring rations up to No Man's Land?"

"Yes, when we have to," said Lieut. Black, "Men can't fight on empty stomachs."

And as the Infantry was very hungry our boys divided the rations with them as far as they would go; and from that moment, whenever help was required—in fighting or in any other way—they always rallied round the Canadians.[277]

It was quiet that night, but the fighting picked up at daybreak on March 25, and the Yukon Battery had to retreat to a new defensive line. According to Captain Meurling, "Our guns had orders never to retire until out-flanked and this was always complied with—with the result that we lost heavily from machine guns and snipers all through the day."[278] Sergeant Anthony Blaikie, who had received both the Military Medal and the Distinguished Conduct Medal, was one of those killed. Lieutenant Black reported that their position was under fire from all directions and both flanks, so they picked up their gun to withdraw.

Blaikie was killed instantly, and another member of the gun crew was shot in the stomach. Sergeant Blaikie, reported Black, was a great loss: "Cool and resourceful, he made an admirable N.C.O.; his decorations were a witness to his great personal courage, which was never more in evidence than on this occasion. As a man he was marked by an unusual honesty and integrity of character. He had a 'hunch' before going into this fight that it would be his last."[279] Blaikie was a member of the Fraternal Order of Eagles. Today, a memorial marker in the public cemetery in Dawson City lists him and five other brothers of the Dawson lodge who died while in service to their country.

On the night of March 25, Captain Meurling assembled his men and moved them from Roye to Bouchoir, which they reached at 7:00 a.m. on March 26. From there, they were moved to Le Quesnel and were ordered to take a twenty-four-hour rest, but after only twenty minutes, they were sent to Fouquescourt, where the Germans had broken through the line. Captain Meurling now had twelve guns under his command, each operated by half-strength crews of two men each. About 1:00 p.m., the general called upon Captain Meurling to fill a gap near Bouchoir. Meurling managed to assemble four more machine guns with assorted gunners he could "scrape up from any old unit in the neighbourhood" and send them in under the command of Lieutenant Lyman Black. They arrived just in time to beat off an enemy attack on the crossroads between Folies and Arvillers. According to Meurling, "This undoubtedly saved Divisional Headquarters and prevented the position being outflanked. The General thanked me, saying that but for my guns, the position would have been lost."[280]

Later in the day, they checked a German advance against Hangest. Heavy action then developed at Rouvroy and Warvillers, where six of their sixteen guns were damaged, leaving ten men to handle eight guns. Desperately undermanned, Captain Harkness took a motorcycle to round up more gunners. A blast from a nearby shell left him dazed and shaken up, but he was able to inform Captain Meurling of their dire situation. Meurling, who had encountered him while driving on the road to Le Quesnel, sent three men forward to help out the undermanned units. Another four reinforcements were found, but the ranks were thinning: he had to settle for two truck drivers, a cook and a sick man. That was enough to keep the Germans at bay for the remainder of the day.

Meurling was then able to report:

I received orders at 8:00 a.m. to withdraw to Brigade H.Q. which had moved... to HEBECOURT, where we arrived about 9:30 a.m. Everybody at once went to bed, as no man had had any rest since the morning of the 22nd—with the exception of two hours on the morning of the 24th and two hours on the morning of the 26th. For three days we had not tasted government rations. The men, however, fed well. I requisitioned everything I wanted without scruple—from sardines to champagne—for I knew these would do better work in the stomachs of my men than in the hands of the Boche. Sgt. Peppard, my Q.M. Sergt., did great work in foraging. A sort of kitchen was fixed up in one of the cars, where food was cooked and sent up in sandbags to the guns, where the men were to be seen at times holding large pieces of bread and steak in one hand and working their guns with the other.[281]

The remaining men of Meurling's tattered company rested for twenty-four hours, but instead of being removed to the rear to recover, they were again called upon for help. The Germans had advanced farther between Luce and Somme and were threatening to take Amiens. This could not be allowed to happen. The only thing between the Germans and the threatened city was a force under the command of General A.B. Carey. On March 28, Meurling cobbled together thirty-two guns and enough men to put two on each gun. Lieutenant Black was positioned on the heights east of Hamel with four guns, Sergeant Major Forrest at a crossroad 2.5 kilometres south of Hamel and others at strategic locations.

As the Germans manoeuvred for advantage, Meurling repositioned his mobile force. Heavy fighting occurred over the next twenty-four hours, but the machine gunners held the line. Sergeant Major Forrest was now in charge of eight machine guns, as an officer had been wounded earlier in the day. The heavy fighting continued into March 30; after three days of continuous fighting, the Canadians, now praying for reinforcements, still held the line. Meurling received a plea from General Carey: "For God's sake, hold the line another day." The following day, the request was repeated. Meurling held the Germans at bay, mostly by bluff, moving the guns up and down along the line, and firing short bursts from different positions to convey the impression of a larger force. If only the Germans had known! Finally on April 1, several divisions came in to beef up the line.

General Carey thanked Meurling, acknowledging that if it hadn't been for the Canadian (and Yukon) machine guns, the line would have been broken. The reinforcements were three tattered divisions, and the machine gunners had to remain in their defensive positions until April 3, when they were finally replaced by British and Australian machine gun companies. They returned to camp at Hébécourt, where they rested and reorganized the decimated remains of the Yukon Battery (only ten soldiers survived) and the Eaton Battery (fifteen survived).

If they thought they would get some rest, they were sadly mistaken. On April 4, they received word that a German attack was expected at the village of Villers-Bretonneux. Captain Meurling sent out a number of machine gun crews to take up positions, and a number of guns were placed in armoured cars to patrol the roads to the village. That afternoon, while unloading ammunition from a three-tonne truck, four men were killed and twenty-six wounded when a shell exploded on the truck and set it afire. That left Meurling with only enough men to man two machine guns.

That also left Lyman Black without either a machine gun or a crew. In his own words, he later told his stepfather, George Black, that the enemy artillery fire had made a direct hit on the truck with his crew in it:

There was a perfectly good armoured car standing there fully equipped, guns, ammunition and crew, so I hopped on to it and out the road we went between the lines on a good road in "no man's land" that the enemy was advancing at right angles to in bunches. Before they realized what was coming we were onto them pouring in burst after burst of machine gun fire annihilating a group here and a group there and back to our lines without a man getting hit. The other cars were then put at the same work and did mighty well. This was the first time a Canadian armoured machine gun car was taken into the scrapping and made to do the work for which it was designed. It was swell fun, the best I ever had in my life. Captain... gave me fits for doing it, and Captain... patted me on the back as the cars were of his unit, and it made a name for that unit. I suppose I ought to be jealous, but I'm not, they all look alike to me and I consider I would have been bone head not to do what I did."[282]

For his action, Lyman Black was awarded the Military Cross May 4, 1918.[283] In its citation for the decoration, the *Edinburgh Gazette* reported: "For conspicuous gallantry and devotion to duty. When the enemy was rapidly advancing he handled his motor machine guns with great daring, time after time checking the enemy's advance and giving the tired infantry time to reorganise. On another occasion he rushed his machine guns up to hostile cavalry, causing them enormous casualties."[284]

Joe Newman, a Londoner who was mining near Dawson before enlisting, wrote in a letter published in the *News*:

Lyman, since he has had his commission, has not been in charge of any Yukoners of the Seventeenth Yukon Machine Gun Company. There are not many of us who would not serve under Lyman. There might be two or three but the rest of us would only be too pleased to serve under him. He has proved himself what he is, and has got where he is on his own merits, under heavy shell fire, and has proved that he is capable of taking charge of men... Lyman has got to the top on his own merits. For a time he was O.C. of what was left.[285]

Lyman may not have commanded any Yukoners from the 17th Canadian Machine Gun Company, but that was about to change. During his actions on April 4, however, that was the last thing on his mind. The Yukon Battery, or what was left of it, was not yet finished. They were stationed near Villers-Bretonneux for several more days, providing barrage fire. One of these fusillades broke up a mass of German soldiers who were preparing to attack.

What remained of the Yukon Battery was finally relieved of duty on April 11. The bulk of the Canadian Army remained at their posts in the region of Vimy Ridge and experienced routine front line activity. During their three weeks of uninterrupted battle, however, the Yukon men had played an important role in allowing infantry units to regroup. They slowed down and eventually stemmed the German advance at Villers-Bretonneux, and in part prevented the capture of the vital transportation centre of Amiens. Three weeks may not seem like a long time, but to the men of the Yukon Battery, it must have seemed like a year.

Within a few weeks, the now depleted Yukon Battery was no more. It was amalgamated with George Black's 17th Machine Gun Company to become part of a new unit: the 2nd Canadian Motor Machine Gun Brigade. When the transfer was made to the new unit, only one officer, Lieutenant James A. McKinnon, and three other ranks, William Kenneth Currie, Ernest Lawrence Peppard and Aubrey Forrest, remained from the forty-nine who posed beneath the "Dawson to Berlin" banner back in 1914. The rest had been killed, wounded, taken prisoner or transferred to other units. Of the latter three named, one would not survive the end of the war.

ZEEBRUGGE-OSTEND

AS THE BATTLE on the Western Front continued in early 1918, another important front was about to open up. The German submarine fleet had posed a constant threat to transatlantic shipping throughout the war. The British Navy was about to put a big dent in this activity. As quickly as the British could sink the German submarines, new ones were being built to replace them. The Americans had entered the war and started to ship large quantities of men and equipment to France, so it became necessary to shut down one of the greatest threats to this shipping: the submarine pens on the Belgian coast. Zeebrugge and Ostend were satellite ports of the major trading centre of Bruges, and of considerable strategic importance to the Germans. Bruges was close to the troopship lanes across the English Channel and allowed much quicker access to the Western approaches for the U-boat fleet than their bases in Germany.

The British plan was to obstruct access to the canals leading inland by sinking obsolete British cruisers at the mouths of the canals. After several cancelled missions, the attack of Ostend took place on April 23. Things went terribly wrong, as the smokescreen laid down by the British blew back on them when the wind changed. This made them easy targets while blinding them at the same time. Nevertheless, the British commanders attempted to enter the mouth of the canal with the block ships. The German commander of the defences at Ostend had anticipated the British attack and moved the harbour buoys into shallow water so that when HMS *Brilliant* and HMS *Sirius* attempted to enter the canal, they ran aground instead.

Artillery and long-range machine gun fire riddled the wrecks, and the combined crews were ordered to evacuate as the officers set the scuttling charges, which would sink the block ships in their current, useless locations. As men scrambled down the sides of the cruisers into motor launches that would relay them to the offshore squadron, Lieutenant Rowland Bourke, commanding Motor Launch 276, picked up thirty-eight seamen and Commander Goodal, who was the last to abandon ship, and towed another disabled motor launch out into safer waters. For this, Bourke was awarded the Distinguished Service Order (DSO).

Rowland Bourke was born in London, the son of Dr. Isadore Bourke. Dr. Bourke moved his family to Dawson City during its heyday and established a medical practice and a hospital that was later converted into a hotel. Although Rowland Bourke was in Dawson City, little is known about his time there. Bourke was an unassuming individual of slight build and extremely poor vision. Somebody described him as "the kind of chap with whom girls danced out of kindness."[286] When war broke out, he attempted to enlist in the Canadian armed forces but was rejected. Instead, he returned to England and enlisted in the Royal Naval Volunteer Reserve. When the raid on Ostend was planned, he volunteered the motor launch he commanded for duty.

In Bourke's case, it wasn't his poor eyesight or slender build by which he was measured but his courage. And his courage would be tested again very soon. Another assault on the harbours of Zeebrugge-Ostend was planned for May 9 and 10. Bourke was able to repair his damaged launch, and was accepted as a standby for the operation. As was later reported, he had followed HMS *Vindictive* into the canal mouth at Ostend where the cruiser was sunk, and was withdrawing from the harbour, when:

> Hearing cries in the water he again entered the harbour, and after a prolonged search eventually found Lieutenant Sir John Alleyne and two ratings, all badly wounded, in the water, clinging to an upended skiff, and rescued them. During all this time the motor launch was under a very heavy fire at close range, being hit in 55 places, once by a 6 inch shell—two of her small crew being killed and others wounded. The vessel was seriously damaged and speed greatly reduced. Lieutenant Bourke, however, managed to bring her out and carry on.[287]

This episode displayed daring and skill of a very high order, and Lieutenant Bourke's bravery and perseverance undoubtedly saved the lives of Lieutenant Alleyne and two of the *Vindictive*'s crew. Bourke was presented with the Victoria Cross by King George V at Buckingham Palace on September 11, 1918. And he was later proudly remembered in the *Dawson Daily News* and at public events as being a Dawson Boy.[288]

Rowland Bourke, whose father was a doctor in Dawson City, was rejected by all branches of the Canadian Armed Forces. He went to England, joined the Royal Naval Volunteer Reserve, and was later awarded the Victoria Cross. IMPERIAL WAR MUSEUM Q 91466

AMIENS AND THE HUNDRED DAYS

BY MARCH OF 1918, it had been nearly eighteen months since the last of the Black contingent had steamed away from Dawson City. Training in Victoria, then in England left the men prepared but impatient and eager to go to the front. At last, orders were given to proceed to France. The men moved from Witley to Seaforth on March 20 in preparation for shipping out and arrived at Le Havre on March 25. They moved to Dieppe the following day, then on to Verdrel. On March 31, George wrote to his wife, Martha:

> We've been a long time getting over here, but since arriving no time has been lost getting forward. As I write this the din of battle is deafening, but I can say nothing except that we are in the midst of the real thing.
>
> I have been unable to get any news of Lyman. His unit was away south when we were at their base and the information I did get was most disquieting. I am fearfully worried about him. If anything has gone wrong you will have been advised before this reaches you. If you have not, it is almost certain that he is all right. I do hope so.[289]

The 17th Canadian Machine Gun Company was moved up near the line and started rotating in and out of action on the front. While Lyman and the other members of the Yukon Battery were fighting a hard battle in front of the advancing German army at Villers-Bretonneux, the main contact the 17th had with the enemy was from shelling and the occasional lobbing of gas shells into the Allied line. Their initial welcome to trench warfare was relatively gentle, and much time was spent drilling and training to the rear of the battle zone. During April and May, George was the commanding officer, but in early June, the 17th was incorporated into the newly formed 2nd Canadian Motor Machine Gun Brigade. The former Yukon Battery became "A" Battery, and Black's 17th Company became "C" Battery. Captain Meurling, now Major Meurling, became the brigade commander.

It took the new brigade a couple of weeks to reorganize, after which they settled into a routine of drill and training. This was part of a larger reorganization instituted by General Arthur Currie among all Canadian forces. In addition to divisions of motor machine guns, each consisting of five eight-gun batteries, the brigade established a Machine Gun Corps Mechanical Transport Company to maintain its fleet of transport vehicles. By the end of the war, the Machine Gun Corps had increased in size to include 8,771 officers and men.[290]

By June 22, the brigade was stricken with Spanish influenza, and a number of men were taken ill. To accommodate the number of sick in the unit, and isolate the sick from the general population, the Chaplain Services tent was converted into an infirmary. Less than a week later, however, the ranks were so depleted another battery had to step in to take over some of their duties. The number of men that were taken ill in the 2nd Brigade at any time was one hundred, but only two were sick enough to be sent to hospital. All the men recovered after three days, weak but otherwise fit for duty.[291] Harry Melin, an unmarried Montenegrin labourer from Dawson, died of pneumonia, the only fatal case among the three hundred victims in the entire brigade stricken with what became known as the "Three Day Fever."[292] The pandemic was so virulent and widespread that within a year more men had died from influenza than all the soldiers on both sides of the conflict who were killed during the war.[293]

In mid-July, the brigade was posted to Hermaville, where they continued drill, training, inspections and battery duty. Black's men must have wondered if they were ever going to see action on the front. Activity to that point had been quiet on the Canadian sector for the past few months, probably because the Canadians had proven themselves to be the most determined and tenacious fighters among the Allies. They were well equipped, up to full strength and well rested. But the Canadian Corps had big plans in which the entire Canadian Expeditionary Force would be involved in a massive Allied assault on the German line.

The assault was prepared using meticulous planning and deception. As misdirection, meetings were held for a planned attack on Orange Hill, east of Arras, about 10 kilometres south of Vimy, and the plans were very realistic, but all of this activity was a blind for the real objective. Strict orders were given to all soldiers not to talk about their activities to anyone, and a number of misleading communications were designed to misdirect the attention of the Germans, who knew that if the Canadians started to redeploy, something big was about to happen. On July 29, Canadian divisional commanders were finally let in on the secret: the German line east of Amiens was the real target. The movement of 100,000 men, plus their equipment, artillery, ammunition and supplies, 65 kilometres southwest of Vimy to the secret marshalling area was a logistical challenge. The movement took place at night; despite the planning, the traffic jams were enormous. Heavy deployment of aircraft to the skies over Amiens prevented the depleted German air reconnaissance from detecting the massive movement that was afoot below. If the Germans had known that the Canadians were massing, they could have blown them to smithereens with artillery fire.

Besides being fresh, well equipped and well prepared, the Canadian force faced an enemy from which its elite fighting elements had been stripped out of regular units for their spring gamble. The Germans had also been weakened by the attack of the virulent influenza pandemic, and few defensive preparations had been made along this relatively quiet section of the Western Front. Their main strength was the deployment of highly effective machine gun positions across the planned field of battle. The Canadians had moved into place the largest tank force used to date in any battle. These lumbering monsters were slow and vulnerable, but they instilled terror in the enemy. Behind the Canadian line was the artillery; guns were placed 5 to 10 metres apart. They would provide the barrage support behind which the Canadian troops would advance at the rate of 200 metres per minute.

The battle was to be known, informally at least, as "Llandovery Castle," a reminder of a hospital ship that had been torpedoed by a German submarine. Only six of the ninety-four Canadians survived the sinking; all fourteen Canadian nurses on board perished. The Germans then gunned or rammed many of the lifeboats full of the wounded or defenceless. Brigadier George Tuxford, a Saskatchewan farmer before the war, gave orders that "Llandovery Castle" was to be their battle cry as they moved forward onto the Germans. He wanted those words to be the last thing the enemy heard before they were run through by bayonet.

Tuxford had a Yukon connection. During the Klondike stampede, he and two other family members spent more than a year moving a herd of cattle 4,000 kilometres from Moose Jaw, Saskatchewan, to the Klondike to cash in on the high prices that were being paid by the beef-hungry miners in the goldfields. His account of this adventure later made up an entire volume of his memoirs.[294]

The Canadian battlefront was 8.5 kilometres wide and their target was a line 14 kilometres into enemy territory. Any confusion or foul-ups would have a devastating impact upon the success of the Canadian assault. The

Waiting along Arras-Cambrai road to go into action, September 1918. YUKON ARCHIVES
GEORGE BLACK FONDS 81/107 #187

Canadian armoured car headed into combat, battle of Amiens, August 1918. YUKON
ARCHIVES GEORGE BLACK FONDS 81/107 #198

Canadian armoured cars going into action, battle of Amiens, August 1918. YUKON ARCHIVES GEORGE BLACK FONDS 81/107 #163

German prisoners acting as stretcher bearers. YUKON ARCHIVES ROY MINTER FONDS 92-15 #264

assault began at 4:20 a.m. on August 8, as 2,000 artillery pieces opened fire at once along the breadth of the Allied assault. Of these, 646 were Canadian. Shrapnel, smoke, and high-explosive and gas shells were intended to stun and confuse the enemy. According to one soldier, the sound was deafening and the sky was "a furnace of orange lightning," as the fury of the guns was unleashed.[295] The Germans were caught entirely by surprise, which was compounded by a heavy fog that lay over the battlefield and hid the advancing Canadians.

The role of the Yukoners and the 2nd Canadian Motor Machine Gun Brigade was to act as an independent force that would pass through the 3rd Canadian Division and secure the flank to the south of the Amiens-Roye road. Their armoured cars would serve as a link between the most advanced cavalry and the leading infantry, and provide supporting fire as they advanced. They received orders to move forward on the morning of August 9. The attack of the previous day had advanced farther than expected, and the various batteries of the brigade advanced along the Roye Road with the 5th Canadian Mounted Rifles on their left and the French 55th Infantry Division on their right. One battery was sent into Le Quesnel with orders to advance toward the village of Folies, while another was sent into Arvillers to the south. A third battery was sent forward into the settlement of Bouchoir. They encountered heavy opposition and were tied down for several hours, until the 5th Canadian Mounted Rifles, supported by tanks, broke down the enemy machine gun nests and moved forward. They settled in at sunset, but early the next morning they attacked Bouchoir, where the Germans were heavily entrenched. At 6:30 a.m., they received orders to withdraw the batteries back to Hamon Wood in the rear, but before that was done, the German resistance collapsed and they moved forward, taking the little village of Le Quesnoy.

The attack was a huge success. As described by historian Tim Cook: "As the Canadian Corps advanced through a covering fog the morning of August 8, the Germans were unprepared for the battle and the Allied forces, along a broad front, made the largest advances in a single day of battle since the opponents had become entrenched along the Western Front. Within 6 days, the Germans had retreated 15 miles. The morale of the German High

Command was badly shaken. In General Ludendorff's words, August 8 was the 'black day of the German Army.'"296

It was the start of the offensive that would become known as the Hundred Days. Sergeant David Fotheringham, a Mountie from the Yukon, described it from a more personal point of view:

> We went into the line on the eighth, in support of the French, and worked with them right along. The Huns were driven back several miles; in fact, they went so fast that it is hard to keep up to them. Talk about the dead. Why, the ground simply was strewn with them for miles. A good many of them are not buried yet. We got the greatest praise and honor shown by the French army. They awarded a good many of the boys in the brigade the Croix de Guerre, the highest order…
>
> [T]he Yukoners stood the test wonderfully. I don't think that any of them shirked their duty, and I must say that we were up against the hottest shell fire, gas and machine gun cross-fire that could happen anywhere.297

Of the three hundred men in this brigade, after two days of intense fighting, five men were killed and fifty-five were wounded, including George Black. Among the dead were Sergeant Charlie O'Brien and Corporal Angus McKellar. O'Brien was a Dawson schoolboy, one of forty-nine who enlisted over the duration of the war. His father was T.W. O'Brien, the Klondike brewery king, who had died two years earlier. Angus McKellar had been a member of the first detachment of North-West Mounted Police that had established a police post in the Yukon at Forty Mile before the gold rush. Single when he enlisted, he was now one of the newly wed soldiers. Both were killed near Bouchoir when an enemy shell made a direct hit on their armoured car. The driver of their vehicle had one arm shot off, and showed great composure in turning the vehicle around and moving back from the action, but he died later in the day. Sergeant Major Aubrey Forrest, originally of the Yukon Battery, received a wound in the abdomen during the attack and was moved to a clearing station, where he died of his wounds twelve days later.

George Black was more fortunate. He sustained a bullet wound to the thigh. As he later wrote:

My headquarters were in the edge of a small wood, just abreast of the battery. Mr. Hun quite correctly surmised that there would be something doing in that wood. Infantry and tanks were massing there to tear into him while we strafed him with the machine guns, so he anointed us with shrapnel and machine gun searching fire.

It was not only uncomfortable, but decidedly unhealthy. He knocked down a lot of trees, some of which fell across the main Amiens-Roye road, and a little squad of axe men under Corporal Dick Armstrong promptly beat it out and removed those trees so that when the time came for our cars to advance they could do so unimpeded by those trees, anyway. Of course the Boche didn't fire at them. Oh, no! But luckily he didn't get any of them. I can't remember who were in that squad, otherwise I'd give you their names. I was too busy except to make general mental notes. Why I didn't get my block knocked off or get pulverized into hash instead of only a measly machine gun bullet slipped through my thigh I'll never understand. Well the tanks started ahead, the infantry right behind them; the Hun began to go; the battery to move ahead when I sustained a puncture.[298]

He later wrote to his mother-in-law:

My "wounds" (that's a strong word for it—I've been worse hit in civilian life) consist of a slam on the left leg with a chunk of shrapnel, that didn't break any bones, but rather messed up the hide and my breeches, but wouldn't have been sufficiently serious to stop me just then, had not the swine punctured my right leg with a Machine Gun Bullet (he had some to spare from the amount we were anointing him with). It is just a clean bore and will heal rapidly—not very painful but most annoying.[299]

Black saw only a few hours of front line combat; he was quickly removed to a clearing station on the Somme. The following day he was sent by train

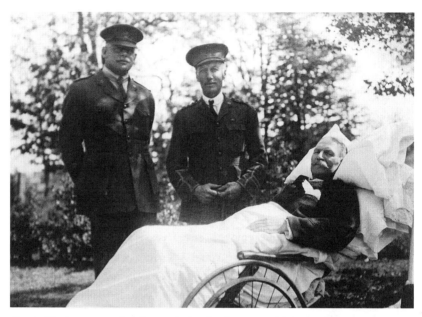

George Black was wounded during the battle of Amiens, and was sent back to England to recuperate. YUKON ARCHIVES GEORGE BLACK FONDS 81/107 #48

to Abbeville, then forwarded to Bolougne. On August 12, he was transported across the English Channel to Dover and taken to the Royal Free Hospital in Hampstead, London. Martha received a notification that he had been wounded, followed shortly thereafter by a letter from George reassuring her that he was not seriously injured—that it was a regular handpicked blighty.

After a convalescent period, George Black was back on duty by early October, stationed in reserve. When he returned to his unit, the war was over and he was called upon to command his unit as a force of occupation. He would have only one more battle to fight before returning to Canada, but it was of a different sort that would not occur until the late spring of 1919.

Other Yukon soldiers also wounded in this phase of battle were sergeants Hamilton Daglish and Frederick Annand, and privates Walter Sharpe, Eugene Villeneuve and Frank Sohier. Sohier had a lot at stake: a miner at the time of enlistment, he had been born in France and had a sister who lived in Flanders.[300]

The success of the offensive at Amiens caused a change in Allied thinking about the war. Whereas before authorities were planning for the war to continue into 1919 or even 1920, they now saw an opportunity to bring it to an end swiftly. They decided to continue applying pressure on the Germans with a series of offensive attacks. The French Army struck between Compiègne and Soissons on August 20, while the British Army attacked several points along the Western Front. The Americans entered a major offensive in mid-September, but the Germans were not about to capitulate at this stage of the war, and there would be many more lives lost before the guns were silenced.

After the initial success at Amiens, the Canadians, 100,000 strong, were returned to their position at Arras, southwest of Vimy, in preparation for the next big offensive. The ensuing three months were an inexorable march back through France into Belgium toward the conclusion of the war. Yukoners participated in this march but at a terrible price; the route to the Belgian city of Mons represented the bloodiest weeks of the war for the Yukon and was marked by a trail of graves. Again, there was a diversion, a deceptive feint designed to convince the Germans that the attack was to be north of the Scarpe River. But the Germans must have known that the Canadians, being at full strength and with a proven record of battle victories, would be the first choice of the Allies to punch a hole through their most heavily fortified position.

It was the German intention to hold on to the series of strongly defended trenches to the east of Arras, a total of 30 kilometres in depth. First, there was the Hindenburg Line, then the Fresnes-Rouvroy Line and, last, the Drocourt-Quéant Line. Behind these defences was the unfinished Canal du Nord, and farther east, the city of Cambrai, a key transportation hub for the Germans. The ultimate target for this attack: the Red Line, a line chosen by the Allies that ran along the defensive works behind the Drocourt-Quéant Line and the town of Dury.

The British and the French had the utmost confidence in the ability of the Canadians to capture these important features. Said Marshal Foch, the general-in-chief of the Allied armies, "I think the Canadians are the force on which I can rely to clean up between Arras and the Hindenburg Line...

the Canadians know the ground so perfectly and they are so determined that I think I can trust them to do so."[301]

The Canadians were backed up by 762 artillery pieces, whose primary objective was to neutralize the German artillery, and a light bomber squadron that would attack from above. The attack started at 3:00 a.m. on August 26. It was dark, with a full moon, but it was also raining heavily. When the artillery opened up their barrage and lit up the skies, the attack began. The first Yukoner to fall was Private Stephen J. McNeill, a forty-seven-year-old gold miner originally from Nova Scotia, who was killed in action during the attack south of Vis-en-Artois, which was taken by the night of August 27.

Slowly, they moved forward until they reached the Drocourt-Quéant Line on September 1. This German defence line was one of the most heavily protected along the Western Front. The Canadians took it—but at a cost. They lost 297 officers and 5,325 other ranks, either killed or wounded. Four of these were Yukoners, who fell on September 2. Lieutenant Robert Hartman of the 102nd Battalion "was in charge of two Stokes trench mortars during an attack made on the enemy's position East of Dury, when he was severely wounded in both legs by enemy machine gun bullets. Whilst a comrade was in the act of dressing his [sic], a shell landed almost on top of them, killing both instantly."[302] Sergeant John J. Melville, formerly of Atlin, had already been awarded the Military Medal for his bravery, but on this day, it was of no help. "During the attack south west of Dury he was in charge of a company of Lewis gunners. And after reaching the final objective, while searching for suitable positions for the guns, he was hit and killed instantly by enemy machine gun bullets."[303] Alfred Clinton Totty, son of an Anglican missionary and a First Nation mother at the settlement of Moosehide, near Dawson City, was one of the few Yukon recruits of First Nation ancestry. He was with the 78th Battalion of the Canadian infantry during the attack of the Drocourt-Quéant line when he was killed by a machine gun bullet to the throat on September 2. He was buried two days later with fifty-one of his comrades at Dury Mill cemetery.[304] Saletto Michunovich was a miner back in the Yukon. Born in Montenegro, he volunteered as a member of the Black contingent and was later transferred to the 1st Canadian Motor

While acting as a gunner on armoured car No. 5792 during the attack north of Villers-les-Cagnicourt, Private Saletto Michunovich was instantly killed when the car was hit by a shell. CANADIAN WAR MUSEUM CONTROL NUMBER: 19930013-846 IMAGE NUMBER: 0.2595

Machine Gun Brigade. While acting as a gunner on armoured car Number 5792 during the attack north of Villers-lès-Cagnicourt, the twenty-eight-year-old Michunovich was killed instantly when his car was hit by a shell and blown to bits.[305]

The next logical move was for the Allies to take Cambrai, as it was such an important transportation hub for the Germans. The Canadians were the best choice: they were considered the best fighters on the Allied side of the conflict; they were at full strength; and, politically, it was better for the British to have Canadians slaughtered than more Englishmen. After the massive losses at the Somme and Passchendaele, Britain had lost about as many men as the public would accept. The attack would take place at the only point on the Canal du Nord that was dry: a 2,600-metre-wide stretch through which General Currie would throw his army. It was a big gamble, but he hoped it would pay off. The Canadians were assigned the task of taking Bourlon Wood, located 3 kilometres west of Cambrai.

The capture of Bourlon Wood was essential to the successful advance of Allied forces toward Cambrai. The attack commenced with a ferocious barrage at 5:20 a.m. on September 27. The fighting was intense, but the Canadians advanced: "Creeping from tree to tree, bush to crater, routing enemy artillery positions and machine gun nests... Enemy strongholds fell one by one, or surrendered when they encountered Canadians in front, around, and behind them. Several counterattacks were beaten back throughout the day, and by dusk the fortress of Bourlon Wood had fallen to the Canadians and would not be recaptured."[306]

But the battle took a heavy toll on Yukoners. James Watters, an Atlin man, was killed at Vimy the first day of the attack, as was Marshall Tibbets Stevens. Better known to his friends as "Steve," he was a native of Andover, New Brunswick, who came to the Yukon in the early days and had mined for many years on Gold Run Creek. He later worked for the Canadian Klondyke Mining Company as winchman on one of their mammoth dredges. For several seasons, immediately before enlisting, Steve was associated with the Milvain brothers in their dredging operations in the Sixtymile district, west of Dawson City. He was considered one of the most experienced and competent dredge men in the camp, and was a close personal friend of Captain George Black.[307]

Lieutenant Alfred Cronin of the 54th Battalion, a displaced Liverpudlian from Whitehorse, had been a clerk before he enlisted. He was killed instantly near his objective on the north side of Bourlon Wood when he was hit by a shell while going to the aid of a wounded comrade. He was thirty-four years old.[308] Patrick John Martin, formerly from New Brunswick, was working as a miner near Dawson when he enlisted with the Black contingent. Now serving with the 102nd Battalion (Central Ontario), he was killed by machine gun fire while taking part in an attack between Inchy-en-Artois and Bourlon Wood. Martin was forty-three years old.[309]

Two more Yukon men were killed on September 28. The first was Private Ambrose George Crisfield, a miner from Dawson City. Some years earlier, he was trapping with Jim Christie when Christie was attacked and mauled by a grizzly bear. Originally from England, he enlisted early in 1918 in Vancouver, and had been in France for less than a month when he died. Like Christie, he was a sniper with the Princess Patricia's Canadian Light Infantry. He and a comrade were detailed to sniper work on the right flank of their company. Just after passing through the wire in front of the Douai-Cambrai road in the vicinity of Raillencourt and Sailly, Private Crisfield was instantly killed when the enemy opened up machine gun fire. He was thirty-six years old.[310]

Also among the fallen was Lieutenant Colonel Charles James Townshend Stewart. His name is among the many on the memorial triptych now displayed at the Dawson City Museum. Stewart was one of twelve children born into a wealthy Nova Scotia family. He joined the North-West Mounted Police for a five-year term in 1896, and had posted to detachments at Lower Laberge and Tagish during the Klondike gold rush. He also served as an officer in the Imperial Yeomanry in South Africa. When he returned to Canada in 1904, he "disappeared into the Yukon."[311] He seemed to have wanderlust that made him the stereotype of the northern wanderer. In the ensuing years, he shifted from one thing to the next. He worked for the railroad, and nearly died of starvation while trapping in the Hudson Bay region. He drifted from one job to another, making a living playing poker and leaving a trail of "legends and stories." Described as restless and susceptible, he had a contempt for red-tabbed staff officers.

Yet when war was declared, Stewart was one of the first to enlist. He joined the Princess Patricia's Canadian Light Infantry (PPCLI) in August 1914. Commissioned as a lieutenant, he was wounded several times, and twice decorated with the Distinguished Service Order. He rose through the ranks until he was appointed lieutenant colonel and commanding officer of the PPCLI on March 31, 1918. A fellow officer said that Stewart had the most pronounced character he had ever seen. His strength and vitality were impaired by his chain smoking and love of whiskey, and he was an excellent bridge player. Wild and reckless in his personal life, his energy, resourcefulness, tactical knowledge and complete disregard for danger made him an excellent and successful leader on the battlefield. But his luck ran out September 27, 1918. While advancing with his battalion near Raillencourt, he was killed by a German shell. He lies buried in the Ontario Cemetery, near Sains-lès-Marquion, west of Cambrai.[312]

Frank C. Slavin, son of the famous Australian prizefighter, was a student of mining engineering before enlisting in the 72nd Battalion (Seaforth Highlanders). They were operating in the vicinity of Sancourt when he was killed. He was twenty-six years old.

After Cambrai fell, the Allies expected to dig in for the winter, but the Germans were demoralized and weakened. "The Powers figured that we had them on the run," wrote some Yukon members of the 2nd Canadian Motor Machine Gun Brigade, "and that we would keep them that way."[313] Lieutenant Norman Watt, former territorial councillor, was wounded protecting the flank of the 51st (Highland) Division. The rest of the men advanced into the town of Denain, where the villagers greeted them with joy. At the time, the Canadians were advancing to capture Mons before the expected armistice. The Belgian city had been taken by the Germans at the beginning of the war, and there was symbolic value to recapturing it before the conflict ended.

The Townsend brothers described the kind of reception they encountered when they entered villages just liberated from the Germans. In a letter from Norton's brother, Alfred, dated October 27, 1918, and later published in the *Dawson Daily News*, the war was almost over. "We were chasing Fritzies through a lot of French towns and villages," he wrote. "Fritz was going pretty fast so he did not have much time to destroy the houses or put up much of a fight, so we got along with very few casualties."[314] All the girls and women ran out and kissed and hugged the soldiers.

Norton's letter expanded upon this theme: "A good bit of the time we were just a few hundred yards behind the Germans and under fire at that. The people came out of their cellars—cheered, danced, cried and sang all at once. Old women and girls cried and kissed and hugged one till you didn't know if you were yourself or not. They cut all the badges and buttons off our clothes—stripped us of everything for souvenirs. The cruelties they suffered under the Germans are unbelievable."[315]

Norton's letters continued during the period that his unit occupied Germany after the war. Both he and his brother survived and returned to civilian life in the Yukon. The brothers served in different units but crossed paths occasionally during the war, incidents to which they referred in their letters home.[316]

The 2nd Canadian Motor Machine Gun Brigade moved inexorably east toward Belgium. They were sent to Naves, then Denain and Valenciennes, where the Germans were putting up a stubborn resistance; it took three days for the latter place to fall. "We entered the town with bands playing," reported one letter to Dawson. "The town was decorated with flags that had been concealed since 1914. From Valenciennes we had no heavy fighting except rear-guard actions which the Huns were putting up to enable them to get their heavy guns back."[317]

According to intelligence reports, the Germans were now weak, exhausted and demoralized. Their defences were diminishing, reduced primarily to machine guns that held the Allies back while they retreated. Orders were given for the Allies to push their advantage and break through the rear guard if possible. Various batteries from the 2nd Canadian Motor Machine Gun Brigade were dispatched with some guns mounted on motor-cycles to probe and test the enemy resistance. If the enemy was falling back, they were to press forward. The roads were in terrible condition, as the retreating German troops had blasted huge craters in them up to 4 metres deep and 6 metres across. Somewhere between Valenciennes and Mons, on November 7, the Canadians entered Belgium.

In the end, as historian Tim Cook has noted, during the fighting at Amiens and the Hundred Days: "30,000 prisoners were taken. For the 102,000 members of the Canadian Corps, there were 11,822 casualties, mostly infantry in combat along the front lines. Ten Victoria Crosses and 3,000 other medals were awarded to members of the Corps during this battle."[318]

ARMISTICE: TRIUMPH AND TRAGEDY

NEWS SWIRLED ABOUT that the war was about to end, but rumours like that had been common since the beginning of the war. By November 10,

When Canadian troops entered Mons, Belgium, on the last day of the war, Lieutenant Lyman Black (on motorcycle) was chosen to lead the motorized machine gun component. YUKON ARCHIVES GEORGE BLACK FONDS 81/107 #197

General Currie had still not received any formal notification that fighting was to cease, and the retreating Germans were still resisting the advancing Canadians. Between November 7 and 10, more than six hundred Canadians were killed or wounded just in the vanguard of the Canadian force that was moving toward Mons. Sadly, a stray shell landed among a body of men on November 8, killing six and wounding six more. They were members of the 42nd Battalion and had survived thirty-seven months of continuous struggle on the battlefields. Walter Sharpe, who was born in London, had been employed as a cook in Whitehorse when he signed up. He was wounded on the last day of the war.[319]

The Yukoners encountered sporadic fighting with the Germans as they entered Mons at nine o'clock on November 11, but nobody in the machine gun unit was killed that day. At 11:00, the armistice began and the guns fell silent. The last Commonwealth soldier to be killed during the war was Private George Price, a conscript from Saskatchewan, who was shot and killed by a sniper just a few minutes before 11:00.

As the Canadians made their way through Mons, the Highlanders marched their pipe band through the narrow streets. Lieutenant Lyman Black, who had left high school in Dawson City three years before to enlist, was now a battle-scarred veteran of the war. He led the machine gun contingent on his motorcycle through the city square in the centre of Mons.

They were met by ecstatic citizens:

The liberators were hounded, kissed, hugged and back-slapped. The Belgians ... broke out their hidden bottles of wine "They were wild with delight," wrote Private Jerry Mansfield. "They kissed us, they cried over us, they whole-heartedly welcomed us. They hemmed us in and crowded around us ... They showered us with such poor gifts as they had, flowers, blessing, sweet biscuits, wine and this cheap bit of ribbon." Embarrassed Canadians returned the gestures tentatively, then affectionately, passing out kisses and cigarettes, the only things they had in abundance. At least three large Canadian flags were hung from windows ... as the citizens of Mons desperately tried to replicate the Red Ensign. Marching through Mons after the armistice, the citizens greeted the Canadians with songs, including the popular "It's a Long Way to Tipperary." One exhausted Canadian was heard to mutter, "It's been a bloody long way to Mons."[320]

Back in London, Martha Black was drawn to the window by the peal of church bells, the sound of factory whistles and hands clapping. On the streets below and on the balconies around her, she could see the signs of celebration: little boys tooting whistles, uniformed lift girls dancing to jazz music, people cheering loudly and waving flags. On one balcony, a happy young woman was locked in the arms of a sailor; together, they turned to Mrs. Black, blew her a kiss and shouted, "Good Luck."[321]

She later received a letter from Colonel Meurling, who had commanded the Yukon machine gunners through their years in the war, which said: "It may interest you to know that I have given Lyman command of the armoured cars in the official entry into Mons. I thought it might be of interest to Yukon to have the youngest member take part in such an historical event."[322] Not everyone was so happy with the big news, of course. Martha Black saw one "sad-faced young woman" with a wide black armlet on the sleeve of her uniform, and no smile on her face.[323]

The end of the war brought both joy and sadness for the Yukon. News of the armistice reached Whitehorse at 10:00 a.m. on November 11 and quickly spread throughout the town. As the *Whitehorse Star* reported:

> Soon the flags were flying from every flagstaff, and the doorways and show windows of every business house were being decorated with bunting and the flags of the allied nations. J.B. Watson, Dominion telegraph operator, mounted to the cupola of the post office and played several cornet solos, among the selections being "O, Canada," "Rule, Britannia!," and "God Save the King." In the front window of the dry goods department of Taylor, Drury, Pedlar & Co. a life size effigy of the bust of the Kaiser, the artistic handiwork of Charles Atherton, head of the grocery department... was displayed—and attached to the effigy were two cards, one bearing the inscription "Hock der Kaiser," and the other, "What Shall We Do With Him?"[324]

The businessmen of Whitehorse quickly met in the Red Cross room on Front Street to plan a celebration. Since there were numerous people from Carcross and Skagway who wanted to join in the celebration, the event was postponed until the following day. Forty-three Skagway and Carcross residents arrived in Whitehorse on the train from Skagway the following afternoon at 4:30. Everybody in Whitehorse was there to greet them amid blowing whistles, ringing bells and a brass band. The meals and hotel rooms were covered by the celebrating Whitehorse community.

A fine dinner followed at the Whitehorse mess house, and at 7:00, the effigy of the Kaiser was carried up the street in a torchlit parade from the Taylor Drury Pedlar store and placed atop an 8-metre-high pile of cordwood, which was set afire in the ball field. The festivities then moved inside the North Star Athletic Association hall, where Fred Maclennan made a speech, which was followed by local talent performing a number of songs and recitals. The schoolchildren concluded with "Rule, Britannia!" and "O Canada," which was followed by a dance that lasted until the late hours of the morning. At 9:30 the following morning, the woozy out-of-towners were poured onto the train and sent back to Carcross and Skagway.[325]

Dawson City was caught up in the excitement as well. The town went wild in celebration. The word was out at 9:40 a.m., and church bells started ringing; everywhere whistles were blown, guns were fired and every other sort of noisemaker was brought into action. School was let out and children poured into the streets. They marched about town setting off firecrackers for hours. Everywhere homes were festooned with streamers and flags.

In the afternoon, returned soldiers and others formed a parade several blocks long, headed by Sheriff George Brimston. Bert Houghtaling and Miss Bessie Sinclair followed, beating on bass drums. Then came returned soldiers carrying a coffin containing an effigy of the Kaiser, and a long line of men hauling a cart in which sat Hughey Hamilton, a Crimean War veteran. Alex Sealey followed, carrying an effigy of the Kaiser; then came a long line of what the *Daily News* termed "women representing all the patriotic societies of the town." They were followed in turn by blocks of gaily adorned automobiles, and then others carrying large British and American flags.[326]

The parade led to the Arctic Brotherhood Hall, where, in a crowded, informal meeting chaired by Sheriff Brimston, returned veterans and relatives of war veterans were asked to take the platform. Speeches were given by Colonel Knight, acting chief executive; Judge John Black; and other dignitaries.

As word spread, people throughout the Yukon celebrated the end of the war. But there was also a heaviness of heart that word of the armistice couldn't lift.

Freeze-up had occurred just a short time before, and it was part of the annual cycle of Dawson City that a large number of people had left town on the last boats of the season to spend the winter Outside.

On October 15, the last two river steamers of the navigation season, the *Casca* and the *Yukon*, packed to capacity, had been sent on their way to Whitehorse by hundreds of well-wishers. The two sternwheelers arrived in

Whitehorse four days later, and the passengers were quickly transferred to the train for the 175-kilometre, seven-hour journey to the coast. The train delivered a record number of people to Skagway, where the population doubled in size with the arrival of the transient residents.

Every hotel room in town was booked and every restaurant filled to capacity as the throng awaited departure for the Outside. In the meantime, the travellers were entertained by two dances and a fundraising film night at the Skagway Popular Picture Palace.[327] Some last-minute arrivals felt fortunate that they could book passage on the *Prince Rupert*, leaving a day before the *Princess Sophia*, which had been booked to capacity well in advance.

Amid the noise and confusion of the crowded dock, passengers boarded the *Princess Sophia* the afternoon of October 23. At ten in the evening, she slipped away from the dock in the darkness and headed down the Lynn Canal. An hour later, she rounded a point, and the weather changed. It started to snow and the wind picked up to 80 kilometres per hour.

In the era before radar and global positioning systems, pilots had to guide their vessels by knowledge and experience, with a little blind luck thrown in. Unfortunately, the blind luck failed the ship's captain, L.P. Locke, on this fateful evening. Just after two in the morning, passengers were jolted from their slumber when the *Sophia* ran head on into Vanderbilt reef, in the centre of the channel. In the pitch darkness, with heavy snow and strong winds, the *Sophia* had drifted off course and directly onto this well-known hazard.

The ship sent wireless messages stating they were grounded on the reef. Over the next two days, several ships were dispatched to the reef to assist in the transfer of passengers to safety. At low tide, the entire vessel could be seen resting on the exposed reef, balanced on an even keel. Unfortunately, although the rescue ships could get close enough to communicate by loud-hailer with the *Princess Sophia*, the wind continued unabated, and the waters were too rough to allow the use of lifeboats.

At one point, the passengers of the *Princess Sophia* appeared on deck, some carrying suitcases, and it looked as though they were preparing to abandon ship. The passengers must have been in a state of confusion, balancing between hope and panic. The presence of rescue ships nearby would have reassured them, but the weather frustrated any hope of transferring to safety. One passenger, Joe Maskell, fearing the worst, wrote to his fiancée, Dorothy Burgess, who awaited him in Manchester, England. "I made my will this morning to you, my own true love..."[328] he began, but the letter was not delivered until months later. Another passenger, Auris McQueen, writing to his mother in a more optimistic tone, anticipated rescue and speculated: "As soon as this storm quits we will be taken off and make another lap to Juneau."[329]

The storm didn't quit. On the morning of October 25, the wind shifted and rose to gale force. It was estimated that it was gusting as high as 160 kilometres per hour. The attending ships made for cover in nearby bays. The high tide, the powerful winds and the churning waves finally had an effect on the stranded passenger ship. At 4:50 p.m., the *Princess Sophia* sent out a distress signal: "Ship Foundering on Reef. Come at Once." This message was followed a half hour later by a much more ominous transmission: "For God's sake hurry." There was water coming into the radio room. But the rescue ships could not make headway against the powerful storm.

When the storm died down and the rescue ships were able to return to the reef, the *Princess Sophia* was gone. All that remained above the water beside the reef was the top of its mast. The *Princess Sophia* had gone to the bottom, and all the passengers had perished.

Gone were some of the Yukon's most prominent—and promising—citizens. Scotsman William Scouse, one of the most successful mine operators in the Klondike, had perished. He came to the Klondike the summer of 1896. Joe Ladue tipped him off, and he and his partners were able to stake 15 Eldorado, which made him a rich man. In recent years, he had spent his winters with Mrs. Scouse in Seattle but continued to work his mines in the summertime.

Walter Harper was the son of Arthur Harper, one of the original locators of Dawson City, and a First Nation mother. He had received a good education Outside, and then returned to Alaska. He was the guide who led Hudson Stuck on the ascent of Mount McKinley,[330] and was the first man to set foot on the summit of North America's tallest peak. Walter and his

The plight of the Yukon during the war years was made worse when 343 souls were lost in the sinking of the *Princess Sophia* during the last days of the war. YUKON ARCHIVES, ROY MINTER FONDS, 92/15, #375.

new bride, Frances, were headed Outside, he to join the American army and study medicine, and she, a nurse, to work with the Red Cross.

All seven members of the O'Brien family perished in the wreck. William, a cousin of Charlie O'Brien, was a member of the Yukon Territorial Council. Arriving in Dawson in 1901 at age twenty-two, he at first worked for his uncle, Thomas W. O'Brien. He was involved in the construction of the Klondike Mines Railway and the management of the fleet of O'Brien and Moran river steamers.

Very active socially, O'Brien's last charitable act was singing at the fundraising event in Skagway the evening before the *Princess Sophia* sailed. He married Sarah McKinnon of Detroit. Together, they had five children, aged two and a half to fourteen, all of whom were with them on the *Sophia*.

Others were not so prominent. Kakuzo Tsuji and George S. Shimada both worked together in a hand laundry in Dawson, after which Tsuji cooked for the Yukon Gold Company. Shimada had been the chief cook on the steamer *Dawson* before leaving for the winter. There were hundreds of similar stories.

Except in the Yukon and Alaska, the sinking of the *Princess Sophia* vanished rapidly from public attention, the story overwhelmed by the news of the pending armistice. A world that had been battered by conflict and death for four years seemed determined to celebrate and look forward to the future, rather than remember one of the worst marine disasters in West Coast history. Today, the tragedy is remembered in various books and in songs by Steve Hites of Skagway and Dan Halen of Whitehorse, and by a prominent memorial on the Dawson City waterfront.[331]

JOE BOYLE AND THE QUEEN OF ROMANIA

WITH TRUCES ESTABLISHED between Germany and both Russia and Romania in late December of 1917, animosities were reduced, and the larger threat became that between the Bolsheviks and Romania. For Joe Boyle, the primary purpose for being at the Eastern Front seemed to have vaporized. He could no longer advance the Russian conflict with Germany. Furthermore, his official status in representing Canada was in question. In late January 1918, the Governor General of Canada, the Duke of Devonshire, received a cipher telegram from Colonial Secretary Walter Long, a friend of Boyle, that disowned Boyle, stating that he "evinced utmost repugnance to cooperate with Inter-Allied representatives and refuses to recognize any party. His independent action has caused much trouble to Allied Railways Mission and his presence in Russia has been the source of constant embarrassment to British representatives."[332] In response, a few days later, the Governor General sent Boyle instructions recalling him from Russia to Canada. There were two problems: first to deliver the order to him, and second, getting the maverick Canadian to comply with any instructions from a government that employed him in no official capacity.

However, Britain had not established diplomatic recognition of the new Bolshevik regime in Russia, and her diplomats were restricted to Petrograd and isolated from diplomatic affairs.[333] Boyle, in contrast, seemed to have the freedom to travel widely and, for the moment, had gained the respect of the Bolshevik regime, which opened doors for him. Recognizing this, Romanian prime minister Ion Brătianu asked him to go to Petrograd on behalf of the Romanian government to assure Leon Trotsky, the Russian commissar for foreign affairs, that "Jassy wished to avoid friction and misunderstanding between Roumania [sic] and the new regime in Russia."[334]

This suited Boyle's purposes well, as he had a deeply hidden secret: he was running a spy network. In 1917, he began to organize an intelligence network consisting of units, each headed by "one good man," who would select ten others, preferably engineers—all of the men had to be officers, of independent means—ready to take on any job required and do exactly what they were told, without asking questions who gave the orders or what relation their work had with any other work. Absolute secrecy and obedience were to be observed—no written orders or reports, no questions asked. As soon as a man in any unit showed sufficient initiative and ability to handle men to warrant starting him out, he was to be, in turn, deputed to raise and take command of a unit of another ten men.[335]

Boyle referred to these as "destruct units," among whose assignments would be the sabotage of industrial production in Russia. By March 1918, he had forty-four units, with 484 members, financed by the British and the French.

Before departing on his diplomatic and intelligence mission, however, at the request of the general commanding the Russian 4th Army in Romania, he investigated the food shortages they were experiencing. The problem—a shortage of meat—was diagnosed, along with a solution. Boyle told them to slaughter half their horses to provide meat for the soldiers and the civilian population. Since it was winter, the meat could be kept frozen until needed, and the amount of fodder required would also be reduced, so there would be enough to feed the remainder of the horses.

Boyle left Petrograd later in January with two tasks: to improve the efficiency of the rail transportation system, and to discuss Russian-Romanian relations with the current commander of the southern front. A third task was asked of him. Since transportation had broken down, he was asked to take diplomatic mail pouches with him and deliver them to Jassy. Ironically, he was being asked to serve the diplomatic service at the same time that the Governor General was trying to order him back to Canada!

Boyle's achievements over the following months were breathtaking in their scope. In February, he travelled by train first to Sebastopol and then to

Odessa, for the purpose of establishing a peace treaty between Russia and Romania. The strategy was to keep the Russian hostilities focussed upon the Germans, whose forces would be divided between two fronts. In Odessa, on February 20, he met Dr. Christian Rakovsky, who commanded the Rumcherod, a short-lived organ of Soviet power in southwestern Russia. The negotiations that followed were challenging. When Rakovsky was hostile to Romania, Boyle focussed on the others attending the three days of meetings and eventually got them to agree to peace terms. Rakovsky at first refused to sign the treaty in a marathon negotiating session, until, at five in the morning, he finally gave in and added his signature.[336]

The treaty had three provisions. First, Romania would progressively withdraw troops from Bessarabia, except for troops to protect the vital railway lines. Second, if a peace could be negotiated with the Central Powers, then the Russian armies within Romania would withdraw. Third, safe entry would be granted for Romanian troops in Russia if they were forced to retreat from their homeland in front of a German advance. Rakovsky had once been imprisoned in Romania for subversive activities and was now an avowed enemy of the Romanian government. He had arrested a number of prominent diplomats, ministers, industrialists and aristocrats to be held as hostages in the relations between the two countries. The treaty also provided for a prisoner exchange.

Boyle, accompanied by his interpreter, returned to Jassy, where he conferred with Alexandru Averescu, the war minister, and with great difficulty persuaded him to present the treaty before the cabinet. The cabinet resisted at first, being more concerned about their treaty with Germany, but eventually signed the document. Boyle then returned to Odessa in an airplane provided by French general H.M. Berthelot to have the treaty ratified by the Rumcherod.[337]

The Germans were advancing and it appeared that Jassy, which had for some time served as the temporary capital of Romania, would be captured. Allied staff located there were in a panic to leave as quickly as possible to avoid capture. It was a terrible time for Romania, as everybody seemed intent on abandoning ship before the German army arrived. It was under these circumstances that Joe Boyle met Queen Marie of Romania. The first encounter was at a luncheon on March 2. It was a courtesy invitation to an unknown Canadian who was doing so much for Romania. She remembered: "Although full of anguish, I had a busy day and made the acquaintance of a very interesting Canadian, a certain Col. Boyle, who is working for us in Russia, trying to better our situation and especially our transport. A curiously fascinating man who is afraid of nothing and who, by his extraordinary force of will and fearlessness manages to get through everywhere, a real Jack London type."[338]

They met three more times over the next week. And then, on March 9, as the various Allied missions were abandoning Romania, and German elements were already insinuating themselves into the court and government, he came to see her. Queen Marie stayed up late at her palace so that she could receive and bid farewell to the departing diplomats. It was a miserable stormy evening that expressed the circumstances well. She was alone in her anguish, when Boyle, obviously having braved the storm and dripping wet, waited awkwardly in the reception hall until she greeted him. "Have you come to see me?" she asked. "No ma'am," Boyle replied. "I have come to help you. And my God, woman, do you need help."[339]

They talked for hours, pouring out their inner feelings, and an irresistible bond was formed between them. "We understood each other from the first moment we clasped hands, as though we had never been strangers," she was later to write.[340]

It was an unlikely pairing. Boyle had never had much time for the women in his life. He had abandoned his current wife in Dawson, never to see her again, when he departed for London two years before. Queen Marie was the granddaughter of Queen Victoria, and at age seventeen had married into the royal family of this distant and minor nation. Boyle was, in fact, smitten by this beguiling member of the royal family.

Immediately after this rainy encounter, Boyle flew to Odessa with instruction from the queen and others to ensure the safety of the seventy Romanian hostages arrested by Rakovsky and being held there in Turna Prison. They were to be exchanged for four hundred Russian prisoners being held in Romania but were not able to leave by train for Romania as planned. Instead, the prisoners were released and taken by truck to the waterfront.

When Boyle reached them, they had been loaded onto two boats at the dock; he immediately saw the danger in the situation. Boyle confronted the officer, a man named Dichescu, in charge of the hostile Romanian revolutionary battalion (also known as the death battalion) to stall any action to leave port with the hostages until he had had time to speak with the Rumcherod.

After a lengthy search, he located a member of the council and obtained a document that turned the prisoners over to Boyle's custody. Armed with this document, he returned to the waterfront and prevailed upon Dichescu to release the hostages. The Soviet was unable to command his soldiers to release the prisoners. Much confusion followed; shots were fired, two hostages were killed and seven more were lost in the excitement.

They eventually got underway, but instead of going west to Romania, the ship headed east through stormy seas for three days before landing at the small coastal Crimean port of Theodosia. Unfortunately, they found themselves caught between the Bolsheviks and their civil war combatants, the White Russians. Here they were herded off their boat and taken to an abandoned sanatorium.

Convinced that the prisoners were doomed to be executed, Boyle enlisted the aid of a Bolshevik official named Breshenan. With a bribe provided by the British vice-consul in Theodosia, Boyle was able to secure a small freighter called the *Chernomore* to take the hostages to Romania. They got away safely and headed for Sebastopol. There he was able to arrange with the German general in command of the southern front for safe passage to the port of Sulina, but the general failed to inform the Austrians, who held the port at the time.

The *Chernomore* arrived at Sulina, but it was three days before they were able to proceed up the Danube to the railhead at Galaţi, where there was a waiting train. But the stationmaster had not arranged for passage for the freed hostages in Boyle's care. The train left the station without them, but after Boyle sent a heated telegram to Jassy, the train returned two hours later and room was made available for all of the freed hostages. From there, the train travelled non-stop at top speed until it arrived in Jassy, where the engineer had been ordered to deliver them in time for lunch.

Joe Boyle with Queen Marie of Romania (left, dressed in peasant attire) and Princess Ileana, Queen Marie's daughter (right), in Romania, 1918. Boyle was recovering from a stroke. YUKON ARCHIVES OXFORD HISTORICAL SOCIETY COLLECTION 84/078 #108

News of this heroic rescue reached Romania before Boyle and his party of newly freed hostages; the streets were packed with cheering crowds. "People had given up the prisoners and their saviour for dead," said the grateful wife of one of those rescued.[341] The next day, March 25, at a luncheon celebrating the escape to freedom, Boyle was awarded the Romanian Star of Freedom. He was proclaimed a hero in the Romanian newspapers and hailed as "The Saviour of Romania." He was thanked publicly at a luncheon at the Romanian Jockey Club on April 11.[342]

Britain, which had been discontented with Boyle, made an about-face and rescinded the recall order from the Canadian Governor General to Boyle, "so long as his services were considered useful."[343] No less a luminary than Leon Trotsky, the Russian commissar for foreign affairs, frequently asked about Boyle.

Things were not going well for Romania, however. Germany had advanced into Bessarabia and taken the port of Odessa. They were moving toward Kiev and Crimea. Meanwhile, the Germans had installed a new pro-German government in a rigged election in Romania. They had taken control of the oil fields, and the postal service, telegraph and telephone (thus isolating Romania from the outside world). They forced peasants young and old into servitude; disobedience resulted in imprisonment or execution. And they publicly condemned the king and queen to strengthen their own control of the country. And things only got worse for Romania as Germany's position in the war deteriorated.

Queen Marie withdrew to a small cottage at Coțofănești to distance herself as much as possible from the Germans and the actions of their puppet government. "Undeniably my wooden abode was an adorable retreat and everyone who saw it loved it as I did," she wrote. "Many came to visit me in my solitude, especially those, who like me, were sick of what was going on in our official world. My doors were hospitably open to every visitor, and my table stretched according to the number of my guests."[344]

Joe Boyle was now outside the puppet government circles and spent his days sharing his lifelong love of horse riding with Queen Marie. He had meetings with members of the former Romanian government and continued his spy activities. Nor did the situation seem to stifle his movements. Toward the end of April, he was in Bessarabia, where, under royal orders, the Romanian air squadron made two planes available to Boyle and his interpreter. During this time, he was constantly travelling. The German puppet prime minister, Alexandru Marghiloman, was powerless to intervene, as the Germans were preoccupied elsewhere.

The Romanian royal family did what they could to defy their German masters. Some of it was merely symbolic. After many delays, in early June, Romania held a day of mourning to honour the fallen. Despite strictures that no Allied officers would be allowed to attend, Boyle accompanied Queen Marie, at her invitation, to a mass in Jassy Cathedral. He did so in full military regalia, proudly displaying the decorations he had received from the Russians.

According to historian Leonard Taylor, "Several days later, personally confronted by [German General] von Mackensen, Boyle was ordered to remove his uniform. He coolly refused, saying it could be taken from him only by force, and that he would shoot the first man that attempted it. The General did not pursue the issue."[345]

Boyle was tireless in his personal campaign, exuding the energy of a much younger man, but this drive took its toll upon him physically. While attending intelligence meetings at Kishinev, in Bessarabia, Boyle suffered a debilitating stroke in his hotel room shortly after his arrival. He was paralyzed on the right side.

The first two weeks he was in grave condition, but he slowly improved. By the end of July, when he was able to be moved, Queen Marie arranged for him to be transferred to the Romanian summer palace near Bikaz, in the hill country west of Jassy. He arrived August 1. Slowly, he began to recover. His sense of humour returned, and he began to tell stories of the Klondike again. He became friends with Princess Ileana, Marie's youngest daughter.

"Each day," said Boyle biographer Leonard Taylor, "Marie had breakfast with him, and, unless the weather was inclement, she and her children joined him for a drive... Frequently they carried a picnic lunch brought from the palace. It was exactly what Boyle required: quiet, the care and loving attention of good friends, good food, and an opportunity to rest, which had escaped him all his previous year."[346]

Boyle next took on the task of helping the Red Cross recover medical supplies that had been confiscated by the Romanians. He wanted them to be the basis upon which Marie could start a medical organization (the Order of Maria Regina), and to divert some of the supplies to the White Russian armies battling the Bolsheviks. Boyle was able to find the $250,000 to pay for the purchase of the supplies.[347]

His health steadily improved, and it wasn't long before he was travelling widely on one assignment after another. In September, he helped arrange for Grand Duchess Maria Pavlovna to escape to Romania from Odessa. At the beginning of October, he went on a secret mission 2,500 kilometres to Ekatrinburg, deep in the heart of Russia, to determine the fate of the Romanoffs, the Russian royal family. As the war concluded, he celebrated the armistice in Jassy at a dinner party hosted by General Ballard at the British embassy, which was also attended by Queen Marie and two of her daughters.

A week later, Boyle sailed to Yalta on the Crimean Peninsula to facilitate the escape of Dowager Queen Maria Feodorovna to Romania, an offer she refused to accept. By the time Boyle had returned to Romania, the German-backed Romanian prime minister, who had resigned during the final days of the war, had been replaced by pro-Allied general Constantin Coandă, in Bucharest. It was at the Cotroceni Palace in Bucharest that Boyle reported on his activities in the Crimea.

The honours for Boyle and his wartime feats poured in. He received the French Croix de Guerre from General Berthelot, and the Order of Maria Regina (for his efforts to acquire Red Cross supplies). Sir George Barclay, the British ambassador, recommended Boyle for recognition. As a consequence, he was awarded the Distinguished Service Order (DSO), which was announced officially on the 1919 royal birthday honours list. Dubbed the Duke of Bucharest by the press, he was granted the title of Duke of Jassy by the Romanian royal family, and given a sizeable estate in Bessarabia, in gratitude for all he had done for this tiny nation.[348] The one thing that Boyle did not receive was recognition from his mother country.

1919 AND BEYOND

OCCUPATION

THE WAR MAY have been over, but it was not finished for the Yukon men and women who had gone overseas. For some, the process of returning to Canada and demobilizing would be a slow and often frustrating period; for others, there was occupation duty. The 2nd Canadian Motor Machine Gun Brigade was one of the units assigned the latter.

In preparation for the advance into Belgium and Germany, Harry Meurling, now lieutenant colonel of the brigade, instructed them regarding this assignment:

> The Brigade is about to advance... into country lately held and occupied by the enemy and even into the enemy country itself.
>
> It may also fall to the lot of the Brigade to be sent to different points to keep order, quell disturbances, etc., etc., and, in view of the more or less disorganized state of the enemy forces, to help the friendly population against straggling bands.
>
> This means that, in order to successfully impress the population, both friendly and hostile, with the efficiency of the Brigade, and its power and intention to carry out its mission, every officer, N.C.O. and Man must do his utmost to practise the kind of discipline that has carried us so successfully through the past years and must keep up to the highest standard his training in technical matters.[349]

Meurling cautioned the men to be on their best behaviour and ever alert for the "inherent German cunning and double dealing."[350] They had to maintain discipline of the highest standard and turn away from temptations that they might encounter.

He concluded:

> You are men entering enemy country as an advanced guard of Free Men, not as the Germans entered France and Belgium, filled with lust and greed and the destructive discipline that is based on slavery and compulsion.
>
> See to it that you act as free men, that you show what effect freedom has on intelligent men, which is to breed sympathy, tolerance, respect and fair play towards all.
>
> That is what the Canadians, who during the last four years have laid down their lives and their blood, demand from those that are left behind.
>
> They paid for the name; it is up to you to uphold it.[351]

The men marched across Belgium, and crossed the Rhine into Germany, to "hold certain parts in order to secure the fulfillment of the terms of the Armistice Preliminary to the Peace Treaty."[352]

"We are all being fitted out in good order with clothes, etc., for our advance into Germany," wrote Norton Townsend to his mother on November 15. "[W]e are to follow up behind the Germans. I wouldn't miss it for anything. It will be a great trip. The people are simply mad over us during the last few days." He later added: "We are all talking of coming home now but I guess it will be some time yet."[353]

The brigade advanced, crossing into Germany on December 10 and reaching their barracks at the outskirts of Bonn four days later. Writing to his father in mid-December, Norton Townsend stated: "It is a kind of strange sensation to sit and try to talk to them and drink their coffee. But they are as fine and all give us the big smile though the Lord only knows what is at the bottom of it. All seam to be fead [sic] up and glad it is over…

Zowitza Nicholas left Dawson to study nursing in Seattle. She joined the American nursing corps and served in France, where she was called "The Angel of Ward 7" by one of the soldiers she cared for. DAVID E. CANN

They admit themselves that we had them beat every way the last few months. Their artillery men say that when they would send 10 shells over we would send 200 back."[354]

Although the German armies had been beaten in the field, the war had no direct impact upon the people back in Germany, except for a few aerial bombings, which may have made them feel that they had in fact not been beaten but betrayed by the politicians. Thus were sown some seeds of discontent that would grow into the next world war.

It is hard to say how the Germans felt as they watched Canadians march into their homeland. Norton Townsend watched the Canadian troops march into Bonn in the pouring rain on December 14 with bayonets fixed and flags flying. "There is no doubt about it being our day," he wrote.[355] The men were billeted with German families along the way, and now fourteen of them were lodging in a house much like Government House in Dawson City, but with more style. The established routine included regular battery duty, training, lectures and continued machine gun drill and practice. More attention was paid to health, cleanliness and appearance; bathing and regular changes in underwear were duly logged, and one day, the 2nd Brigade officers engaged the officers of Canadian Corps headquarters in a game of indoor baseball (the brigade beat headquarters 25 to 9).[356]

George Black rejoined the brigade on Christmas day, when voluntary Christmas Mass was celebrated and a Christmas dinner was enjoyed by all. As Norton Townsend described it to his mother, "We had a leg of mutton, potatoes with boiled ham and cabbage on the side lots of nuts, apples and oranges. When they [the Germans] saw our oranges and dates they went crazy [as they] had not seen either for three years." He added: "Captain Black is back with the Brigade, everyone is glad to see him back again, he is a good head and hard to beat, the only one around here in his class at all is Lyman."[357]

Zowitza Nicholas was also resting after the cessation of combat. She had left Dawson City sometime before to study nursing in Seattle. A former Dawson high school student, she came north with her parents during the gold rush when she was just five years old. Her father took the name John Nicholas when he immigrated to the United States from Greece. Her mother, Jennie Wilhelmina Erickson, was a Swedish immigrant who married John in 1891. John had worked as a barber from his arrival in Dawson until his death in December 1917.

In the summer of 1918, Zowitza shipped out as an army nurse and was stationed at Base 50 Red Cross Hospital at Mesves, France. It was one of more than one hundred hospitals established by the US Army to tend the wounded. After the armistice, she was granted leave and travelled widely through occupied Germany, Belgium and France. She travelled from Nantes to Paris, then Metz, Koblenz, Cologne and Brussels, visiting cathedrals, art galleries and museums. She travelled with another nurse to Nice, where they spent several days enjoying the warm Mediterranean climate. But it is the description of her journey from Brussels to Paris by train that stirs the emotions. The ten-hour journey took her through the battlefields of France and Belgium. There, she saw the barren wasteland that had been created by war. She saw countless bridges destroyed by the conflict; she witnessed overturned locomotives in the ditches beside the railroad tracks. She observed the wire entanglements, mowed-down trees and shell holes, big and small. She saw trenches, trenches and more trenches. Small white wooden crosses populated the landscape, some single; others clustered together. One had a helmet hanging from it.

"It is hard to believe that the mass of stone was once a town or a house or that people ever lived there and worked," she wrote in a letter to her mother:

There are rods of twisted iron ... and then there is the inevitable pile of stone. Stone and red bricks; perhaps a piece of wall standing, perhaps not, and more piles of stone. Town after town is like this—no people there—not a sign of life ...

At one place I saw a man with a long stick or rake—I don't know which—digging and pushing and scraping aside a mass of stone. I wonder if he was intending to build himself a home, or if he was only looking for riches that were once his treasures.[358]

She didn't describe the horrors she saw in her hospital. Sixty years later, though, she remembered her work. Many soldiers died of influenza in the closing weeks of the war. "The room was so full of coffins that we had to step over them," she recalled. "I could never get over the terrible things that happened to those poor boys."[359] She was remembered as the "Angel of Ward 7" by one soldier she cared for in the winter of 1918. Sixty-five years later, he tracked her down to thank her in suburban Los Angeles, where she continued to nurse until 1979.[360]

The 1918 Spanish influenza epidemic that struck the soldiers in combat continued its spread around the world. The pandemic broke out on the eastern American seaboard in early September. The deadly virus spread rapidly, and within weeks, reports from various cities and military camps confirmed the news that this influenza was highly contagious and killing people in large numbers.

Private Russell McCollom, formerly a steam engineer and miner in Dawson, would die of bronchopneumonia, probably as a secondary infection from the deadly virus, very early in 1919. He was buried with thousands of others in the military cemetery at Étaples, on the coast of France. Hugh McDonald, whose father was an Anglican missionary and his mother First Nation, was another victim of the flu. McDonald was serving with the 49th Battalion at Passchendaele when, on October 30, he earned the Military Medal. For forty hours, without any break, he was the only runner who survived the attack to carry messages from the battlefield through heavy enemy barrage. For hours, he coolly helped dress and evacuate the wounded from the field. Because of his fearless actions in the field, he was eventually commissioned. He was wounded twice but survived the war, only to be taken by influenza and pneumonia. He died at No. 1 Casualty Clearing Station and was buried near Mons. McDonald was twenty-three years old.[361]

The influenza pandemic was a bitter pill for the men who had survived the brutality of the war. The death toll rose rapidly as this invisible scourge made its way around the world. Back in Canada, it would take almost as many lives as the war had. It was a deadly postscript to a deadly war.

The residents of the Yukon learned about the plague from reports in newspapers, and letters sent from friends and loved ones Outside. Were they, too, to be stricken by the deadly virus? By November 1918, the *Dawson Daily News* issued reports of influenza cutting a swath around the world. Dr. Alfred Thompson confirmed the dire situation in a letter he wrote to one of his colleagues in Dawson City. Members of his own family Outside had also been stricken.

Seattle had fallen to the flu in October. By mid-month, 75 residents had died; by the end of the month, 350 had succumbed. Alaska was not spared, either. Juneau reported three cases at the end of October. There were eight cases on December 14 and more than one hundred a week later. The remote city of Nome was hit as well, despite the quarantine of all passengers arriving by boat. There were no cases on October 22, but by November 8, there were more than three hundred. The December 23 issue of the *Dawson Daily News* reported that there had been one thousand deaths in the Nome area. Even if this number was exaggerated, it must have terrified Yukoners.

Fairbanks placed sentries on all the trails into town and imposed a five-day quarantine, but the dreaded flu still appeared. Influenza knew no boundaries; anyone could be stricken, regardless of race, gender or social class, though some groups were hit harder than others. Indigenous communities throughout Alaska were decimated. In one settlement, only a half dozen survived. In another community, twenty-two of twenty-four adults perished, leaving sixteen orphans. Of ten villages visited by one doctor, three were wiped out entirely, and the other settlements suffered 85 percent mortality. Many children whose parents had died then starved or froze to death.

The *Dawson Daily News* and *Whitehorse Star* reported the mounting death toll from around the world. Yukon citizens waited with uneasiness. They could feel the circle of death closing in from all directions.

Finally, the Yukon took action on November 9, when R.B. Knight, acting gold commissioner, issued a notice to the assistant medical health officer for Whitehorse, Dr. W.B. Clarke, to take all necessary steps to prevent the spread of influenza. Dr. Clarke was in close communication with Dr. Gable, the medical health officer in Skagway, where all incoming passengers were placed in quarantine for five days. No cases had been reported so far.

Fearing the worst, the government started making preparations. Thinking that contagion could be spread by handling incoming mail, Dr. Gable at Skagway had all mail from Juneau and Haines fumigated. Outside mail, which took more than five days in transit, was not considered to be a health risk.

If the pandemic reached the Yukon, would the territory be prepared for the onslaught? In Dawson, territorial secretary J. Maltby asked Mother Superior Mary Mark what the capacity of St. Mary's Hospital was if they had to deal with an outbreak in the gold rush capital. Ninety beds, and eight staff, was her reply.[362] Maltby also contacted local businesses and determined that fifteen additional beds, fifteen mattresses and twenty-five sets of blankets were available if needed. With an estimated 10 percent of the population likely to be stricken with the flu, would this be enough?

Dawson City continued to function normally. Christmas was enjoyed without the spectre of death, and New Year's Eve was celebrated with the annual masque ball at the Arctic Brotherhood Hall.[363]

Early in the new year, 1919, word was received that the "Copper River Indians," the Ahtna, located west of the Yukon in Alaska, were suffering from influenza. Instructions were sent out to discourage any contact with them that winter. When a report reached authorities that a party of Chilkat Tlingit from Haines had set out to visit the Indigenous community of Champagne, west of Whitehorse, the Mounted Police were sent to intercept them. A temporary quarantine station was set up in the village until January 17. Travellers were also intercepted at the town of Forty Mile, where only the mail carrier was allowed to proceed into the Yukon.

Advice from Ottawa was confusing regarding a serum treatment for influenza. Although it stated that there was no serum to treat the illness, an unproven product developed in Kingston, Ontario, was sent to the Yukon as a precautionary measure. At the end of January, the annual winter patrol to Fort McPherson carried one hundred doses of the serum, wrapped in buffalo robes with a small charcoal foot warmer to prevent the vials from freezing.

Pressure mounted to remove the quarantine in Skagway, which occurred February 22. But a month later, with an outbreak of fifty cases in the coastal Alaskan port, an incoming train was intercepted by the local Mounted Police, and a temporary quarantine was established in Carcross for the thirty passengers. The line of defence was drawing closer and closer to Whitehorse.

This temporary Carcross quarantine station proved inadequate and inconvenient; requests were put forward to move the quarantine station to Whitehorse. Meanwhile, Alaska governor Thomas Riggs imposed a five-day quarantine on all outgoing and incoming traffic at Skagway. Despite large alarmist headlines on the front page of the *Dawson Daily News* on March 21, Dr. Clarke, who was reported to have been stricken, had only suffered from a minor cold. Three people in Skagway, however, died from the deadly virus.

Finally, inbound passengers were allowed into Whitehorse for their quarantine period. On April 18, the quarantine was lifted in Skagway, and Whitehorse followed suit on May 2. During the critical period, November 1918 to May 1919, not one case of influenza was reported anywhere in the

Yukon. By the spring of 1919, the dangerous virus that had swept the globe had mutated and lost its potency. The Yukon seemed to have been spared.

Before freeze-up each autumn, when river transportation came to an end, Dawson City stockpiled essential supplies in large warehouses in sufficient quantities to last through the winter. During the height of the pandemic, the gold rush town was secure in its isolation. With only one means of access from Outside, via rail to Whitehorse, and then five days by sleigh over the snow-covered winter trail to Dawson, it was possible to control the spread of infection in the territory.

That, combined with the coordinated efforts of the administration during this period, meant that the Yukon was one of the few jurisdictions on the planet that was not ravaged by the pandemic. How ironic for the young men overseas who succumbed to influenza; if they had remained at home in the Yukon, it would have been one of the few places on the planet that was spared this final indignity.

HOMEWARD BOUND

THE PRESENCE OF a force of occupation in Germany brought home the fact that the Allies had won the war, but for the men stationed there, it must have been hard not to think of what would happen when they returned home. In preparation for their return to Canada, educational classes commenced in January, with subjects such as agriculture, bookkeeping, gas engines and mathematics. It was known as the Khaki University and was aimed at everyone from the illiterate to the university level.

As a distraction, the Canadians played each other and the Americans in matches of football, baseball and other sports; at one event, the Canadians beat the Americans at "divisional sports." On January 22, the entire 2nd Canadian Motor Machine Gun Brigade assembled for a group photo, followed by another of officers only, with the Bonn Bridge in the background.[364]

The withdrawal of the brigade from Bonn began on January 26, with a 110-kilometre march back to Namur, in Belgium. After billeting at Fieron that evening, they arrived at Verdrin, 5 kilometres north of Namur, the following day. The 320 officers and men were then transported to Aubin-Saint-Vaast, France, by train on February 18. Next they were transferred by rail to the port city of Le Havre on March 5, where they rested, bathed, deloused, received new clothing and moved into better quarters in preparation for shipping back to England. They boarded the SS *Dieppe* on the evening of March 7 and sailed for Weymouth that night.

The men of the 2nd Canadian Motor Machine Gun Brigade were at last on their way back to England, some of its Yukon members having been at the front since 1916. Those early birds had seen action at the Somme, Vimy, Passchendaele and Amiens, as well as during the Hundred Days. They had seen the worst combat of the war; they had seen their comrades fall to the sniper's bullet, the machine gun's chatter, the whirring of shrapnel or the deadly fumes of poison gas. They had endured the ceaseless barrage of enemy shells in the trenches and in No Man's Land. They had survived the rats, the lice and trench foot, all the while wondering if they would ever see home again. And now they knew.

They arrived at Weymouth and disembarked at nine o'clock in the morning on March 8. They received a haversack lunch at Alexander Gardens and left by train for the Canadian Machine Gun Depot (CMGD) at Seaford, Sussex, where, after rattling along for 200 kilometres or more, they arrived at four in the afternoon. They were greeted by the CMGD band and marched to their new quarters. After a few days' rest, they went on leave for two weeks; when they returned, they prepared for discharge and embarkation. More than a dozen documents had to be filled in and hundreds of questions answered. They were subjected to a medical board, and many, fearing that their return to Canada might be delayed by any medical problems, lied about their condition—which they would later regret when they applied for disability pensions back in Canada. As noted by Tim Cook, "A persistent cough from relentless minor gas poisonings was shrugged off; an old bullet wound through the shoulder that never fully healed was downgraded to a nonchalant stiffness; recurring nightmares were kept from probing committee members who were forced by sheer numbers to race through their patient files."[365] Many men had much-needed dental work before their final departure. For some, this meant multiple extractions—often without the benefit of novocaine. Day by day, battery by battery, the men were processed. The officer in charge of the Khaki University gave them a lecture on civil re-establishment and land settlement.

On April 3, the brigade was presented with the regimental colours in a formal ceremony at Seaford. The weather was warm and sunny, with a clear blue sky and a light breeze—the first nice day in the longest time— which bode well for the ceremony, and the men. Martha Black accompanied Lady Perley, the wife of the Canadian High Commissioner, on the two-hour trip by automobile from London. They were met upon their arrival by the general officer commanding and the staff of Canadian headquarters, which included Colonel Anderson, the camp commandant; Lieutenant Colonel Meurling and Major Trench, his second in command; Colonel (Canon) Almond; and Captain George Black. It must have been a proud moment for the Blacks, as their son Lyman was one of the two colour-bearers. The colours had been sponsored by the chapters of the IODE in Dawson City and Whitehorse, and were embroidered by members of the School of Art Needlework, Kensington. Mrs. Black had gone down to the school to sew in a few stitches personally.

After the colours were presented, Lady Perley spoke of the honour and pleasure it gave her to present the colours to a unit of whose fighting record everyone had a right to be proud. Lieutenant Colonel Meurling responded, noting that the brigade had been right in the thick of things through all of the battles of 1918, up to the armistice, at which point they were holding the line 6 kilometres east of Mons.[366]

A few days later, the men were granted leave while waiting for their departure. Finally, after several delays, the men of the 2nd Canadian Motor Machine Gun Brigade, including a large number of men from the Yukon, boarded the SS *Minnekhada* on May 3. George Black, however, was not among those returning to Canada. Because of his legal background, he was delayed for court martial work.

Martha Black had kept herself busy in England while her husband and son remained across the English Channel in France in late 1918 and early 1919. After George was transferred back to the brigade, then stationed in

George Black (extreme left), Lyman Black (seated extreme left) and other officers of the 2nd Motor Machine Gun Brigade in Bonn, Germany, after the Armistice. YUKON ARCHIVES GEORGE BLACK FONDS 81/107 #137

Germany, she spent her Christmas with friends from Brighton. During the winter and spring, she kept up her speaking schedule, including a three-week tour of Wales. Throughout these months, she also continued to administer the Yukon Comfort Fund.

By March, Mrs. Black was worn out by her gruelling schedule and had to cancel some speaking engagements, but she was back at it again in early May. In June, she was sent across the English Channel to inspect the graves of American soldiers. She was to look into reports of fraudulent antics. It was said that photographs were taken of a single grave marker, with different nameplates mounted upon it, and the photos were then sent to different families back in the US.

"Far from this being the case," she reported, "the cemeteries of France are growing into fields of beauty each day, tended by battalions of devoted men and women who have volunteered from all services to do this special job. As the work proceeds each grave is marked and numbered to correspond with maps, so that when the relations of the dead men are able to come they will have no difficulty in finding it."[367]

When she returned from France in early July, she was off to Liverpool for ten days for the Western Command. "A pretty strenuous life for a real

Lady Perley, wife of the British High Commissioner to Canada, presenting the colours to the 2nd Motor Machine Gun Brigade, April 3, 1919. Lyman Black kneels in the foreground. TORONTO PUBLIC LIBRARY

grandmother," she wrote, "but it is better to wear out than to rust out."[368]

After she returned to England, she wrote of the tour:

> I had a perfectly wonderful trip and saw a great deal of the devastated regions, Poperinghe, Ypres, Bailleul, Bethune, Arras, Vimy, Lens, etc., etc., then Etaples (not so desolate as other places) Amiens, and finally Chateau Thierry and Rheims. I was three days between Lens-Arras-Vimy, and at the time Peace was signed [June 28, 1919] was wandering over the Vimy Ridge between that town, or the place where it was, and Arras. The more I saw of the country the greater was my admiration for the wonderful men who fought for us over there. And aren't the French magnificent in the spirit with which they are working to restore what seems devastated beyond repair.[369]

RIOTS AND DISCONTENT

NOW THAT THE war was over, the Canadian government was faced with the immense logistical challenge of returning a quarter of a million men to Canada, amid "storms, strikes, shipping shortages and the consuming impatience of every man to get home."[370] While waiting to be returned to Canada, the men were transferred to several demobilization camps, including one at Kinmel Park, Wales. They occupied temporary quarters until their turn came up to be transported back to Canada. While they waited, many men were subjected to the influenza pandemic, which, before it ran its course, had infected half the population of England. The coal shortage only compounded the harshness of the coldest winter in living memory.

Meanwhile, the Canadian government had to compete with the United States and other nations for transportation. After one returning ship delivered troops to Halifax under horrible conditions, Canada imposed a standard that reduced the volume of flow. During the winter months, Halifax was the only port open to arriving soldiers; the CPR became the bottleneck, because it could transport no more than twenty thousand soldiers and ten thousand wives and children out of the Maritimes per month. Of course, there was also conflict between officials who felt that the most employable soldiers should be returned first, to stimulate the economy, whereas General Currie argued that the men who had been first over should be shipped home before the recent arrivals. In the end, complete units from the four divisions went home first, while reserve units, conscripts and the logistical support returned piecemeal.

Discontent fomented among those detained in the demobilization camps because of the deplorable living conditions, cold weather, unfair treatment and "rumours that Americans were monopolizing ocean shipping."[371] These poor conditions were exacerbated by a dock strike that tied up the troop ship SS *Cassandra*, while a carpenters' strike stopped the refitting of bunks and toilets on another vessel.

Once George Black returned to England, he was asked by former Yukoner Fred Wade, now agent general for British Columbia, to represent several British Columbian soldiers who were being court-martialled for their involvement in the Kinmel Park camp demobilization riots. The events would stir the captain's blood almost as much as the war had.

Early in 1919, Kinmel Park camp was a "random mixture of combatants and non-combatants, conscripts and 'Old Originals,' mixed with the professional misfits who drift to the rear of any army. The camp staff, resentful of the delay in their own homecoming, took little interest in men passing through the camp. Neither did the officers... Only a bully or a fool would have asserted his authority with demobilization only weeks away."[372]

February shipping delays kept the malcontents penned up at Kinmel. Cold weather, relentless rain and shortage of fuel made life miserable for the men in the damp frame huts. Food was monotonous, in part because of a lack of good cooking staff. By the end of February, seventeen thousand soldiers had accumulated in camp, some of whom had been stuck there for six weeks, and the paperwork was slow to be sorted out. While veterans who had come over in 1915 and 1916 waited in the dismal conditions at Kinmel, raw conscripts were being shipped back with a heroes' salute at Liverpool. Most of the men were dead broke and could not even break up the boredom with a trip to the canteen.

The evening of March 4, most officers were out of camp and the military police were patrolling nearby towns. Soldiers in the camp invaded and looted a canteen in the section reserved for men from eastern Ontario and western Quebec. Next the crowd attacked another canteen, and then swarmed into the neighbouring "tin town," where locals sold things to the soldiers from makeshift shops. At midnight a mob broke into the quartermaster's stores. They were driven off by a few officers armed with sticks, but when the lights went out, these men withdrew and the stores were looted.

Commanding officer Colonel Malcolm Colquhoun ordered all supplies of liquor to be drained at once and ammunition withdrawn, but they missed two carloads of liquor and beer. The soldiers, however, found it; soon the drunken mob drove back the twenty-five troopers from the reserve cavalry sent in to restore order.

As the men sobered up, things calmed down somewhat, but a mob of six hundred to one thousand men stalked the camp, assaulting anyone who tried to stop them. In some cases, men were out to settle old scores.

Finally, Lieutenant J.A. Gauthier rallied a few hundred men and they confronted the rampaging mob in a field. Gauthier and a few supporters twice raced toward the rioters, grabbing gang leaders. Suddenly, shots rang out from the mob, and one of Gauthier's party fell, mortally wounded in the neck. They dove for cover, and some of Gauthier's men returned undirected fire. This sobered the crowd, which quieted down and withdrew. In the end, five soldiers were dead and twenty-five others were wounded—five by gunshots, two by bayonets.

Fifty-one Canadian soldiers were eventually brought before a court martial and charged with mutiny; George Black was assigned as legal counsel to represent some of them. The trials began on April 16 in Liverpool and lasted until June 6. Of those brought up on charges, seventeen were acquitted and three more were reprieved by higher authorities. Sentences of the remainder ranged from ten years for a Czech-born soldier and seven for a Romanian-born private to a few weeks for others for minor offences. Twenty-five were convicted of joining in on a mutiny, and five others were convicted of not doing their utmost to stop it.

The harshest sentences seemed to be handed out to those with foreign-sounding names. The British press got a hold on the story, and in the absence of accurate information, sensational but inaccurate accounts filled the newspapers.

The actions of the court seemed designed in part to satisfy British public discomfort about the wild Canadians, and the punishments meted out were draconian. Most of the men should have been charged with drunkenness rather than mutiny, and the president of the court martial seemed deaf to the pleas of qualified defence witnesses who testified to the medical unfitness of one of the accused. As the trial progressed, the court seemed to tire of the process and appeared unable to approach the proceedings with openness and fairness. The convictions (and infrequent acquittals) were churned out like hamburger from a meat grinder.

In response to the riots, the Canadian government, which had previously been unable to arrange enough transportation, was suddenly able to make four additional ships available to transport soldiers back to Canada.

George Black was incensed by the entire proceedings, charging that ordinary soldiers could never get a decent break from the senior officers who formed the court. "In some cases exaggerated ideas of their own importance as officers fogs their vision and warps their judgement as to make them positively dangerous where it is necessary to weigh evidence and pronounce on the guilt or innocence of the accused persons," he charged.[373] Black sided with the plight of the enlisted men. Acting as defence counsel for Charles Sherstotoff, a Doukhobor, he asserted that "it was a case of mistaken identity and that he was a poor ignorant foreigner who had accepted the responsibilities of citizenship in the country of his adoption and had fought as a volunteer."[374]

With the trials complete, Black had only a couple of weeks left before sailing back to Canada. He departed on the Cunard liner *Caronia* on June 25 and arrived in Halifax on July 2. Martha was still in France and unable to obtain passage on the *Caronia* with him and would follow shortly. She thought that she might return to Canada mid-August, but if she accepted an offer from the imperial government to lecture to the army of occupation (in France and Germany), she would not book passage to Canada until near the end of September.[375] In the middle of August, Martha set sail aboard the SS *Melita*, arriving in Quebec City on August 21. After visiting family in Chicago, Denver and Los Angeles (the latter where her father died in late October), she joined George in their new home in Vancouver in early December.

Before going on to Vancouver, Captain Black stopped in Ottawa, where he made his feelings known at the highest levels of government. In a letter to the minister of justice dated July 29, he called the court martial a mockery of justice. Three men who were initially convicted were released, he wrote, when it became apparent that the "impropriety of the verdicts and that they were not sustained by the evidence was so palpable that the General Officer Commanding, in Chief, Western Command, England, being the officer who convened the Court, declined to confirm the findings and the accused were set at liberty."[376]

He further stated that the servicemen convicted "do not deserve the punishment imposed upon them, and the Government of Canada should have them released without delay," and cited a number of reasons. As he explained, the military structure follows junior officers into court, where they are subservient to the will of those superior in rank. Many soldiers were convicted by a narrow vote and without due regard to doctrine of reasonable doubt. Four men charged with mutiny could only be reasonably charged with unlawfully possessing goods. Four men were convicted, but two were given twelve months whereas the other two were only given six months, which smelled of discrimination.

In other cases, the men were acquitted of mutiny but were charged with failure to do their utmost to suppress a mutiny. It was shown that these men were in the presence of officers and NCOs and obeyed orders given them. One accused, who could not speak English, did not have the evidence against him interpreted or explained to him. The same court tried case after case for several weeks. Black argued that what the court heard in one case was carried over to the next trial and affected the judgement of the court. The court became worn down and the trials routine.

In Black's opinion, there was no conspiracy or organized lawlessness, only spontaneous insubordination because of drunkenness. The poor conditions in the camp and the delays in sailing certainly didn't help matters.

"The worst that can be said," wrote Black, "is that some were guilty of riotous, insubordinate and rowdy conduct which never would have assumed any serious proportions had the men received proper treatment and had adequate precautions been taken by those in authority."[377]

George Black was back in Vancouver by July 29, and suffered the disappointment of missing the celebration honouring the returned Yukon soldiers that occurred a couple of months earlier. On May 19, when two hundred Yukoners of Vancouver held a banquet at the Citizens' Club in honour of the "returned remnant" of the shattered 2nd Canadian Motor Machine Gun Brigade, only two of the original members of Boyle's Yukon Brigade were in attendance.[378] A handful more had proceeded north a few days before. These were all that were left of the original fifty men, said Lieutenant Colonel Harry Meurling as he spoke to the crowd on hand: "It was that adaptability and resourcefulness which carried the brigade through against almost overwhelming odds... It was indeed the 'Spirit of the North' that each man typified as he helped to hold the line against hordes of

Boches without rest or supplies, decimated until it was a case of one man to one machine gun, fighting day and night and never giving up."[379]

He summarized the brigade's record, which commenced on the Somme in 1916 and was carried through Vimy Ridge, Lens, Hill 70, Passchendaele, through the March and April retreat of 1918, and many minor actions. With supporting batteries, the brigade held the Somme-Havre Line against four entire divisions of Germans in March of 1918, and when the pressure was relieved, answered an SOS call, travelled 196 kilometres with all their equipment and slung their guns into action on the Somme—all within twenty-two hours.

Then there was a period when for six days and six nights the battery fought the rearguard action, holding back overwhelming hordes of Germans, without supplies, rest or even water at times. Daily the word would come to hold the line, and a rest period of twenty-four hours could be arranged, but all the rest the men got was an actual twenty-four minutes break.

Another time, on another front, the battery withstood five days and nights of constant and terrific fighting, suffering heartbreaking losses and decreasing in numbers so greatly that it was often necessary for one man to operate each gun.[380]

When the cheers subsided, the meals and drinks consumed and the speeches over, the returned veterans turned their backs on the war and attempted to pick up where they had left off five years before. Only a small portion of those who left the Yukon to fight the Germans returned after the war. There just weren't the same opportunities as before, and many who returned from Europe were physically diminished by gas, shrapnel and the horror of it all.

One of the first veterans to return to the Yukon was F.N. Wright, who planned to be a fireman on the steamer *Selkirk* upon his return. His injuries may have made that an impossibility. Wright had been in heavy combat on the Western Front, and had been wounded and sent back to a convalescent hospital in Vancouver. He was wounded in the leg and now had a considerable limp and some pain, but he was not looking for anybody to support him.

D.W. McLeod, who had just returned to Dawson City from Vancouver, saw hundreds of wounded men in hospitals in Vancouver, and more in

Victoria. The worst of them were the soldiers who had been gassed. Some would recover, but others were slowly slipping away. Wracked by recurring bouts of coughing, there was little the nursing staff could do but take them outside into the fresh air, where, if the treatment was not effective, the suffering patients were at least freed from the four walls of their ward for a while. It was difficult to see the young men who had left two or three years before, strong and vibrant, returning reduced in health to such a condition. How many of these Yukon men would ever return to the Yukon?

REMEMBERING

ON APRIL 9, 1919, the people of Dawson City were treated to a special event. Sponsored by the IODE, a special showing of slides taken by George Black of the 17th Canadian Machine Gun Company training in England was presented at the movie theatre in the DAAA building. Those who were featured in the slides included Councillor N.A. Watt, now a seasoned officer; Sergeant Dave Fotheringham, whose wife, Marie, had published a book of poetry in Dawson to raise money for the war effort; and Reverend Buck, now a captain in the Chaplain Service, and wearing the Military Cross. The audience also saw Charley Barwell, Al Roth, Alfred and Norton Townsend, Charlie and Jim O'Brien, and little Jimmy Matthews. Charlie O'Brien was dead now, and Jimmy Matthews, the youngest of the Dawson boys to enlist at the age of sixteen, was wounded in the head at the second Battle of Arras, on August 28, 1918.[381]

The veterans had been trickling back into Dawson slowly in the later years of the war. This trickle turned into a minor flood after breakup of the Yukon River in the spring of 1919. Dozens of men returned on the riverboats as soon as they started steaming to Dawson. One returning veteran, Charles Moore, couldn't wait to get home, so he chose to make his own way back from the coast. Moore, who had been awarded the Distinguished Conduct Medal, floated down the Fiftymile River from Whitehorse on a raft, perhaps because he was short of cash. Lake Laberge was full of ice, so he walked around it. At the lower end of Laberge, he built another raft and floated as far as the Big Salmon River, where he obtained a small boat, in which he floated back to Dawson City. Upon arrival, he settled in at the Great War Veterans' Association (GWVA) headquarters.[382]

As soon as the veterans had started returning to Dawson, they had formed a veterans association, known as the Returned Soldiers' Club, in space provided free of charge by Dr. Alfred Thompson, at the corner of Queen Street and Second Avenue. By the spring of 1918, there were a dozen members, but anticipating a large influx of returning vets after the war, and realizing the need for larger accommodations, they transformed it into a branch of the GWVA at a meeting held in Dawson City on October 18, 1918.

On November 24, 1918, members of the Yukon Order of Pioneers held a memorial service at the Pioneer cemetery in honour of both the fallen in the Great War and the victims who perished aboard the *Princess Sophia*. The list of the *Sophia* drowned was ten times longer. Three veterans were also honoured: Anthony Blaikie, Peter Allan and Angus McKellar.[383]

A ladies auxiliary was formed in December, and within a short time, they did what they did best, raising $1,500 to secure and furnish a larger headquarters for the GWVA at the corner of Duke and Third. The aims of the GWVA included preserving the memory and dignity of all soldiers, especially those who died in service; the erection of monuments to remember the fallen; the provision of suitable burial for veterans; and the establishment of an annual memorial day. By August 1919, the GWVA of Dawson had eighty-six members, and a smaller chapter in Whitehorse had sixteen.[384]

The memorialization of veterans involved the entire community. On St. George's Day, April 23, 1919, the flag of St. George was flown at several places in Dawson, and the *Dawson Daily News* remembered, incorrectly, that a Dawson man, Rowland Bourke, had earned the Victoria Cross on this date the previous year off the coast of Belgium (he earned the DSO on that day).[385] On June 19, 1919, the IODE sponsored an Empire Peace Day celebration in the Arctic Brotherhood Hall, which was decked out with numerous flags for the occasion. Both the community and visitors danced until just before midnight, when gold commissioner George Mackenzie took the stage and spoke about the achievements of the Canadians in the war, and about the Yukon, which he noted had offered up more volunteers and donated more money per capita than any other part of the country. At midnight, whistles blew, cannons fired and a variety of noisemakers, confetti and streamers were employed. The people sang patriotic songs, and then they danced some more.[386]

George Black arrived in Vancouver on July 29, and intended to set up his law practice in that city—but first, he had to return to his beloved Yukon. He was in Whitehorse in early August, speaking highly of the men he had served with in France:

> We went through some very trying experiences, but always pulled together. There was no jealousy, bickering or disloyalty to the unit. We all did the best we could for each other... They were true comrades. Each was a personal friend. Although our casualties were heavy, yet considering the style of fighting and the desperate tasks the motor machine gunners had to perform, it is lucky they were not a great deal heavier.
>
> In coming through Southern Yukon I was glad to learn that every returned soldier from that district has been placed in a situation and that employers are making it their business to provide opportunities for them.[387]

Black continued to rail against the courts martial he had been involved in related to the Kinmel Park camp riots, stating that the army was unfit to administer justice and should never be resorted to when the regular courts were available.

He left Whitehorse on August 6 aboard the steamer *Casca* and arrived in Dawson City on August 8 at 2:30 p.m. Now dressed in civilian clothing, the citizen soldier was greeted by a large crowd on the waterfront. He was in good health and walking erect, shaking the hands of many old friends.

Three days later, a big reception was held in the Arctic Brotherhood Hall, honouring the returned veterans. Of the hundreds who had left the Yukon during the war, one hundred had come back to the North upon their return from overseas. Most of them were already back on the creeks pursuing their mining, either unable to attend or uninterested in attending the function that had been planned for them. As always, the hall was a spectacle of colour. As reported in the *News*:

> The stage was a bower of beauty. Evergreens flanked the two sides, while in the rear was a forest scene upon canvas, making it appear as though the eternal verdure clad hills were stretching away there interminably. In the foreground were gorgeous full blown plants, including fuschias [sic], geraniums, and quantities of sweet peas, asters and other beautiful flowers from Dawson's gardens. A huge Union Jack draped gracefully from one side of the proscenium arch, and the Stars and Stripes from the other, while about the balconies were flags of all the Allied nations.[388]

The celebration started with the usual speeches. Dr. Thompson acted as chairman and spoke about the work of the Allies during the war, praising Yukoners for their part. Vocational training would be available to returned soldiers, he stated, and the government would advance money for homesteading: $4,500 for land, $2,000 for livestock and equipment, and $1,000 for buildings. Pensions for veterans had been increased by 20 percent.

George Black was greeted by an ovation when he marched through the crowd to the stage at the front. He spoke of the fighting of the Yukon contingent and expressed his appreciation for the work of the patriotic organizations at home that never forgot about the Yukon men fighting overseas. He thanked the IODE, the American Women's Club, the Klondike Knitting Klub, the Yukon Patriotic Fund and others.

Black's speech was followed by musical performances. Captain Charles Thornback sang "The Hills of Donegal," accompanied by his wife on piano. Mrs. George Mackenzie sang "Sing on, Sweet Bird," followed by "The Bonnie Banks o' Loch Lomond." Finally, Miss Rynetta Malstrom of Seattle sang "Lassie o' Mine" and "I'm Forever Blowing Bubbles." After the formalities had been completed, the four-piece orchestra tuned up and the crowd danced until after one o'clock in the morning. Many people crowded around to meet Captain Black and the other returned veterans.[389]

Discovery Day 1919, Sunday, August 17, had sombre overtones as the Fraternal Order of Eagles, Dawson Aerie No. 50, held a memorial service to commemorate lodge members who had lost their lives in the service of their country. On the hillside overlooking the Klondike Valley, a large gathering witnessed the unveiling of a monument honouring the six members who died while in service. Dr. Alfred Thompson delivered the eulogy, followed by Reverend W.W. Williams, and then flowers were placed on the graves of Eagles and others in the cemeteries.[390] The special Discovery Day edition of the *Dawson Daily News* included a list of more than seven hundred names of men who had enlisted, as well as a number of articles about the war by some of the veterans.

On August 20, there was a meeting of the Yukon committee of the Canadian Patriotic Fund in the administration building, where George Black resolved that money that was given to the national body, more than $36,000, should be returned from the large surplus of $7 million that remained at the national headquarters. Dr. Thompson was asked to send a telegram directly to the minister for immediate action. A month later, the Soldiers' Civil Re-establishment Department advised they would be refunding $6,000 of the money raised locally in the Yukon, to be used as the Yukon committee saw fit. The exact amount returned by Ottawa, $6,604.32, was added to the balance of $3,538.37 held in the fund's local account. A committee of five was established to accept applications for loans from the fund, not to exceed $500, and grants of up to $50 to be given to disabled men in need. Early in 1920, the Yukon Patriotic Fund had $10,000 to distribute among the unemployed soldiers of the territory.[391]

George Black returned to Vancouver—his job as the territorial commissioner had been abolished, and he was unemployed. He had plans to establish a law office in Vancouver; although the economy and the population of Dawson were once robust enough to support a huddle of lawyers, the number had shrunk to a small handful. Nevertheless, Black's triumphal return to the Yukon in August of 1919 was an affirmation of his strong ties to the territory and acknowledgement of those with whom he had served

Celebrations and other events to memorialize the war and war veterans filled the summer of 1919, but in fact the process had started even before

Unveiling the cenotaph in Whitehorse, June 9, 1920. YUKON ARCHIVES RYDER COLLECTION 80-154 #4 (TOP) AND #6 (BOTTOM)

the war was officially over. In September 1918, the Whitehorse chapter of the IODE complained that the names of several southern Yukoners had been omitted from an honour roll being set up by the Dawson branch of the British Empire Club.[392] On November 15, the Yukon chapter of the IODE was having a temporary memorial cross prepared as a tribute those who had "made the supreme sacrifice." It was their intention to place it in the Whitehorse cemetery within two weeks. Memorial services would be conducted in the rooms of the IODE, followed by a procession to the cemetery where the cross would be unveiled.

Something similar happened in Dawson City. By October of 1918, a shrine had already been installed on the wall at the post office. Sponsored jointly by the British Empire Club and the IODE, it came in the form of a triptych, made from material removed from the famous old battleship *Britannia*. Inserted into the panels were the names of hundreds of Yukon men who had served and died in service to their country. The latter were denoted with a cross printed in the margin beside their names.[393]

Not long after that, a number of letters were written to the *News* suggesting that some souvenirs from the war would make a permanent reminder of the war. Machine guns, German colour standards or gas alarm horns were suggested as possible choices. The response was slow in coming, but eventually the idea took root. By the summer of 1920, three German artillery pieces were shipped to the Yukon: one 155 mm, a second 115 mm and a third 77 mm in size.[394] When they reached Whitehorse on September 13, one of them was retained by the little town, and the other two were forwarded to the Yukon capital. Additional trophies were soon on their way; at the end of September, four machine guns were forwarded to the Yukon, two for Carcross and two for Dawson City, while a trench mortar had been dedicated to Whitehorse.

The biggest memorial event of that summer was the dedication of a cenotaph on June 9, 1920. The service was held beside the Whitehorse Public Library, where the granite monument was placed. The dedication ceremony commenced at 8:00 a.m. The veterans left the NSAA hall ten minutes earlier, followed by the IODE. Regent Mrs. C.J. McLennan was escorted by Robert Lowe of the Yukon Territorial Council, on behalf of the gold commissioner. After that came the Girl Guides, and the schoolchildren. The Masons and the Moose arrived at the same time, having marched from their respective halls. The veterans stood facing the memorial, which was the work of A.E. Henderson, and the rest of the crowd stood behind the veterans and around the sides of the memorial.

Bishop Stringer gave a "soul-stirring"[395] speech, then the regent of the IODE placed a wreath, which was followed by little boys and girls, who placed flowers, wreaths and crosses under the bronze plaque with the names of the fallen: Albert E. Browne, Percy A. Butler, George M. Chapman, Alfred Cronin, Bruce Fisher, William Hare, Joseph Joyal, Arthur G. McLelland, Harold A.E. Newton, Frank Polley, George V. Raymond, Hugh Stewart and Hilliard Snyder. Robert Lowe read a telegram from gold commissioner George Mackenzie. He referred to the cheerfulness with which many of the men had left the Yukon, never to return. After the hymn "For All the Saints," several schoolchildren recited a poem penned by a Whitehorse resident, and Lieutenant Frank Berton read out the roll of one hundred names of the Whitehorse volunteers. "When the name of a dead hero was called no reply came except a tap on the muffled drum."[396]

When the roll call was completed, J.B. Watson played the last post on the bugle, and the spectators sang "O Canada" and "God Save the King." The crowd then turned and faced the road as the veterans marched past.

The large field guns—the artillery piece and the trench mortar—soon joined the cenotaph and were placed at the entrance to the library. After the old library burned down during World War II, the cenotaph stood in the centre of a large vacant lot at the corner of Second Avenue and Elliott Street. A new memorial, bearing the World War I plaque, was unveiled in front of the new federal building, constructed at Main and Fourth, on October 24, 1954. This memorial was demolished in 1989, before the construction of the new federal building, and the bronze plaque was saved. The plaque is now mounted on a granite memorial that stands in front of Whitehorse City Hall, beside a second memorial to the fallen of World War II.

The two field pieces, one a howitzer seized after the Battle of Vimy Ridge, the other a 600-kilogram trench mortar, never found a permanent home over the decades. At one point, they were stored in the old telegraph office at the MacBride Museum. When new Legion facilities were built, the museum asked the Legion to take them away. For a while, they were stored on the property of a Legion member at Little Atlin Lake. In the mid-1980s, they were stored in the government compound in Marwell, after which the inmates at the Whitehorse Correctional Centre restored them. In 1989, a permanent home was still being sought for them.[397] Eventually, they were placed at the Cadet Summer Training Centre by Mary Lake, south of Whitehorse.

A few months after the initial unveiling of the cenotaph in Whitehorse, at two o'clock on November 11, 1920, gold commissioner George Mackenzie unveiled a bronze tablet in the Dawson Public School. Upon it were engraved the names of students from both Dawson schools who were killed during the war: Stuart Ross Cuthbert, Donald Chester Davis, Francis E. Gane, Oswald Grant, Harry McLennan, Charles Thomas O'Brien, George Vail Raymond, and Frank C. Slavin. The plaque was inscribed by Dawson jeweler Charles Jeanneret:

> To sometime students in the Dawson schools who gave their lives in the Great War, this tablet was erected by their fellow pupils on November 11, 1920.
> Greater love hath no man than this.[398]

Mackenzie, who was the former principal of the school, mentioned other fallen Dawson students whose names were not inscribed on the plaque: Ross Hartman, Alex McDonald, Thomas Taylor, and two sons of Sergeant Major Bowdridge of the Royal Northwest Mounted Police.[399]

On September 17, 1921, another plaque was unveiled in the flag-draped lobby of the Canadian Bank of Commerce in Dawson, honouring three employees of the bank who enlisted in the war effort: Lieutenant Albert Edward Browne, who was killed on April 5, 1918; John I. Miller; and Frank H. Thompson. Inscribed on the large plaque were the names of the three men, plus the following: "In memory of the 1,701 men of the Canadian Bank of Commerce who served in the Great War, 1914–1918."[400]

In February of 1924, Mrs. Frank (Laura) Berton gave an inspirational address in the DAAA building at an event sponsored by the IODE. At its conclusion, she invited Mr. Mahon, the superintendent of schools, to step forward. She presented seven framed pictures of the works of British and Canadian artists depicting views of the various battles in which Canada's

Unveiling the cenotaph in Dawson City, September 1924. YUKON ARCHIVES ROY MINTER
FONDS 92/15 # 507

"gallant troops took part." Five were to be placed in the Dawson Public
School; the remaining two were to go to St. Mary's (Catholic) School. The
Dawson Daily News reported that one veteran was so pleased with the idea
that he offered a picture of the Black Watch (Royal Highland Regiment) of
Canada, which was gratefully accepted.[401]

The GWVA in Dawson had long been preoccupied with re-establishing
returned soldiers into civilian life, but by January 1923, they met to discuss the issue of some sort of memorial to commemorate the war dead. A
motion to set aside fifty dollars for the purpose was approved. They met
with various community groups, including the Royal Canadian Mounted
Police (RCMP), and various patriotic, fraternal and social organizations, and
formed the Yukon Memorial Committee. William Rendell and Frank Berton were appointed to prepare plans and a cost estimate.

The funds, a total of $2,700, were raised by advertising in the newspa-
per and receiving donations from the public. Consisting of a granite obelisk
mounted on a granite base 7 metres high, the memorial was unveiled on
a cool windy day in September 1924. The cenotaph was positioned in the

centre of a lawn on a large lot to the north of the administration building. Attached to its base was a bronze plaque with the names of seventy-one dead, a list that had been compiled locally by Arthur Coldrick, and then verified in Ottawa. The obelisk was draped with two large Union Jacks and guarded by four returned soldiers, standing at the four corners. At 3:30, 150 schoolchildren took their place on the east and south sides of the memorial. Martha Black, carrying the standard of the national body of the IODE, accompanied by Miss A. Vale, with the flag, and Vice-Regent Mrs. A. McCarter, assumed a position north of the monument.

The colours of the 2nd Canadian Motor Machine Gun Brigade, which had been brought back to the Yukon in 1922 by Lord Byng, the Governor General, were then carried in by Lieutenant Phil Creamer and Lieutenant F.G. Berton, escorted by the RCMP. The colours were positioned on either side of the monument, while the Mounted Police and veterans stood facing the memorial on the west side. The schoolchildren sang "O Canada," accompanied by John Dines, Claude Tidd and W.F. MacKenzie.

George Mackenzie gave a short speech explaining the history of the project and thanked the public for their contributions to the memorial fund. George Black, by this point serving as MP, then gave a stirring speech about the men who gave their lives during the war.[402] And with that, the memorialization of the war dead had been fulfilled.

As the years progressed, the population of Dawson City declined. By the 1980s, the cenotaph stood in an overgrown lot. During the 1990s, the community, with support from various levels of government, restored the landscaping of the park, and today the cenotaph stands proudly in the same spot that it has been on for more than ninety years.

CLOSURE

LIFE IN THE Yukon was never the same after the conclusion of the Great War. The population tumbled from 27,000 in 1901, to 8,500 ten years later, and halved again by 1921, to 4,157, a level that would remain stable for the next two decades. Of these, 1,500 or so residents were First Nation people. The precise number of Yukoners who served may never be determined. Many served in the forces of other nations, including Britain and America. Some names listed in memorials in various communities included former Yukoners who were not resident in the territory any longer, whereas some residents were inadvertently overlooked. George and Martha Black, and other officials, often repeated the figure of 600, but that clearly understates the number who served. The Dominion government assembled a "Domesday Book" of all who served; the number from the Yukon (2,427) was grossly overstated.[403] In the end, a list of nearly 1,000 names has been compiled of those whose service can be verified in one way or another (see the Appendix).

With a population hovering somewhere between four and five thousand, that number represents a significant portion of the population of the territory. Some went into the navy, others into the Royal Flying Corps; others went to the Balkans and Africa. But the bulk of the Yukon recruits joined the army and were sent to the killing fields of France and Belgium. Whatever the precise number, it represented a percentage of the population far in excess of the national average, as patriotic Yukoners very proudly mentioned often during and following the war. They shared this distinction with their Alaskan neighbours to the west, who also enlisted in numbers far greater than was noted in the lower forty-eight states.[404] But the impact of such a massive loss of labour capital would be significant to the economy of the territory.

As a result of the cuts made by the wartime Borden government, the territorial budget had been reduced drastically and the civil service was slashed. For twenty years, the Yukon languished in a frigid no man's land of its own, kept alive economically by the one surviving dredge company. The gold fields that had yielded 1 million ounces of gold in 1900 produced only 26,000 ounces in 1926. The silver mines of the Keno area that boomed after the war were the other mainstay of the economy during the interwar period from 1919 to 1939.

Laura Berton, the wife of the mining recorder and war veteran Frank Berton, saw the difference:

At first glance Dawson looked exactly as it had on the day I first saw it from the decks of the riverboat—the same grey-roofed buildings, the same helter-skelter of cabins. But on second glance there was no doubt at all that we were living in a decaying town. The population had now sunk to eight hundred, though there were buildings enough for ten times that number. Dozens more houses were standing empty, dozens more lots were vacant, dozens more buildings were slowly falling to pieces... The north end of town had become a desert of boarded-up cabins. For Dawson had shrunk in towards its core.[405]

What a contrast she noted: many of her old friends, including Mr. Bragg, the school superintendent, were gone. The only place that seemed to be growing was the hospital, which was housing an increasing number of aging sourdoughs.[406] Government House, which had housed the commissioner, was closed, and the position of commissioner had been abolished. The war had taken its toll, especially on the youth and vitality of the community. On top of all that, the sinking of the *Princess Sophia* had taken almost 10 percent of the remaining population of the territory to the bottom of Lynn Canal. Many of Berton's old associates in Dawson had been killed during the war. Life in the Klondike, she said, carried on as before the war, but in a much-modified way:

In Dawson, shrunken by war and disaster and old age, the pre-war pattern of social life went on, though on a smaller scale. The engraved calling cards still piled up in little mounds in the silver salvers, and the eight-course dinners with candle light and wine still continued behind the log and frame walls...

But the social lines had blurred slightly as the population shrunk. There was only one chapter of the I.O.D.E. and everybody belonged to it, whether they were, in the words of the national regent, "the best people" or not. The Mounted Police constables were now more or less accepted at the dances and in the homes of the townspeople and a new phrase "scarlet fever" was brought into use to describe the malady of any girl who had a Mountie for a beau. At the formal balls in the A.B. Hall the

After the war, George Black was elected to Parliament six times, serving a total of twenty-three years, one month and ten days. From 1930 to 1935, he was Speaker of the House of Commons. NED BLACK COLLECTION

Martha Black served as Member of Parliament for the Yukon from 1935 to 1940. She was only the second woman to be elected to the House of Commons. LIBRARY AND ARCHIVES CANADA C-081812

Grand March was no longer led by the town's elite, but by anybody who happened to get in line first. And the female teachers now lived alone, without stigma.[407]

The women of the Yukon were the beneficiaries of social change as a result of the war. They had mobilized and organized, and campaigned while the men were overseas: first for prohibition, and when that failed by a slim margin, they lobbied for the vote, which was granted by the federal government in the spring of 1918, and came into effect the following year. During his federal election campaign in 1921, George Black made frequent references to welcoming women voters, who attended his rallies in significant numbers. Not content with hearing what the candidates had to say, the women organized committees and became active in the campaign. When George Black spoke to a crowd at the headquarters of GWVA, Mrs. Mary Walker presided. More than seventy women attended that evening, and all took a keen and intelligent interest in the matters before the electors, and listened with closest attention throughout his speech.[408]

Those who survived the war returned to ordinary lives, attempting to pick up where they had left off a half decade earlier. Originally George and Martha Black had moved to Vancouver. George lost a run at a seat in the provincial legislature in 1920. He was more successful a year later, when he was drafted to run as a candidate for the Conservative party in the Yukon riding. He was elected and re-elected several more times over a parliamentary career that lasted from 1921 to 1949. He never forgot veterans and championed their cause in many ways. The most noteworthy of these may have been when, as a rookie member of parliament, he left his seat in the House of Commons and took the train to Edmonton, where he assisted in defending one of the veterans who served with him in France. George Wuksanovich was charged with killing a man in Jasper with a knife during a labour dispute. When the man was found guilty, George spoke to the court, giving Wuksanovich a character reference, and commending him for his service to the Crown during the Great War. Memories of the war were already starting to fade; despite Black's character reference, George Wuksanovich was sentenced to ten years hard labour, in order to teach foreigners that you couldn't do that sort of thing in Canada.[409] Black embraced an abiding respect for the men who served their country in times of war, even those charged with murder. "[If] I found pure gold in the Yukon," Black later said, "I also found it in the mud of Flanders, where I mined it from the hearts of men I had brought with me from the Far North."[410]

Martha Black, who accompanied her husband to England and did so much to support her Yukon boys and promote the Yukon, later stepped in to run as the Conservative candidate in the Yukon when George was unable to for health reasons. She spent five years as the Yukon's member of parliament, from 1935 to 1940. Over the years, she rose to iconic stature in the Yukon and was recognized as a person of national historical significance by the Historic Sites and Monuments Board of Canada. A plaque commissioned by the board in her honour is mounted on a large boulder beside Government House (now known as the Commissioner's Residence), where she had been chatelaine from 1912 to 1916. She lived ninety-one years, and George lived ninety-two. Their son Lyman never returned to the Yukon. He remained in the PPCLI until he was killed in an automobile accident in 1937.

Joe Boyle remained in Europe after the war, continuing to act as an agent on behalf of Romania, but his position became more tenuous in peacetime. Internal politics, scheming opponents of the royal family and a critical press painted him as an outsider interfering in the internal affairs of the country. Boyle's relationship with Queen Marie was damaged when she learned that Joe was still married but had not told her that wife number two was waiting for him back in Dawson City. After his withdrawal from Romanian affairs, Boyle was employed by British oil interests in negotiating oil deals in Eastern Europe. Despite declining health, his determination never seemed to fail him. He eventually became confined to bed, in the care of his friend Edward Bredenburg. Outwardly, Boyle remained full of confidence and optimism. Although bedridden, he spent his time on business reports and correspondence. He indulged in the works of Robert Service, whose poems he loved, and in the evenings he and Bredenburg would talk about good times in the Klondike and make plans for a return visit.

He frequently wrote letters to Queen Marie but, as his health declined, resorted to dictation to his friend Bredenburg's son, Anthony. The young Bredenberg also wrote letters to the queen, updating her on Boyle's declining health. Boyle, aged only fifty-six, passed away quietly on the morning of April 14, 1923. He was buried a few days later in St. James parish churchyard in the London suburbs. Several hundred people attended. A short time after that, a white stone cross was placed on the grave, a gift of Lord Beaverbrook. Months later, Queen Marie visited the site in person. She was not impressed by the tiny stone memorial. She returned at a later date with a large stone slab, which was laid upon the grave. Upon it were engraved words inspired by the poem "The Law of the Yukon" by Robert Service:

Lt.-Col. Joseph Whiteside Boyle CBE, DSO
November 6, 1867–April 14, 1923
Man with the heart of a Viking
And the simple faith of a child

The stone slab was followed by an ancient weathered Romanian grave-stone in the shape of a cross and a large cement urn that was placed on the slab over his grave. "He was all strength and honor," she later wrote, "and he had given me his faith and I had given him my trust. We clasped hands at the hour of deepest distress and humiliation and nothing could part us in understanding... No one knew his heart better than I."[411] Whenever she visited relatives in England, Marie would make a pilgrimage, heavily veiled in black, to Boyle's grave and place flowers in the urn that had special meaning between the two of them. She intended for the grave to be cared for and the flowers replaced, but this practice was curtailed when Queen Marie's husband, Ferdinand, died, and her son Carol ascended the Romanian throne.

Boyle's remains were later repatriated to his birthplace, Woodstock, Ontario, with military honours. He was finally recognized for his accomplishments as a true Canadian hero; in 1984, the Historic Sites and Monuments Board of Canada unveiled a plaque in his honour near one of the monster gold dredges he had built seventy years earlier. Dredge Number 4, located on Bonanza Creek, is now a national historic site and is receiving ongoing repair and restoration as a proud symbol of Canada's rich history.

Robert Service lived happily in France for the rest of his life. During World War II, he escaped the Nazis and relocated to California. He continued to write throughout his life, until he passed away in 1958. His writing was never considered to be mainstream poetry in literary circles—rather, rhyming verse or doggerel—but his works had a universal appeal. He found his inspiration in the people and events that he saw around him. This may have been, in part, his motivation for volunteering as an ambulance driver during the war. The poem "The Man from Athabaska," from his wartime volume *Rhymes of a Red Cross Man*, may have been inspired by an encounter that he wrote about in a newspaper article on December 18, 1915.[412]

A half century later, this poem, and others from that book, inspired 1960s folk singer Country Joe McDonald to adapt them to music and record them on his album *War War War*. In an interview in 2015, he related how, in 1965, he was working for a small company in Los Angeles that breaded fish sticks. On the way to catch a bus after work, he bought an old copy of the book, complete with coloured plates, which he happened to see in a small bookstore. Time passed and he became a folk singer. In a fit of inspiration, he put the poem "Jean Desprez" to music and performed it at local hootenannies, where it proved to be a popular selection with its dramatic surprise ending.

A century after the poems were written, these songs are still poignant statements. In recent concerts, McDonald compared the Athabasca oil sands with the desolation of wartime No Man's Land. Service's poem "The Man from Athabaska" is yet again bridging the generations and drawing attention to a contemporary issue.

"Grizzly Bear" Jim Christie survived the mauling, and four years in the trenches and No Man's Land. Upon demobilization, he was fifty-one years old. He took his scars and his medals back to the Yukon, but he didn't remain there for long. By the early 1920s, he had moved on to a position as a forest ranger in Jasper National Park.[413] Laura Berton remembered visiting him years later, when he was a white-haired, agile little man in his seventies, living peacefully on Salt Spring Island with his wife. According to Berton, "only a slight scar [was] visible on his scalp as evidence of the terrible winter when... he fought for his life after his famous battle with a grizzly."[414]

Christie had hoped to see the king and queen during their royal visit to Vancouver in late May 1939, but that was not to be—he was too ill. He died of cancer in Shaughnessy Military Hospital on June 1, 1939.

One warrior from the Yukon was only belatedly awarded his medal for gallantry. Lieutenant A.W.H. Smith had been recommended for the Military Cross by General Plumer, for bravery in the field in 1918. For some reason, the decoration was never presented to Smith. Twenty years later, it came to the attention of George Black, who investigated and confirmed the

George Shaw (left) of Historic Sites and Monuments Board of Canada and Pierre Berton unveil the plaque commemorating Joe Boyle at Dredge Number 4 on Bonanza Creek, Discovery Day, 1986. GATES COLLECTION

award. He brought it to the attention of his wife, who was the member of parliament for the Yukon at the time. Authorization was given to Mrs. Black to make the presentation to Smith, and she did so on the afterdeck of the CPR steamship *Princess Louise* in a surprise ceremony in Alaskan waters near Wrangell in the summer of 1938.[415]

As the years slipped by, the memories of the war faded, and the veterans slowly aged. Announcements in the newspapers kept Yukoners apprised of the veterans who never returned. Harold Walter Butler, who served in the Black contingent during the war, married Edith Cornelia Whitaker in Los Angeles in 1920, reported the *Dawson Daily News* that year.[416] Marcel Schmidt, who spent eight years in the Yukon and had enlisted with the

Black contingent, wrote the *News* that he was having a hard time convincing the sophisticated people of Rhode Island that the temperature falls below minus forty, and that he had seen thousands of caribou in the Sixtymile region. He asked for verification of these facts in order to convince the doubting Thomases of Rhode Island that it was true.

Jack Suttles, who was known as "the Kentucky Minstrel," and who sent movies of the Yukon boys of the Black contingent to Dawson during the war so that they could be viewed in the community theatres, wrote from his home in Olin, Jackson County, Kentucky. He had every intention of returning to the Yukon after his discharge in 1919, but by the time he was ready to use the ticket, it had expired, and he never returned. In 1923, he wrote to the *Dawson Daily News*:

> I still have a duplicate of the reel of moving pictures of the Yukon boys that was taken at Sidney, B.C., by myself, as a present to the Daughters of the Empire at Dawson. This reel was used only once, and that was in Seaford, England, for the benefit of the Yukon boys who had not yet seen their own pictures. I would like to know if the reel would be of any value to any of the moving picture men at Dawson or Whitehorse or elsewhere. I would let them go for what they cost me, as I cannot use them on a farm in the moonshine mountains of Kentucky.[417]

There is nothing to indicate that anybody ever took him up on his offer, nor what happened to the films. They would have served as a vital link between the men in uniform and those who remained back in Dawson City.

The many specially prepared newsreels that were shipped in and shown in the theatres of Dawson City through the war years formed part of an amazing discovery sixty years after the war ended. Dawson City was the end of the line for the old black-and-white silent films and newsreels that were shipped north, and it was too costly to return them to the distributor Outside, so they were stored in the basement of the old Carnegie Library on Queen Street, across from the DAAA building. Eventually, they were used as landfill in the abandoned indoor swimming pool at the DAAA, where they lay frozen in permafrost for fifty years, until they were recovered and restored in 1978.[418] A century later, the old newsreels of the war that flickered on the theatre screens of Dawson City are again available for viewing by another generation.

In 1914, the first of the northerners left for Europe in glorious celebration. What they found when they got to France beggared the imagination: trench warfare and the massive slaughter made possible by new technologies. There is no doubt that tens of thousands, maybe even hundreds of thousands, of Allied soldiers were sent to their deaths needlessly as they were pitted against the firmly entrenched German lines. These soldiers endured constant gas attacks, shelling and shrapnel, lice and rats and trench foot. These conditions they experienced from day to day, week to week, month to month. As the years dragged on, the horror of what they were doing was etched in their souls for a lifetime.

The men who had been shattered emotionally, if not physically, may have found the Yukon that they returned to after the war to be something of a quiet refuge from the horrors that they had experienced in Europe. It is hard to say how many of them suffered from post-traumatic stress when they returned home, but those who did might have healed slowly in the sanctuary and solitude of their cabins on mining claims scattered throughout the territory. They were torn asunder by deployment, injury, death and capture, and were never the same after the war. There is little in the archival record to reveal the psychological impression that the war made on a generation of northerners—that remains one of the biggest unanswered questions of this account. But we can get a glimpse; in correspondence some years after the war, Martha Black noted that her brother-in-law William, who had been buried by a shell at Passchendaele, was never the same after the war. And George Black had a nervous breakdown in 1935, possibly the result of the psychological scars of the war.

As the years rolled by, the names of the veterans appeared in the newspaper as they passed away. Andy Hart, the former fire chief, died in January 1921. After acting as recruiting officer for the Boyle detachment, he returned to Scotland to enlist in the armed forces. At war's end, he returned to Dawson, dying at age sixty. He is buried in the Pioneer cemetery on Eighth Avenue. Frank Hull, a Yorkshireman, died in 1926 at age thirty-nine while working for the Yukon Consolidated Gold Corporation on Dredge Number 2. Sam Whitehouse lied about his age so that he could enlist at age fifty-one. He died in 1934 and was buried in the family cemetery across the Yukon River in West Dawson.

William Ganderson, an Englishman who enlisted with the Black contingent, returned to Dawson and mined on Hunker Creek. He seldom came into town, and it is said that he took a considerable amount of gold out of his claim below Nugget Hill. He was sixty-three years old when he passed away after a short stay at St. Mary's Hospital in Dawson.[419] Joseph Devine, an Irishman who mined on Gold Run Creek, was found at the bottom of a 30-metre-deep shaft on his placer claim by two neighbouring miners in October 1938. It appeared that the seventy-three-year-old either was overcome by noxious fumes or fell down the shaft. Devine was a very close friend of George Black, reported the *News*, and it was only that summer that Black had arranged for Devine to receive his government pension. Like many of the independent-minded miners in the gold fields, Devine did not wish to receive the pension while he was still capable of working for himself.[420]

Londoner William Sullivan was found dead on his Gold Bottom claim in November 1938. It appeared that he had gone to the creek to fetch some water and had suffered a heart attack or a stroke. Aged sixty-six, he had no known relatives.[421] Robert Allen died a year later at age sixty-nine. Allen, who was both an Eagle and a Mason, served as the land agent in Dawson until his retirement, after which he and his wife moved to Victoria.[422] Frank Berton, who had served as mining recorder in Whitehorse and Dawson for thirty years, died in August 1945 in Vancouver. He had suffered angina in his later years.[423] His son, Pierre, became one of the most celebrated and prolific Canadian authors of the twentieth century, who wrote best-selling books about the Klondike gold rush and the Battle of Vimy Ridge. Stanko Karadich came to Canada as a youngster of thirteen. When war was declared, he returned to Serbia, where he joined the Serbian army. He served with distinction on the Salonica Front but later died of a heart attack at the relatively young age of fifty-five.[424]

Each year, the number of veterans who served in the war continued to dwindle as they passed away from old age, or in some cases from the effects of wounds suffered during the war. The ranks of the veterans marching in Remembrance Day services thinned, until there were none to remind onlookers of those who served in battlefronts around the world during the Great War.

Those who had remained in the Yukon seemed to keep the sense of high adventure, which was a legacy of the gold rush days. Before the war, it was noted, the population was becoming normalized with an equal ratio of married men with families to single men. After the war, that trend was reversed; by the 1921 census, the number of single men to married men had risen to two to one.[425] Rich men and poor men alike, they shared the common bonds of those who adopted the North as their home, participated in the Klondike stampede and experienced the war.

It is said that as a result of the war, Canada started to forge its own identity as a nation. The independent-minded Canadians proved more adaptable and achieved greater success than the hidebound imperial command of the British. One example illustrates how different the men of the Yukon were from the British mould. In 1918, Lieutenant William Black was on leave in London when he encountered another Yukoner, Felix Boutin. Black was an officer, Boutin a private, but the distinction was irrelevant in their former lives in the Yukon. They were glad to see each other and returned to Bill Black's hotel for dinner and to meet Black's new wife. Shortly thereafter, the military police arrived and took Black away to headquarters, where a major chastised him for associating with a mere private. In response, according to one account, Black told the officer "about the army and the mental capacity of some of its ornaments, that had probably never been stated so frankly by a sub to a major."[426] Bill Black was let off with a reprimand but found, upon his return to the hotel, that Boutin had been taken away and locked up in the guardroom so that he could testify if Black was prosecuted.[427]

By the end of the war, many Yukoners who entered the conflict as British left it feeling more like Canadians. Yet the men and women of the Yukon who served in the great conflict always seemed to have a strong affinity for their adopted northland. In the years that followed the war, the Yukon lost much of its lustre. Remote and isolated, it was almost forgotten by the rest of the country, until a second world war two decades later, and the Japanese invasion of the Aleutian Islands, ignited renewed interest in the North, and the fate of the Yukon was changed forever.

ACKNOWLEDGEMENTS

THERE ARE MANY I would like to thank for their assistance in one way or another. If I had been more attentive to this, especially during my formative period of research, the list would be longer. This is, therefore, only a partial list and I ask forgiveness from those whose names I have forgotten to include.

First, I would like to thank my wife, Kathy, who got me started on this narrative several years ago. Kathy kept me supplied with newspaper articles and references from other sources. She is very good at that. She also listened to me patiently as I talked about what I was learning, and acted as a sounding board as I toyed with ideas about how I would tell the story. And she reviewed various drafts of my manuscript and made them better. I doubt that my initial writing would have ever seen the light of day had she not whipped it into shape.

The Whitehorse Branch of the Royal Canadian Legion gave me encouragement and financial support. Red Grossinger, of the Legion, in particular, was supportive of my efforts. The Yukon Archives contained a treasure trove of old documents that helped me complete my picture of the Yukon during the Great War. All of the staff were helpful in every way. Peggy D'Orsay, the library archivist, stands out for the work she did, especially in compiling the names of the Yukoners who volunteered for service during World War I, both men and women.

The MacBride Museum provided me with access to documents in their collection. Thanks to Leighann Chalykoff, Colleen Dirmeitis and Rose Mary Fordyce. Alex Somerville, director of the Dawson City Museum, provided me with access to the collection and encouragement for what I was doing. Parks Canada in Dawson City has an excellent collection of historical artifacts and archival material. I would specifically like to thank Rose Hebert, Janice Cliff, Elaine Rohantensky and Dylan Meyerhoffer for their assistance.

The staff at both the Whitehorse Public Library and the Department of Energy, Mines and Resources Library (Whitehorse) were helpful whenever I needed them.

The PPCLI Museum and Archives provided me with valuable information about Jim Christie, who served in their unit. Thanks to Jim Bowman and Sergeant Brad Lowes. Thank you also to Karen Storwick, who added more material about Christie, and to Janet Karascz, Christie's great-niece, who shared what she had about Christie.

I visited the Canadian War Museum in 2015. Special thanks to Dr. Dean Oliver, director of research at the Canadian Museum of History, and Dr. Andrew Burtch, then acting director of research at the Canadian War Museum, who opened the doors to me when I was there. Historians Dr. Nicholas Clarke, Dr. Jeff Noakes and Dr. Tim Cook have been particularly helpful and inspiring.

I worked for two years on the organizing committee for the conference on the North in World War I. It was a profound experience. I would like to acknowledge the members for their support and inspiration: Max Fraser, for many stimulating collaborations; Dr. Brent Slobodin and Dr. Ken Coates, who organized the program; Nancy Oakley, former executive director of the Yukon Museums and Historical Association; Sally Robinson, who shared her research with me; Piers McDonald; Marius Curtenau; Joanne Lewis; Dan Davidson and Kelly Proudfoot. At the conference, I had the good fortune to meet and exchange knowledge with a number of individuals, most notably: historian Cameron Pulsifer, curator emeritus, Canadian War Museum, who provided feedback on an early draft of this book; Blair Neatby, who has paid so much attention to the Yukon fallen from World War I; and Tim Popp, who has a remarkable knowledge of the details of Yukon military badges and medals. Historian Dr. Preston Jones wrote an excellent history of Alaska in World War I—I found it inspiring. Professor Ted Cowan introduced me to things about Robert Service that I didn't know.

Mark Zuehlke, whose knowledge of and work with Canadian military history impress me to no end, kindly examined an early draft of my manuscript and provided me with useful comments.

Ed and Star Jones, great champions of Klondike history, kindly provided me with information from their vast collection. Karl Gurcke, historian with the US National Park Service in Skagway, has always been helpful, leading me to useful information and photos, and providing access to the park library resources. David Neufeld, who was my colleague for many years, loaned me useful reference works and shared his knowledge. The late Ian Church shared his copy of Nicholson's account of Canada in World War I, until my wife bought me my own copy.

I would like to thank a number of people who shared information about their Yukon ancestors who participated in World War I: David E. Cann, Harry and Elaine Millar, and Joe Redmond. Evan McDonell allowed me to read and copy a collection of letters from the war. Sarah Tobe and Cynthia Toman kindly shared information. The late Grant Bull shared much genealogical information about George Black. Don Stewart, of McLeod's Books in Vancouver, pointed me to valuable sources and allowed me to copy information from books in his own collection. Stewart Daniel has again taken my sparse information and produced a fine set of maps to accompany this book.

Finally, I would like to thank Pam Robertson, who edited my work. The role of a good editor is to provide insight and ask questions, to root out the bad and recognize the good, to provide a fresh pair of unbiased eyes. After working on this for so long, I became blind to my redundancies and oversights—she spotted and corrected them. She also asked questions that sent me scrambling for answers. All of these things have made this account more readable. Thank you, Pam. Special thanks to Shirarose Wilensky, whose meticulous scrutiny found hundreds of errors, typos and unanswered questions. She put the polish on this little gem.

APPENDIX:
HONOUR ROLL

LISTED BELOW ARE the names of nearly one thousand Yukon men and women who volunteered for service during World War I. It is likely incomplete, but it is as complete as was possible after many months of research. Prime responsibility for the compilation of this goes to Peggy D'Orsay, archivist at the Yukon Archives, with input from many others. We expect that more names will be added as additional information is made available. The names of the fallen, those who died in service, are noted in **bold type**. Thanks must be given to Blair Neatby, of Yellowknife, who has dedicated many hours to gathering detailed background information about the Yukon fallen of World War I.

Adams, George Clayton
Ainsworth, T.H.
Akers, Frederick
Albert, Clarence
Albini, Domenic
Aldcroft, William
Alen, Bob
Allan, Peter
Allan, W.G.
Allen, Arthur James
Allen, Robert Lemon
Andersen, Andrew
   Christian
Annand, Frederick
Annesty, William

Annett, Wilmont Warren
Anstett, Leonard
Anthony, Morris
Armstrong, Nevill
Armstrong, Richard
Arnold, Charles David
Auzias-Turenne, Aimar
Auzias-Turenne, Clarley
Babb, Richard
Baker, John William
Barley, W.G.
Barrett, F.
Barwell, Charles Sedley W.
Bayley, Luke Gilbert
Beaupre, Joseph

Bechevich, John
Bell, J. Laughlin
Bell, William
Bellocchio, Donat
Belney, Louis Eugene
Bennett, L.G., Mrs.
Bennett, Lionel G.
Bennett, R.B.
Berg, Pete Carlson
Berton, F.C.
Betts, H.W.
Bigg, Alexander Aikens
Bindley, Rowland A.
Bingham, Joseph Hadley
Black, George

Black, Lyman Munger

Black, William

Blackwell, Randolph

Blackwell, William A.

Blaikie, Anthony

Bogetto, Anton

Booker, A.

Boulay, Joseph A.

Bouleau, Joe

Boutillier, C.F.

Boutin, Felix

Bowden, Jack

Boyle, Joseph Whiteside

Boyle, William

Brackett, H.

Brady, Peter

Bragg, T.G.

Breaden, James Theodore

Breese, William L.

Bremner, John

Brice, William Galpin

Britton, Frank

Brodie, Robert

Broggio, Lorenz Louis

Brooker, A.

Broom, Charles

Brown, Garnet Leon

Brown, Herman
    Hoffendahl

Brown, William

Browne, Albert Edward

Bruce, Joseph

Brule, Herve

Brun, August

Buck, Frank Hepworth

Buck, Margaret

Buckingham, John
    William

Burden, William Watson

Burgess, Vincent E.

Burke, George

Burnell, Edward Weston

Burns, Charles

Burns, Edith

Burns, Patrick

Busby, Edward Maurice

Busby, Eldon

Bushe, Percy Douglas

Butler, Harold Walter

Butler, Percy

Butterworth, Arthur A.

Cairns, Alexander

Cale, George L.

Cameron, Francis Donald

Campagne, Jean

Campbell, Arthur G.

Campbell, James

Campbell, Lawrence

Campbell, Malcolm

Campbell, S. C.

Campbell, Samuel McK.

Carey, Ernest Frank R.

Carlill, Walter

Carpenter, W.H.

Carrell, James F.

Carroll, James Francis

Carroll, John McLeod

Carter, Arthur

Carter, James B.

**Cassidy, George
    Washington**

Caux, Joseph

Chabot, Joseph Adelard

Chalifour, Amede

Chambers, Frank

Chambers, John Thomas

**Chapman, George
    Merson**

Chapman, H.

Chipman, W.W. (Dr.)

Chisholm, James Hugh

Chisholm, Lawrence
    Dwight

Chisholm, Walter Albert

Chisholm, William

Cholokovich, Mike

Christensen, Charles John

Christie, James

Church, Hubert J.

Church, Orris Eugene

Chute, Frederick Russell

Clarke, W.B.

Clazy, George R.

Close, J. Brooks

Cloud, Edwin Collin

Collier, Harry

Colville, A.C.

Colville, Thomas B.

Condry, Joseph A.

Cook, Henry

Cook, J.G.

Cooper, Francis

Cope, W.H.

Corville, Thomas

Coulter, E.T.W.

Coulter, Samuel

Couture, Alfred

Cowley, William

Craig, W.G.

Creamer, F.S.

Creamer, Phil

**Crisfield, Ambrose
    George**

Cronin, Alfred

Crookshank, J.W.

Crookston, George

Crosbie, Robert

Crowder, Henry Allen
Culbertson, N.E.
Cullin, Wm Wallace
Currie, Daniel
Currie, George Byron
Currie, William Kenneth
Cuthbert, Stuart Ross
Daglish, Hamilton
Dahl, Ole Christian
Darling, John
Datzenic, Waldimir
Davidson, George Edwin
Davies, Ernest
Davies, J.A. (Reverend)
Davis, Donald Chester
Davison, John Anderson
Delavan, John Phipps
Denny, Arthur William
Desales, Frank
Desbrisay, Frank
Deslauriers, Leonard
Desmond, Richard
    Manford
Devine, Joseph
Dewar, Archibald James
Dickson, Alfred
Dines, J.
Dinning, William
Dixon, Edward A.
Doherty, T.
Dooley, Michael
Dooley, Richard
Douglas, Frank Putnam
Douglas, Walter
Douglas, Walter Scott
Douglas, William Lawrence
    Dawson
Dow, J.
Dow, W.

Drake, William Edward
Draper, Peter
Drewes, Charles
Driscoll, D.P.
Drury, John
Dubois, Joseph
Duclos, Alaric R. Theobald
Duff, Thompson
Dunn, Joseph
Dunnet, Sinclair J.
Dupont, Joseph Victor E.
Dycer, E.B.
Dyde, F.W.
Edelston, James
Elliot, William J.
Elliott, Fred W.
Ellis, Robert George
Enevoldsen, Ferdinand
    Eugene
Engelhardt, A.
Espanon, E.
Espenon, Gustave
Etcher, Percy Victor
Etique, E.J.
Ewing, Ralph Crackmay
Falconer, H.
Falconer, Peter
Farr, Joseph
Faulkner, Clair
Faulkner, Jack
Fenwick, Robert
Ferguson, Burnell
    Redmond Brodier
Ferguson, John
Fisher, Alexander Clark
Fisher, David
Fisher, John Bruce
Fisher, Norman
Fisher, Peter

Fitzgerald, Edward
Fletcher, F.W.
Fletcher, Robert
Flick, A.
Forbes, David
Forbes, James Douglas
Forbes, W.H.
Forrest, Aubrey Ernest
Forster, Herbert
Fotheringham, David
    Hetherington
Fournier, Joseph Napoleon
Fowler, Charles William
Fowlie, William B.
Frame, William Jack
Franklin, Ray E.
Fraser, Donald
Fraser, Edward F.
Fraser, Howard F.
Fraser, Margaret
French, John Edward
French, Robert Charles
Fry, John Nelson
Fulton, G.E.
Gairns, William
Gale, E.I.
Galpin, William
Ganderson, William
Gane, Francis
Gatt, Howard
Gay, Henry
Gentry, John
Giberson, C.H.
Gibson, A.
Gifford, Charles M.
Gilbert, Eugene
Gilbert, Reginald
Gill, George
Gillespie, Isaac Laird

Gillies, James
Gillis, Angus Alexander
Gillis, Angus Lauchie
Gillis, Hugh Allen
Glass, Daniel Byron
Gleeson, Daniel
Glorney, Ernest Edward
Godfrey, Ernest
Goetjen, Floyd L.
Goodair, Percy
Goodbow, P.R.
Gourlay, Robert
Graham, A.
Graham, R.
Grant, Oswald
Gray, Jack
Greaves, Robert Bruce
Greenaway, Thomas
Greenaway, Walter
Grenier, George
Grenier, Joseph
Grestock, Howard
Griffith, Richard
Groccaz, E.
Guite, J.P.
Gurr, Bert
Gwillam, Frank L.
Haddon, A.W.
Hair, William
Hale, Martin Larson
Halkett, Duncan William
Hall, Frank
Hall, O.
Hall, Robert
Hall, William
Hallett, Alva
Halliburton, John
Halverson, Richard B.
Hamilton, Hugh C.

Haney, Freeman
Haney, T.A.M.
Hanna, Robert Taylor
Hanratty, Ernest B.
Harding, Charles
Harding, Thomas
Hardy, Conrad
Harkin, Joe
Harknet, George Embry
Harman, Richard
  Browning
Harper, K.
Hart, Andrew
Hart, Colin Dunlop
Hartman, Fred
Hartman, Robert Ross
Harvey, Alexander
Harvey, Harry
Harvey, Thomas
Hawkes, W.G.N.
Hawksley, Stanley G.B.
Hawksley, Cyril Arthur H.
Hay, John Gilmour
Hayes, F.G.
Hayes, H.F.
Hayes, H.G.
Hayhurst, William
Hazen, Larry
Head, Sargeant
Henderson, Harvey
Henderson, Henry Edward
Henderson, Stephen L.
Heneghan, Patrick
Herd, William Frederick
Hickey, Ernest Edward
Hickling, William G.
Higgins, George Gregory
Higgins, Lawrence
Hill, C.H.

Hillicker, Albert F.
Holbertson, E.J.
Holborn, Robert
Holland, Daniel
Holland, Daniel Frank
Holligan, Daniel Frank
Holmberg, Edward
Hooker, James Easton
Hopkins, John
Hornsby, Robert Perry
Hoskings, Arthur
Howard, Gatt
Hughes, Vernon
Hughes, William
Hull, F.
Hulme, Gordon Glencoe
  MacDonald
Hulme, Herbert D.
Humphreys, Joseph
  Hayden
Huppe, Stanislas
Hurst, Fred
Hutchinson, Fred
Hutchison, James
Hutchison, William
Hyde, J.
Inkster, Colin Robertson S.
Ironsides, E.S.
Irvine, James Richard
Irving, James
Iverson, Harry
Iverson, Louis
Jackson, Ivan Daniel
Jamsiewaki, Walter
Jarvis, Benjamin
Jean, Mary, Sister
Jeanneret, Charles A.
Jeckell, G.
Jennings, Charles Edward

Jennings, W.H.

Jensen, George

Johns, F.

Johnson, Alfred

Johnson, Duncan

Johnson, Ernest L.

Johnson, Frederick John

Johnson, Halmar

Johnson, K.A.

Johnson, Walter Scott

Johnston, Duncan

Johnston, Robert George

Johnston, Walter Scott

Johnstone, James Kennedy

Jones, J.A.

Joyal, Eli Felix

Joyal, Joseph

Juraskovich, Marko

Karadzich, Stanko

Kay, Harold

Keddy, Walter Cyril

Keillor, George

Keim, Nicholas

Kelly, W.S.

Kelsey, Thomas

Kennalley, John

Kerr, William

Kettle, Clement

Kilbride, Thomas Fred

King, H.

King, Norman

King, Thomas E.

Kingston, William George

Kirkpatrick, Thomas W.

Kitto, F. H.

Klesinger, A.

Knight, R.S.

Knight, Thomas

La Blanche, Fred

Lacey, James Frederick

Laderoute, Wilbrod

Lagovitch, Spasage

Lamb, Albert E.

Lamontagne, George
   Pierre D.

Langford, Isaac Fielding

Lasnier, Leo

Laverdiere, James

Lawless, Herbert
   Maxwell

Lawrence, Walter

Leblond, George

LeBoeuf, Albert

LeClaire, Jean Baptiste

Leduc, Alphonso

Leggett, William

Levesque, Oscar

Lindsay, George

Lobley, Alfred

Lobley, Harry

Locke, Jack

Long, F. Stanley

Lonnberg, A.P.

Lopez, Edward Pena

Love, John Gibson

Luich, John

Lyons, J.

Macaulay, Cameron

MacBrayne, E.

MacCallum S.P.

Macfarlane, Athol

MacFarlane, J.

MacGregor, D.O.

Mack, A.

Mackenzie, Ed

Mackenzie, Hugh

MacKenzie, John

MacKinnon, James

MacKinnon, Malcolm

MacLennan, Frederick

MacLennan, James

MacLennan, John
   Farquhar

MacLennan, Malcolm

Maddocks, Edward

Mainsfield, James Walter

Maltby, J.A.M.H.

Marcoux, Joseph William

Marshall, George Eric

Martin, A. McN

Martin, Michael Stephen

Martin, Patrick John

Martineau, Jules

Masson, William

Matchett, Harry J.

Matheson, D.A.

Matsumoto, Kazue (Fred)

Matthews, James
   Emmett T.

McAlpine, Frank

McCarter, Arthur Burnet

McCarthy, Joseph

McCarthy, Michael

McCaw, Thomas

McClellan, Arthur G.

McCollom, Russell
   Clarence

McCourt, William Ernest

McCrae, David

McCrimmon, John

McCuish, Neil

McCutcheon, Carleton

McDermid, Dawson Roy

McDermid, Peter Hugh

McDermid, Roy

McDiven, A., Mrs.

McDonald, Alex

McDonald, Daniel Kenneth
McDonald, George Henry
McDonald, Hugh John
McDonald, John A.
McDonald, Kenneth
McDonald, Wilfred
McDonell, Charles Moray
McDonough, Alonzo Patrick
McDougal, Archibald
McDougall, Coll A.
McFadden, Owney
McFarlane, Johnny
McGinley, Barney
McGuire, Tom
McIntosh, Alexander Arthur
McIntosh, David
McIntosh, John W.
McIntyre, A.
McIntyre, Garnet
McIver, Patrick
McKay, W.J.
McKay, W.K.
McKellar, Angus Peter
McKenzie, A.
McKenzie, G.P.
McKenzie, H.F.
McKenzie, John
McKenzie, Malcolm N.
McKinley, A.R.
McKinnon, Duncan
McKinnon, James A.
McKinnon, Peter Dolph
McLaren, Dorothy
McLaren, John Angus
McLaren, Malcolm Earl, Jr.
McLaren, R.

McLaughlin, James
McLaughlin, Lorne
McLean, Archie
McLean, Charles Duncan
McLean, Robert Scott
McLellan, S.G.
McLelland, Arthur G.
McLelland, Pat
McLennan, Harry
McLennan, Jack
McLennan, Purvis
McLeod, David Walker
McLeod, Gundy
McLeod, Henry Gordon
McLeod, Howard
McLeod, Jarvis H.
McLeod, John
McMartin, A.
McMillan, D.J.
McMurphy, W.
McNeil, J.W.
McNeill, Stephen Joseph
McNeill, J.H.
McPhee, J.D.
McPherson, John Angus
McPherson, Pete
McRae, David
McRitchie, John
McRury, Angus
McSmart, Tom
McTavish, John Duncan
Melin, Harry
Melville, John Jeans
Mercure, Richard
Meredith, Edward
Merritt, Cecil Mack
Meyer, Frederick Adolf
Michunovich, Saletto (Charles)

Middleton, Burnett
Mijuskovich, Wido (Mido)
Mijuskovich, William (Bill)
Milatovich, Marko
Miller, Clarence George
Miller, John
Miller, Samuel
Mills, Charles W.
Mills, William Franklin
Milne, C.D.
Milosevich, H.
Milosevich, Milicko
Milton, John Joseph
Milvain, Robert
Miskedoff, M.
Mitchell, Sydney Frederick
Moir, George
Monroe, Alidore
Monroe, E.
Monson, George Thomas
Moore, Charles R.
Moore, Lucien
Moore, Sidney
Moreau, Edward
Morgan, F.
Morgan, Jack
Morgan, Richard O.
Morgan, W.
Morin, George
Morin, Wilfrid
Morishige, Frank
Morison, M.
Morrison, Allan McGillivray
Morrison, Edward
Morrison, Peter
Morrison, Wilfred Angus
Morrison, William Thomas

Morton, Robert
Mounier, Pete
Muir, William
Mulcahy, A.J.
Murata, Frank Sakuju
Murata, Yoshitada
Murphy, Frank
Murphy, John A.
Murphy, Walter
Murray, Duncan
Murray, Neil
Nadeau, Wilfrid
Nagao, Daiken
Naylor, Edgar Herbert
Neelands, Edgerton
    Dolmage
Nelson, R.
Neskadoff, George
Newman, Joseph Henry
Newton, Harold Arthur
    Edward
Newton, J.
Nicholas, Zowitza
Nicoll, Charles K.
Novovich, Milo
Noyd, Amos
Noziglia, Harold
O'Brien, Charles Thomas
O'Brien, James Jonathon
O'Brien, William John
O'Keefe, John H.
O'Keefe, Maurice
O'Leary, Daniel
Oleson, C.R.
Oliver, W.H.
Olson, C.H.
Olson, O.
O'Neill, John Arthur W.
Orr, Jimmy

Osborn, F.H.
Otis, George Eric
Ottley, Sidney F.
Ouvrin, Emile
Overton, William
Owen, "Kid"
Owen, A.W.
Paddock, P.H.
Panet, Maurice
Parovich, Savo
Pattullo, J.E.
Pavely, C.D.
Pavichavich, John
Pearkes, George Randolph
Pearse, F.H.
Pelland, Joseph
Pelland, Lazare
Penderbury, Walter
Pendlebury, H.J.B.
Peppard, Ernest L.
Peppard, Larry
Pepparo, R.L.
Perkinson, J.
Perovich, Ygos
Perron, Joseph Smalophe
Perry, George
Perry, O.B.
Peterson, F.J.
Peterson, H.E.
Phelps, W.L.
Philipovich, Choketa
Phillips, Charles Walter
Phillips, Gerald Basil
Philp, Bart S.
Pieters, Richard
Pilote, Arthur
Pinder, Frank G.
Pinder, W.J.B.
Pinkiert, H.

Pochack, John Peter
Polley, Frank
Polley, Frederick Wells
Pomich, John
Pool, James Ashton
Poole, P.A.
Porter, Bert
Porter, James
Potter, Ed
Poulin, P.J.
Pover, Alexander Crawford
Pratt, S.C.
Pregent, Francois
Priest, John
Pringle, George (Reverend)
Pringle, John (Reverend)
Pringle, John Jr.
Pullen, Royal Rudolph
Purdy, Donald
Putnam, Laurie
    Chalmers
Racine, Victor
Radford, William Gerald
Radosevich, Bozo
Radovich, Guro
Radovich, Kosto
Radovich, Savo
Rae, Samuel
Ralph, Mary (Sister)
Raspopovich, Spasge
Ray, Phillip
Raymond, George Vail
Rector, Charles Edward
Redmond, Charles Francis
Redmond, Ernest James
Redpath, James
Reid, George Thomas
Rich, Gilbert Ray
Rivard, G.R.

Roberts, John Harold
Rogers, Bliss Herbert
Roils, Henry
Ross, Cyril
Ross, Wilbur Alexander
Ross, William
Roth, Alfred
Rouleau, Joseph Armand
Roulston, David
Rowatt, H.H.
Roy, Edgar
Runacres, Edgar
Ryan, E.E.
Ryan, James
Ryder, George
Ryder, Norman
Ryder, William
Ryley, C.J.
Ryley, Charles Sheffield
Salamon, Corona
Salvatore, Jimmy
Samusanka, Saman (Sam)
Sartor, August
Saunders, B.J.
Saunders, Richard
Scanlon, H. Douglas
Scarth, Walter
Scharschmidt, Guy Hope
Scharschmidt, Howard
    Butler
Scharschmidt, Percy F.
Schmitt, Marcel
Scotland, John
Searle, George
Sears, Phil
Seguin, A.J.
Seki, Juan Mien
Selfe, Hugh Ronald
Service, Robert William

Settlemier, Charles Reed
Shand, Alfred Joseph
Shand, William
Sharkey, Owen
Sharp, Melburn
Sharpe, Percy
Sharpe, Walter
Shaw, David Richardson
Sheppard, Edward
Sim, Henry
Simard, Alfred
Sime, W.C.
Simmons, James Aubrey
Simons, Harry Lovell
Simpson, Herbert
Simpson, John Thomas
Sinclair, Fred
Sinclair, Harry Lister
Sinclair, R.
Sirois, Donat
Skelton, H.H.
Skoko, Milan
Slavin, Frank Charles
Slavin, Frank Patrick
Small, Robert Arthur
Smith, A.W.H.
Smith, Clarendon Clark
Smith, Harvey David
Smith, William
Snyder, William Hilliard
Sohier, Frank
Somers, James
Spallworty, H.W.
Sparks, George
Sparrow, John
Spence, E.
Sredanovich, Manojlo
    (Mike Sed)
Stacey, Fred K.

Stallworthy, A.H.
Stangroom, Bertie J.
Stansfield, James W.
Starritt, George
Steeves, Victor Clide
Stepanovich, Fred
Stepanovich, Leo
Stephens, C.
Stevens, A.
**Stevens, Marshall
    Tibbits**
Steward, Hugh
Stewart, Alexander
**Stewart, Charles James
    Townsend**
Stewart, H.A.
Stewart, Hugh Trevor H.
Stewart, Reggie Graham
Stoddard, Thomas C.
Stone, Otis
Strang, Robert
Strang, W.R.
Strong, Harold
Stupich, David
Sullivan, William
Sutherland, Hugh
Sutherland, Louis
    Alexander
Suttles, John Jackson
Tadich, Milos (Michael)
Tanner, Selwood
Tarr, Jack
Taylor, Buck
Taylor, Frederick George
**Taylor, John Albert
    (Jack)**
Taylor, John Sanford
Taylor, Thomas
Teare, Walter

Telford, E.L.
Tennant, Charles
Terrell, Garrett
Thayer, Edward Alding
Thompson, Alfred (MP)
Thompson, Frank H.
Thompson, Marie Louise
Thorn, Frank Percival
Thornback, C.R.
Thruston, E.H.
Tilton, Joseph
Tingley, Paul
Tobin, Henry Seymour
Tolley, Jesse
Tomich, Alexander
Topham, Henry
Torrey, Jesse
Toshtkoff, John Evan
Totty, Alfred Clinton
Totty, Elliott
Townsend, Alfred Henry
Townsend, Norton Turner
Travis, William Allen
Troceaz, Edmond
Turnbull, John
Turner, Frederick
Turner, John
Twirdall, Otto Gerhart
Upp, D. Curtis
VanVolkenburgh, B.
Varicle, Robert
Vaukaire, Gustave
Velge, Montagne Martin
Vella, Ralph
Venn, Hubert John

Vernon, George
Verscoyle, Benjamin
Vichovich, B.
Villeneuve, Eugene
   William
Vinall, Lionel A.
Vlahovich, Eli
Volk, Edgar
Voss, Alpheus
Vovich, Cristo
Vucer, Dusan
Vucer, John
Vucinich, Savo
Vuich, Andrew (Andy)
Vukovich, Boggich
Waddell, Samuel George
Wade, Arthur G.
Walker, G.C.
Walker, Hiram G.
Wall, Charles
Wallace, John
Ward, E.
Waterton, Ralph
Watson, Kenneth
Watson, William Farquhar
Watt, Garnet C.
Watt, John J.
Watt, Norman Allen
Watters, James Bow
Webb, Edward Robert
Webster, Robert
Welsh, Clifford
Welsh, Emery
Welsh, William
Whalley, Charles Edward

Wheeler, Fred
White, Eric
White, Stanley J.
Whitehouse, Samuel
   John
Widman, Charles W.
Williams, C.E.A.L.
Williams, Claude
Williams, Cledwyn I.
Williams, G.N.
Williams, Joseph
Williams, William
   Arthur
Williamson, William
   Hodge
Wilson, Claire
Wilson, Frank
Wilson, Laurence R.
Wilson, "Scotty"
Wilson, Thomas
   Harold
Wolfe, Rudy Victor
Woodburn, Harry
Woods, Alfred
Wright, Frederick N.
Wright, George
Wright, George Elsie
Wright, Joseph
Wright, William
Wuksanovich, George
Wyatt, Fred Filmore
Wyllie, Stewart
Young, Frederick
Young, William Daniel
Zik, Vido

NOTES

Abbreviations:

DDN: *Dawson Daily News, Dawson News, Dawson Weekly News*

LAC: Library and Archives Canada

WS: *Whitehorse Star*

YA: Yukon Archives

YN: *Yukon News*

INTRODUCTION

1 For a detailed description of the lifestyle of these early miners, refer to Gates, Michael. *Gold at Fortymile Creek*. Vancouver: UBC Press, 1994.

WAR IS DECLARED

2 See Yukon Archives photo YA 92/15 PHO 535 #314.

3 "Dawson Stirred By The News of the War," DDN, August 4, 1914: 04.

4 Black, Mrs. George (Martha Louise). *My Seventy Years*. As told to Elizabeth Bailey Price. Toronto: Thomas Nelson and Sons, Ltd., 1938, 224–25.

5 "Brilliant Scene At The Shriner Ball," DDN, August 7, 1914: 02.

6 Berton, Laura Beatrice. *I Married the Klondike*. Toronto: McClelland & Stewart, 1961, 128.

7 "Germany Declares War On The Russians," DDN, August 1, 1914: 01.

THE VOLUNTEERS

8 "Volunteers," DDN, August 7, 1914: 04.

9 "Yukon's Member Going To Ottawa and Then To War," DDN, August 11, 1914: 01.

10 "Walking From Dawson For Battle Front," DDN, September 9, 1914: 04.

11 "Dawson Lads Are Called To The Front," DDN, September 19, 1914: 04.

12 Dobrowolsky, Helene. *Law of the Yukon: A Pictorial History of the Mounted Police*. Whitehorse: Lost Moose Publishing, 1995, 76.

13 "Dawson Lads Are Called To The Front," DDN, September 19, 1914: 04; "Writes Dawson Of Experience At The Front," DDN, December 15, 1914: 02.

14 YA, 351.740 62 Roy 1915.

15 "Whole Family Of Yukoners Has Enlisted," DDN, May 26, 1916: 04.

16 "Three Yukon Brothers Are With Colors," DDN, November 20, 1916: 04.

17 Winegard, Timothy. *For King and Kanata: Canadian Indians and the First World War*. Winnipeg, MB: University of Manitoba Press, 2012, 122.

18 *Skagway Alaskan*, April 24, 1917.

19 "Dawson Girl In France In Uniform," DDN, September 18, 1918: 04; "Dawson Girl Is Going To Siberia Soon," October 4, 1918: 04.

20 Armstrong, Nevill A.D. *After Big Game in the Upper Yukon*. London: John Long Ltd., 1937, 123–124.

21 "Come From End Of Earth To Enlist Here," DDN, May 29, 1916: 01; WS April 7, 1916. Another prospector, Walter Scarth, was on a two-year trapping and prospecting trip on a remote tributary of the Yukon River when he received word of the war. He travelled 1,400 kilometres in an open boat to Nome to catch a ship for Seattle. He took the train to Calgary, where he enlisted in the Canadian Expeditionary Force. *Birmingham Daily Gazette*, September 18, 1915, 08.

22 "Service Flag Is Dedicated to Yukoners," DDN, September 3, 1918: 04.

23 "Tanner of Yukon Is Now With Hussars," DDN, November 26, 1914: 01.

24 "Some Yukoners Are With The Highlanders," DDN, December 29, 1916: 04.

25 "Death-Battle By Man And Grizzly," DDN, January 19, 1910: 04; "Head Is Cracked By Blow," DDN, April 12, 1910: 04; Also: Christie, 1933: 1, 4.

26 Anderson, Torchy. "Noted Princess Pats Sniper, 'Uncle' Christie, a Warrior, Gentleman and Fine Friend," *Windsor Star*, July 22, 1939: 11; Tsukamoto, Suyoko. "Soldier Survives Grizzly Bear Attack in Yukon," *Brandon Sun*, January 16, 2015. Other recruits lied about their age. Lyman Black added a year to his birthdate, and the Townsend brothers, Alfred and Norton, were born only five months apart—if you believe their attestation papers.

27 YA, GOV 1866 file 29600, Black to Ganderson, September 4, 1914; "Claims of Yukon Boys Are Exempted," DDN, October 17, 1914: 01.

28 "Germans Must Not Leave Yukon Territory," DDN, August 9, 1914: 01; "Commissioner on Pro Germans in Territory," DDN, July 12, 1915: 01; YA, GOV 1866 file 29600, Ironside to Black, October 6, 1914. George Black also took pains to write a character reference for one Louis Schreddenbrunner, asking Superintendent Moodie to allow the man, who had been naturalized in the United States, to be allowed to continue his work as fireman on the steamers between Dawson and Fairbanks.

29 DDN, October 13, 1914 (cited in Rodney, William. *Joe Boyle, King of the Klondike*. Toronto: McGraw-Hill Ryerson, 1974, 110).

ON THE HOME FRONT

30 As noted at www.iodeontario.ca/iode-ontario---a-proud-history.html.

31 YA, 351.740 62 Roy 1914.

32 Rodney, William. *Joe Boyle, King of the Klondike*. Toronto: McGraw-Hill Ryerson, 1974, 110.

33 "Yukon to Help Families of Those Who Go to Front," DDN, September 4, 1914: 01; "To Raise Cash for Patriotic Fund," DDN September 10, 1914: 04.

34 "Let Klondike Give Her Nuggets," DDN, September 7, 1914: 02.

35 "Whitehorse Contributes to the Fund," DDN, September 11, 1914: 01; "Whitehorse Alive," WS, September 11, 1914: 01; "Those Who Gave," WS, September 18; "Additional Subscriptions," WS, October 16, 1914: 04; "Patriotic Fund," WS, November 6, 1914: 04.

36 "Yukon to Remember Boys at Front," DDN, November 12, 1914: 04.

37 Moore, Mary MacLeod. "War and War Work in the Arctic Regions," *Canada*, March 17, 1917: 305.

38 "Moosehides Aid Britain in the War" DDN, December 9, 1914: 04; "Yukon Indians Give in Aid of the Empire," DDN, December 23, 1914: 01; December 30, 1914: 04; "Indians Contribute," WS, February 5, 1915: 04.

39 "Public School Children Swell Patriotic Fund," DDN, June 1, 1915: 03.

40 Moore, "War and War Work," 305.

41 "Will Gather Garments For the Belgians," DDN, November 13, 1914: 04; "Many Bundles Gathered for the Belgians," DDN, November 16, 1914: 04.

42 "Yukon's Aid in the Empire's Great Struggle," DDN, December 23, 1914: 06.

43 Ibid., 04.

44 See Jack Suttles's contribution, for example: "Klondike Minstrel Going to Front," DDN, May 22, 1916: 03.

45 "Charity Movies," WS, February 12, 1916: 01.

46 "Trophies of the War Are Received Here," DDN, April 19, 1915: 04.

47 "'Women in War,' Excellent Paper By Martha Munger Black," DDN, July 20, 1915: 03.

48 "Dawson's Great War Veterans Hold Meeting," DDN, November 11, 1918: 04.

49 YA, GOV 1866 file 29600D.

50 "Dawson to Help Swell Fund for Christmas," DDN, November 18, 1914: 04; "Concert for Christmas Fund Success," DDN, November 26, 1914: 04.

51 "Large Sum Is Raised for Patriotic Fund," DDN, July 12, 1916: 04.

52 "Large Sum Is Netted for Patriotism," DDN, July 21, 1916: 04.

53 "Splendid Total of $95,000 Is Raised by Yukon Patriotic Fund," DDN, August 17, 1917: 04.

54 YA, GOV 1866 file 29600A; DDN November 3, 1915: 04.

55 "Great Record Is Made by the Yukon," DDN, March 14, 1916: 04.

FIFTY BRAVE MEN

56 *Yukon News*, January 30, 2009; yukon-news.com/letters-opinions/swiftwater-bill-klondike-casanova-or-gold-rush-gouger/.

57 See Reddick, Don. *Dawson City Seven*. Fredericton, NB: Goose Lane Editions, 1993.

58 "Boyle Offers to Equip Force—Minister Accepts Offer," DDN, September 4, 1914: 01.

59 "When Yukon Goes to War," DDN, September 26, 1914: 02.

60 Ibid.

61 "Yukon's Boys to Sail for War on Seventh," DDN, September 26, 1914: 04.

62 "Mascot Chosen for Boyle Detachment," DDN, September 26, 1914: 04.

63 "It's a Long Way to Dear Old Klondike," DDN, October 8, 1914: 04.

64 "Dawson Honors Boys Who Are Going to Front," DDN, October 7, 1914: 04.

65 "When Yukon Goes to War," DDN, September 26: 02.

66 "Women of the Yukon to Work for Warriors," DDN, September 26, 1914: 04; "Patriotic Service League Is Formed," DDN, September 29, 1914: 04.

67 "Dawson Honors Boys Who Are Going to the Front," DDN, October 7, 1914: 04.

68 Ibid.

69 Ibid.

70 "Young Lobley in First US Draft," DDN, October 17, 1917: 04. Harry Lobley was rejected from service when he arrived at the coast but was later accepted into the first US draft for the front.

71 A "tiger" is defined in the *Oxford English Dictionary* as a "loud yell at end of burst of cheering." The *Gage Canadian Dictionary* describes it as "an extra yell at the end of a cheer."

72 "Dawson Honors Boys Who Are Going To The Front," DDN, October 7, 1914: 04.

73 Ibid.

74 "Anxious To Enlist," WS, March 12, 1915: 01; YA, GOV 1654 file 29600C.

75 Rodney, William. *Joe Boyle, King of the Klondike*. Toronto: McGraw-Hill Ryerson, 1974, 104.

76 *Polk's 1915–16 Yukon Gazeteer and Directory*: 801.

77 "Given Good Time," WS, October 23, 1914: 03.

A NEW KIND OF WAR

78 "Word Received from Boyle Boys in England," DDN, May 16, 1916: 01.

79 Rodney, William. *Joe Boyle, King of the Klondike*. Toronto: McGraw-Hill Ryerson, 1974, 111.

80 Grafton, Charles Stewart. *The Canadian "Emma Gees": A History of the Canadian Machine Gun Corps*. London, Ontario: Canadian Machine Gun Corps Association, 1938, 42.

81 See, for example, Ellis, John. *The Social History of the Machine Gun*. New York: Pantheon Books, 1973, 122–33.

82 Berton, Pierre. *Vimy*. Toronto: McClelland & Stewart, 1986, 48.

83 Ellis, *The Social History*, 1973: 123.

84 LAC. War Diary, Yukon Motor Machine Gun Battery, November 1916, Appendix VIII.

85 Cook, Tim. *At the Sharp End: Canadians Fighting the Great War, 1914–1916*. Toronto: Penguin Canada, 2007, 316.

86 Logan, Major H.T., Captain M.R. Levey, Major General R. Brutinel, Major W.B. Forster, Lieutenant W.M. Baker and Lieutenant P.M. Humme. "History of the Canadian Machine Gun Corps, C.E.F.," 1919. University of British Columbia Archives, Harry T. Logan fonds, D547.M3 L63 1919a. Transcribed by Ron Edwards, Les Fowler, Brett Payne and Dwight Mercer, December 17, 2015, 27: The Boyle Unit was formed in Dawson City as the Boyle Mounted Machine Gun Detachment but was mobilized in England, June 14, 1916, as the Yukon Machine Gun Battery.

87 Logan, Major H.T., et al., "History of the Canadian Machine Gun Corps, C.E.F.," 27.

THE BATTLEFIELDS OF FRANCE

88 LAC. War Diary, Yukon Motor Machine Gun Battery, September 1916.
89 Cook, Tim. *At the Sharp End: Canadians Fighting the Great War, 1914–1916*. Toronto: Penguin Canada, 2007, 447.
90 Foster, Charles Lyon. *Letters From the Front: Being a Record of the Part Played by Officers of the Bank in the Great War*. Canadian Bank of Commerce, n.d., 147.
91 LAC. War Diary, Yukon Motor Machine Gun Battery, October 23, 1916.
92 "Pete Falconer on Fight of the Yukoners," DDN, January 27, 1917: 04.
93 LAC. War Diary, Yukon Motor Machine Gun Battery, November 1916, Appendix VIII.
94 LAC. War Diary, Yukon Motor Machine Gun Battery, November 1916, Appendix VI: 8–9.
95 "Klondiker Is Winner of High Honors," DDN, January 29, 1917: 04.

THE BLACK CONTINGENT

96 Black, Mrs. George (Martha Louise). *My Seventy Years*. As told to Elizabeth Bailey Price. Toronto: Thomas Nelson and Sons, Ltd., 1938, 226.
97 YA, GOV 1866 file 29600, memorandum Hughes to Black, October 5, 1915.
98 "Black to Go as Captain of Company," DDN, November 2, 1915: 04.
99 "Yukon Council Member to Go to Front," DDN, April 18, 1916: 01.
100 "For Yukon Force," WS, January 28, 1916: 04.
101 "Dawson Boys Begin Drills for Service," DDN, February 11, 1916: 04.
102 "Names of the Dawson Men Now Enlisted," DDN, February 15, 1916.
103 *Fairbanks Sunday Times*, April 30, 1916: 02.
104 "Commissioner Black Undergoes an Operation," DDN, May 5, 1916: 01; "Black Was in Winnipeg for Time," DDN, May 10, 1916: 01; "Commissioner Black's Case Is Complicated," DDN, May 12, 1916: 04; "Commissioner Black Making Good Headway," DDN, May 17, 1916: 01.
105 "Governor Black," WS, Friday June 9, 1916: 01.
106 "Commissioner and Mrs. Black Welcomed Back to the Yukon," DDN, June 9, 1916: 01.
107 Ibid.
108 Ibid.
109 YA, 82/234, Martha Black scrapbook, microfilm #62: Undated article, DDN.
110 "Now Lyman Black," DDN, December 30, 1916: 04.
111 "Dawson School Honors Boys Leaving for the Front," DDN, June 9, 1916: 04.
112 "Pride of the Yukon Gets Away for War," DDN, June 10, 1916: 04.
113 Ibid.
114 Ibid.
115 "Dawson Boys Are Given Big Farewell," DDN, July 12, 1916: 04.
116 Ibid.
117 "Mahaffey Boyes Are Given a Big Welcome," DDN, August 3, 1916: 04.
118 "Norman Watt Has Enlisted for the Front," DDN, July 7, 1916: 04, also YN, January 21, 2010, or: www.yukon-news.com/letters-opinions/the-game-that-almost-brought-the-stanley-cup-to-dawson/.
119 "Yukon Boys Are Making Good Showing," DDN, August 18, 1916: 04.
120 "Commissioner Says More Are Wanted," DDN, September 30, 1916: 01.

121 "Bon Voyage," DDN, October 7, 1916: 02.

122 "Farewell Will Be Held for Yukon Boys," DDN, October 5, 1916: 01.

123 "Rousing Farewell Given Yukon's Soldier Boys," DDN, October 9, 1916: 01, 02.

124 YA, Acc# 82/234, Martha Black scrapbook, microfilm #62: Article from DDN, October 13, 1916.

GOING OUTSIDE

125 YA, Acc# 82/234, Martha Black scrapbook, microfilm #62: Article from DDN, October 21, 1916.

126 "Interesting Sketches of Trip on Casca," DDN, October 26, 1916: 04.

127 *Skagway Daily Alaskan*, October 16, 1916: 01.

128 *Victoria Daily Colonist*, November 5, 1916: 19.

129 "Tells of the Life with the Yukon Boys," DDN, August 22, 1916: 04.

130 *Victoria Daily Colonist*, October 29, 1916: 24.

131 "Geo. Raymond Writes of Yukon Boys," DDN, November 17, 1916: 04.

132 "Capt. Black Writes of the Yukon Boys," DDN, December 28, 1916: 04.

133 "Writes of Life in the Sidney Camp," DDN, July 31, 1916: 04.

134 "Yukon Boys Attached to Princess Pats," DDN, January 22, 1917: 04.

135 "Martha Munger Black Addresses Victoria Women's Club," DDN, December 7, 1916: 03.

136 Black, Mrs. George (Martha Louise). *My Seventy Years*. As told to Elizabeth Bailey Price. Toronto: Thomas Nelson and Sons, Ltd., 1938, 234.

137 "Yukon Boys Have a Great Christmas Dinner," DDN, December 26, 1916: 01; "Writes of the Christmas Festivities," DDN, January 15, 1917: 04.

138 "Tells of the Work of the Yukon Boy," DDN, February 10, 1917: 04.

139 Ibid.

140 Ibid.

RHYMES OF A RED CROSS MAN

141 Service, Robert W. *Harper of Heaven*. New York: Dodd, Mead and Co., 1948, 73.

142 Service, *Harper of Heaven*, 74.

143 Ibid., 73.

144 Mackay, James. *Vagabond of Verse. Robert Service: A Biography*. Edinburgh: Mainstream Publishing Company, 1995, 239–40.

145 "Bob Service Writes on the Blood-Red Wave," DDN, March 7, 1916: 02.

146 Ibid.

147 Ibid.

148 Ibid.

149 Ibid.

150 Ibid.

151 Service, *Harper of Heaven*, 84.

152 Cowan, Edward J. "The War Rhymes of Robert Service, Folk Poet." *Studies in Scottish Literature*, Vol. 28, Iss. 1, 1993: 12–22. Not everyone acknowledged Service's writing. Cowan, on page 13, states that "Service was the victim of a strange conspiracy of silence" and "silently edited out by the world of professional criticism which is guilty of either invincible ignorance or, more likely, of monumental snobbery."

153 Service, Robert W. *The Complete Poems of Robert Service*. New York: Dodd, Mead & Co., 1960, 300–302; *Ottawa Evening Journal*, December 18, 1915: 04: Service refers to a man he met in France who was from Athabasca who was trapping when he received news of the war. He enlisted but dreamed of returning after the war. Together Service and this man "yarned" together about the subarctic, through which Service travelled in 1911.

154 Service, *The Complete Poems*, 341–44.

155 Ibid., 87–89.

156 Ibid., 90–91.

157 Ibid., 92.

158 Service, *Harper of Heaven*, 93–94. Dream Haven was a home that Service purchased in the French coastal town of Lancieux, near St. Malo.

BOUND FOR BLIGHTY

159 *Victoria Daily Colonist*, January 17, 1917: 05.

160 "Yukon Boys Pass through Ottawa City," DDN, January 23, 1917: 01; "Dr. Thompson Was with the Yukon Boys," DDN, February 9, 1917: 01.

161 "Pictures of Yukon Boys Tomorrow," DDN, January 16, 1917: 04; "Yukon Boys in Movies Cheered in Home Town," DDN, January 18, 1917: 04.

162 Merrill, Anne. "Yukon M.P.'s Wife Real 'Sour-Dough.'" *Maclean's*, May 1, 1922: 64.

163 Black, Mrs. George (Martha Louise). *My Seventy Years*. As told to Elizabeth Bailey Price. Toronto: Thomas Nelson and Sons, Ltd., 1938, 235.

164 Merrill, Anne. "Yukon M.P.'s Wife Real 'Sour-Dough,'" 64; Black. *My Seventy Years*, 233. Mrs. Black cited Sergeant (Charles Sedley) Barwell as the author, whereas Merrill attributed it to Sergeant Major Sam Rae. As Merrill's article was written closer to the time of the event, and because Mrs. Black could be fuzzy about many of the details in her autobiography, Merrill's attribution is more likely to be accurate.

165 "Interesting Letter from Yukon Boys," DDN, May 23, 1917: 04.

166 "Frank Cooper Writes of Yukon Boys," DDN, June 22, 1917: 04.

167 "Tells of the Work of the Yukon Boys," DDN, May 28, 1917: 04.

168 "Frank Cooper Writes of Yukon Boys," DDN, June 22, 1917: 04.

169 "Tells of the Work of the Yukon Boys," DDN, May 28, 1917: 04.

170 LAC, Service Records of the First World War, Canadian Expeditionary Force: RG 150, Accession 1992-93/166, Box 1713-24; DDN September 19, 1917: 04. A coroner's jury brought a verdict of manslaughter against the driver. *The Surrey Advertiser* (Surrey, England), August 18, 1917: 13.

TRENCH WARFARE

171 Hodder-Williams, Ralph. *Princess Patricia Canadian Light Infantry 1914-1919*, 2nd edition. Toronto: Carswell Printing Co., 1968, 205-206; DDN April 29, 1917: 04; May 14, 19, 1917: 04; June 22, 1917: 04.

172 See: Supplement to the *London Gazette*, March 9, 1917, www.thegazette.co.uk/London/issue/29981/supplement/2486.

173 Williams, Jeffrey. *Princess Patricia's Canadian Light Infantry*. London, ON: Leo Cooper Ltd., 1972, 8-9.

HOME FIRES

174 WS, May 19, 1916: 01.

175 Johnson, Linda. *With the People Who Live Here: The History of the Yukon Legislature 1909-1961*. Whitehorse: Legislative Assembly of Yukon, 2009, 104-105.

176 YN, April 4, 2008: 60.

177 YA, GOV 1661 file 31504, Letter to Commissioner George Black, stamped September 8, 1916.

178 YA, GOV 1661 file 31504, Letter from George Black to Yukon Women's Protective League, September 8, 1916.

179 "Petition for Suffrage Started Here," DDN, November 15, 1916: 04.

180 Ibid.

181 Parliament of Canada, 2015, www.parl.gc.ca/Parlinfo/Compilations/ProvinceTerritory/ProvincialWomenRightToVote.aspx.

MRS. BLACK GOES TO WAR

182 Black, Mrs. George (Martha Louise). *My Seventy Years*. As told to Elizabeth Bailey Price. Toronto: Thomas Nelson and Sons, Ltd., 1938, 249-50.

183 Merrill, Anne. "Mrs. Black and the Yukon 600," *Canadian News*, March 15, 1917, 69.

184 "Work Of Yukoners in England and France by Mrs. George Black," DDN, June 19, 1917: 03.

185 Black, *My Seventy Years*, 252

186 Ibid., 252.

187 Ibid., 254.

188 Ibid., 254-55.

189 "Chronicles by Mrs. Geo. Black on Three Weeks' Trip in Wales," DDN, July 9, 1919: 02.

190 "Klondike of the Past," DDN, August 17, 1918: 07.

191 Black, *My Seventy Years*, 257.

192 *The Geographical Journal*, Vol 50, No. 2 (August 1917: 157); DDN, July 07, 1917: 01; *Toronto World*, June 29, 1917: 10.

193 Black, *My Seventy Years*, 255.

194 Martha Black, Extracts from Letters, n.d., Mary Black papers, Kathy Gates collection, p. 4.

195 Black, *My Seventy Years*, 256-57.

196 "Sketch of the Life at the Witley Camp," DDN, August 27, 1917: 04; also: "Butler Writes of Yukon Boys in Old England," DDN, August 20, 1917: 01.

197 Black, *My Seventy Years*, 276.

198 Ibid., 253-54.

199 Ibid., 250.

200 Ibid., 249-50.

THE BATTLE FOR VIMY RIDGE

201 "Grestock of Dawson Sends Word from Salisbury Camp," DDN, December 1, 1914: 01.

202 "From Dawson Boy," WS, July 30, 1915: 03.

203 LAC, Circumstances of Death Registers, First World War: Frederick Wells Polley.

204 LAC, War Diary Yukon Battery, April 11, 1917: data2.collectionscanada.ca/e/e048/
e001196967.jpg; DDN, June 14, 1917: 04.

205 LAC, War Diary, Yukon Machine Gun Battery, May 3, 1917; also Circumstances of
Death Register.

206 "Yukoners Took in All the Fighting," DDN, July 10, 1917: 04.

207 As noted in the war diary for July 17, 1917. data2.collectionscanada.ca/e/e048/
e001197213.jpg.

DEATH AND GLORY AT PASSCHENDAELE

208 Cook, Tim. *Shock Troops: Canadians Fighting the Great War, 1917-1918*, Volume 2.
Toronto: Penguin Canada, 2008, 319-20.

209 "Seven Yukoners Are Killed in France," DDN, January 5, 1918: 01 The seven men who
were killed were Joe Tilton, William Kerr, Peter Morrison, Peter Allan, Fred LaBlanche,
George Otis and Francois (Frank) Pregent.

210 Cook, Tim. *Shock Troops*, 348.

211 Hodder-Williams, Ralph. *Princess Patricia Canadian Light Infantry 1914-1919*, 2nd
edition. Toronto: Carswell Printing Co., 1968, 1923, 64.

212 Hodder-Williams, *Princess Patricia Canadian Light Infantry 1914-1919*, 85-86; Also
LAC, PPCLI War Diary for October 1915.

213 Williams, Jeffrey. *Princess Patricia's Canadian Light Infantry*. London, ON: Leo
Cooper Ltd., 1972, 23-24.

214 *London Gazette*, April 25, 1918: 5021.

215 War Diary, 5th Canadian Mounted Rifles, October 1917.

216 Ibid.

217 Cited in Cook, Tim. *Shock Troops*, 351.

218 Cook, Tim. *Shock Troops*, 364-65.

THE ADVENTURES OF JOE BOYLE

219 "J.W. Boyle to Leave Tonight for London," DDN, July 17, 1916: 01.

220 Rodney, William. *Joe Boyle, King of the Klondike*. Toronto: McGraw-Hill Ryerson,
1974, 118, states it was September 21, whereas Taylor, Leonard. *The Sourdough and
the Queen*. Toronto: Methuen, 1983, 150, states it was September 13.

221 Rodney, *Joe Boyle*, 118.

222 Taylor, *Sourdough and the Queen*, 172.

223 Ibid., 173.

224 Quoted in Taylor, *Sourdough and the Queen*, 183.

225 Taylor, *Sourdough and the Queen*, 180.

226 Hill, Captain George A., D.S.O. *Go Spy the Land*. London: Cassell and Company,
1932, 86.

227 Hill, *Go Spy the Land*, 92.

228 Rodney, *Joe Boyle*, 146 states that the journey was 1,500 miles (2,500 kilometres),
whereas Taylor, *The Sourdough and the Queen*, 218, states the distance was approxi-
mately 800 miles (1,280 kilometres). The distance on a map, as the crow flies, is closer
to Taylor's estimate.

229 Rodney, *Joe Boyle*, 150, states that the crown jewels were an embellishment to the story.

230 The duration of the journey is in dispute. Rodney, *Joe Boyle*, 146, seems to suggest that the route through Russia to Romania via Kiev, Odessa and Kishineff started around December 6, or perhaps earlier, whereas Hill, *Go Spy the Land*, 139, suggests the journey took nine days. Taylor, *Sourdough and the Queen*, 218, states that the trip took six days.

231 Hill, *Go Spy the Land*, 120.

232 Ibid., 121.

233 Ibid., 131.

234 Ibid., 132–135.

235 Hill, *Go Spy the Land*, 138–139, states that he was at the controls of the engine at this point.

CHANGES AT HOME

236 Elections Canada, 2015.

237 Nicholson, Col. G.W.L. *Canadian Expeditionary Force 1914-1919*. Ottawa: Queen's Printer, 1962, 345.

238 "First Big Meeting of Campaign Last Night," DDN, January 16, 1918: 04.

239 "Last Meeting of Campaign Held Last Saturday," DDN, January 28, 1918: 04.

240 "True Yukoners," DDN, January 23, 1918: 02.

241 "Endorses Capt. Black," DDN, January 24, 1918: 02.

242 "Communications: From Johnny McFarlane," DDN, February 9, 1918: 02; YA Acc 82/234, Martha Black scrapbook, microfilm #6.

243 "Report on the Yukon Comfort Fund Received from Old England," DDN, June 15, 1918: 02–03; "Report on the Yukon Comfort Fund Received from Old England," DDN, June 17, 1918: 02.

244 Smyth, Stephen. *The Yukon's Constitutional Foundations, Volume 1: The Yukon Chronology*. Whitehorse: Northern Directories, Ltd., 1991, 14.

245 "Communication: Soldiers' Vote," DDN, February 16, 1918: 03.

246 The 1902 federal election, which Congdon won, was blemished by Liberal ballot stuffing and questionable voting practices.

247 "Ruling Made at Ottawa on Congdon's Protest," DDN, February 18, 1918: 04.

248 "Thompson Is Member for Yukon," DDN, May 22, 1918: 01.

249 "Noted Yukon Quilt Goes to Mrs. Black," DDN, March 16, 1918: 01.

250 YA, YRG-1 GOV 1866 file 29600A. The total by the end of 1917 had reached $149,212.21.

251 For example, see "Victory Loan 1918," DDN, October 28, 1918.

252 Jones, Preston. *Fires of Patriotism: Alaskans in the Days of the First World War 1910-1920*. Fairbanks: University of Alaska, 2013, 71–74.

253 Johnson, Linda. *With the People Who Live Here: The History of the Yukon Legislature 1909-1961*. Whitehorse: Legislative Assembly of Yukon, 2009, 134.

254 YA, Acc 82/234, Martha Black scrapbook, microfilm #62; LAC RG 85 Vol 851 File 138916, Memo from Clerk of the Privy Council to the Minister of the Interior.

255 Smyth, Stephen. *The Yukon's Constitutional Foundations*, 14–15.

256 "Remember the Boys," DDN, May 15, 1918: 02.

257 Lillian Nakamura Maguire, "Remembering Japanese Canadian Soldiers of WWI," Whatsupyukon, November 9, 2016, 5.

258 "Jeff C. Davis Arrives," WS, October 18, 1918: 01.

259 Coates and Morrison. *The Sinking of the* Princess Sophia: *Taking the North Down With Her.* Toronto: Oxford University Press, 1990, 33–34.

LETTERS HOME

260 "News Picture Gallery Is Growing," DDN, August 31, 1917: 04.

261 The author has a copy of this document in his personal collection, thanks to a private collector.

262 "Story of the 8,000 Mile Trip of Yukon Boys to England," DDN, October 12, 1918: 03.

263 Ibid.

264 Ibid.

265 "Lieut. Watt Writes of the Yukoners," DDN, April 21, 1917: 04.

266 "Yukon Socks Appreciated in England," DDN, April 18, 1917: 04.

267 "Yukon Boys in Hot Fight in France," DDN, April 17, 1917: 04.

268 "Ball Grazes Dawson Boy at the Front," DDN, June 8, 1917: 04.

269 The author has copies of these letters, thanks to a private collector.

270 Letter, Norton Townsend to his mother, August 15, 1918, page 1; private collection.

271 "Dawson Girl Writes from Firing Line," DDN, August 31, 1917: 04.

272 Black, Mrs. George (Martha Louise). *My Seventy Years.* As told to Elizabeth Bailey Price. Toronto: Thomas Nelson and Sons, Ltd., 1938, 239.

273 Black, *My Seventy Years,* 270.

274 "Writes of the Yukoners Now in Europe," DDN, May 4, 1918: 02.

NOT QUIET ON THE WESTERN FRONT

275 Cook, Tim. *Shock Troops: Canadians Fighting the Great War, 1917-1918,* Volume 2. Toronto: Penguin Canada, 2008, 395.

276 Cook, *Shock Troops,* 395.

277 LAC War Diary, 1st MMG Brigade, March 24, 1918: data2.collectionscanada.ca/e/e040/e000987852.jpg.

278 LAC War Diary, 1st MMG Brigade, March 24, 1918: data2.collectionscanada.ca/e/e040/e000987853.jpg.

279 LAC War Diary, 1st MMG Brigade, March 25, 1918: data2.collectionscanada.ca/e/e040/e000987866.jpg.

280 LAC War Diary, 1st MMG Brigade, Appendix 23: Narrative by Captain H.F. Meurling: 3, data2.collectionscanada.ca/e/e040/e000987854.jpg.

281 LAC War Diaries, 1st MMG Brigade, Appendix 23: Narrative by Captain H.F. Meurling, data2.collectionscanada.ca/e/e040/e000987854.jpg.

282 YA, Anglican Church Records, COR 249-15. Letter from George Black to Martha Black, April 22, 1918. The captains referred to by Lyman in his letter were not named.

283 LAC, War Diary, Yukon MMG Battery, May 1918: data2.collectionscanada.ca/e/e048/e001197412.jpg.

284 See: www.thegazette.co.uk/London/issue/30813/supplement/8860; See also DDN, September 19, 1918: 04.

285 YA Acc 82/234, Martha Black microfilm #62.

ZEEBRUGGE-OSTEND

286 See: www.navalandmilitarymuseum.org/archives/articles/local-heroes/commander-rowland-bourke, letter from Lt. Coningsby Dawson to parents, September 1, 1918.

287 Victoria Cross citation, *The London Gazette*, August 27, 1918: www.veterans.gc.ca/eng/remembrance/medals-decorations/orders-decorations/canadian-victoria-cross-recipients/bourke.

288 "Dawson Boy Wins Victoria Cross and D.S.O. Decoration," DDN, December 31, 1918: 03; "Toasts Proposed at St. George's Day Banquet," DDN, April 26, 1923: 02.

AMIENS AND THE HUNDRED DAYS

289 YA, Acc 82/234, Martha Black microfilm #62; DDN, May 14, 1918: 04.

290 Nicholson, Col. G.W.L. *Canadian Expeditionary Force 1914-1919*. Ottawa: Queen's Printer, 1962, 384.

291 LAC, War Diary, 2nd CMMG Brigade, June 7, 1918: data2.collectionscanada.ca/e/e040/e000988527.jpg.

292 LAC, War Diary, 2nd CMMG Brigade, July 14, 1918: data2.collectionscanada.ca/e/e040/e000988551.jpg.

293 Victor Joseph Dupont of Dawson City, another victim of the pandemic, was conscripted for service on July 2, 1918, but died of influenza in hospital in Toronto, without ever having been shipped overseas. LAC veterans' death cards for the First World War: www.collectionscanada.gc.ca/microform-digitization/006003-119.01-e.php?PHPSESSID=i5bbm809c7e2lhsbc7qu32efb0&sqn=1260&q2=36&q3=2865&tt=1304.

294 See Tuxford, Brig. General G.(eorge) S. "The Trail of the Midnight Sun," Volume 2, George S. Tuxford Memoirs, Vol 1-4, Saskatchewan Archives Board, University of Regina, Microfilm R 2.247, n.d.

295 Cook, Tim. *Shock Troops: Canadians Fighting the Great War, 1917-1918*, Volume 2. Toronto: Penguin Canada, 2008, 420.

296 Cook, *Shock Troops*, 437.

297 "Dead Lay Everywhere about Yukoners," DDN, September 26, 1918: 04.

298 Black, George. "Great Fight Made by the Yukon Boys." *The Gold Stripe*, Vol 1, Wednesday, December 25, 1918. Also, letter dated August 13, 1918, from Grey Friar's Hospital addressed to "J.B. and Charlie." Black, Mrs. George (Martha Louise). *My Seventy Years*. As told to Elizabeth Bailey Price. Toronto: Thomas Nelson and Sons, Ltd., 1938, 280, Martha Black later quotes George saying that it was a sniper's bullet.

299 Klondike National Historic Sites, Dawson City, KNHS 201.32a: Letter to Mrs. Munger, August 15, 1918.

300 "Yukon's Second Contingent in the Great World War," DDN, August 18, 1919, n.p.

301 Cook, *Shock Troops*, 458.

302 LAC, Circumstances of Death Register: www.collectionscanada.gc.ca/
microform-digitization/006003-119.01-e.php?PHPSESSID=028f5r8mogpo7mf2v8h-
jq5qmo2&sqn=152&q2=28&q3=2300&tt=971.

303 LAC, Circumstances of Death Register: www.collectionscanada.gc.ca/
microform-digitization/006003-119.01-e.php?PHPSESSID=028f5r8mogpo7mf2v8h-
jq5qmo2&sqn=216&q2=28&q3=2322&tt=799.

304 "Yukon Boy Died Bravely Facing Foe," DDN, March 26, 1919: 04.

305 LAC, Circumstances of Death Register: www.collectionscanada.gc.ca/
microform-digitization/006003-119.01-e.php?PHPSESSID=028f5r8mogpo7mf2v8h-
jq5qmo2&sqn=634&q2=28&q3=2322&tt=799.

306 Cook, *Shock Troops*, 525–526.

307 "Yukoners Are on Casualty List In France," DDN, October 10, 1918: 04.

308 LAC, Circumstances of Death Register, First World War: www.collectionscanada.gc.ca/
microform-digitization/006003-119.01-e.php?PHPSESSID=028f5r8mogpo7mf2v8h-
jq5qmo2&sqn=656&q2=28&q3=2278&tt=787.

309 LAC, Circumstances of Death Register, First World War: www.collectionscanada.gc.ca/
microform-digitization/006003-119.01-e.php?PHPSESSID=028f5r8mogpo7mf2v8h-
jq5qmo2&sqn=842&q2=28&q3=2320&tt=983.

310 LAC, Circumstances of Death Register, First World War: www.collectionscanada.gc.ca/
microform-digitization/006003-119.01-e.php?PHPSESSID=028f5r8mogpo7mf2v8h-
jq5qmo2&sqn=540&q2=28&q3=2278&tt=787.

311 "Stewart, Charles James Townsend," Dictionary of Canadian Biography, www.biographi.
ca/en/bio/stewart_charles_james_townsend_14E.html, accessed October 10, 2015.

312 Ibid.

313 "Yukon's Second Contingent in the Great World War," DDN, August 19, 1919, n.p.

314 "Great Tidings from Yukon's Young Heroes," DDN, December 13, 1918: 04.

315 Letter, Norton Townsend to his mother, November 15, 1918, pages 2–3, private
collection.

316 The Norton Townsend letters, private collection, Vancouver.

317 "Yukon's Second Contingent in the Great World War," DDN, August 18, 1919.

318 Cook, *Shock Troops*, 450–451.

ARMISTICE: TRIUMPH AND TRAGEDY

319 Norton Townsend letter, November 15, 1918: 07, private collection, Vancouver.

320 Cook, Tim. *Shock Troops: Canadians Fighting the Great War, 1917-1918*,
Volume 2. Toronto: Penguin Canada, 2008, 577–78.

321 Black, Mrs. George (Martha Louise). *My Seventy Years*. As told to Elizabeth Bailey
Price. Toronto: Thomas Nelson and Sons, Ltd., 1938, 282.

322 Ibid.

323 Ibid.

324 "Celebrate the Ending of the World's War," WS, November 15, 1918: 01.

325 "Celebrate the Ending of the World's War," WS, November 15, 1918: 01; WS November
22, 1918: 02.

326 "Dawson Is Jubilant In Victory," DDN, November 11, 1918: 02.

327 Coates, Ken, and William Morrison. *The Sinking of the* Princess Sophia: *Taking the North Down With Her.* Toronto: Oxford University Press, 1990, 41.

328 Coates and Morrison, *The Sinking of the* Princess Sophia, 69.

329 Ibid.

330 Mount McKinley was the official name of the peak from 1917 to 2015. The state of Alaska returned to Denali in 1975, and the federal government changed to this name in August of 2015.

331 For a detailed account of the sinking of the *Princess Sophia*, refer to Coates and Morrison, 1990.

JOE BOYLE AND THE QUEEN OF ROMANIA

332 Taylor, Leonard. *The Sourdough and the Queen.* Toronto: Methuen, 1983, 241.

333 At this time, Canada had a limited role in its own foreign affairs. Mark Zuehlke, personal communication, March 3, 1918, states: "Although a small department of Foreign Affairs and International Trade had been created in 1909, its duties were largely to issue passports and liaise with the British Colonial Office and foreign Consuls in Canada as well as manage routine business with the U.S... It is not, however, until the Statute of Westminster in 1931 which formally gave Canada and the other Dominions full control over foreign policy."

334 Rodney, William. *Joe Boyle, King of the Klondike.* Toronto: McGraw-Hill Ryerson, 1974, 152.

335 Taylor, *The Sourdough and the Queen*, 268–69.

336 Ibid., 245–256.

337 Ibid., 257.

338 Ibid., 261.

339 Ibid., 262.

340 Ibid.

341 Pakula, Hannah. *The Last Romantic: A Biography of Queen Marie of Roumania.* London: Phoenix Giant, 1984, 243.

342 Taylor, *The Sourdough and the Queen*, 278.

343 Ibid.

344 Pakula, *The Last Romantic*, 245.

345 Taylor, *The Sourdough and the Queen*, 288.

346 Ibid., 292.

347 Ibid., 296.

348 Ibid., 304–307.

OCCUPATION

349 LAC, War Diary, 2nd Canadian Motor Machine Gun Brigade, November 1918: Appendix VII.

350 Ibid.

351 Ibid.

352 Ibid., Appendix VIII.

353 Norton Townsend letter, November 15, 1918: 05, 07, private collection, Vancouver.

354 Ibid., letter to father, December 14, 1918: 04.

355 Ibid., December 14, 1918: 02.
356 LAC, War Diary, 2nd Canadian Motor Machine Gun Brigade, December 1918.
357 Norton Townsend letter, December 26, 1918, private collection, Vancouver.
358 "Great Adventures of a Dawson Girl in War Zone," DDN, August 18, 1919.
359 *Daily Sitka Sentinel*, November 12, 1982: 14.
360 Ibid.
361 Gaffen, Fred. *Forgotten Soldiers*. Penticton BC: Theytus Books Ltd., 1985. Also:
www.veterans.gc.ca/eng/remembrance/memorials/canadian-virtual-war-memorial/
detail/660280?Hugh%20John%20MacDonald.
362 For information regarding government preparations for the influenza epidemic:
YA YRG-1 GOV 1677 file 5.
363 "Dawson Will Welcome the Year 1919," DDN, December 31, 1918: 03.

HOMEWARD BOUND

364 LAC, War Diary, 2nd Canadian Motor Machine Gun Brigade, January 1919.
365 Cook, Tim. *Shock Troops: Canadians Fighting the Great War, 1917-1918*, Volume 2.
Toronto: Penguin Canada, 2008, 596.
366 *Canada*, April 12, 1919: 47; DDN, June 18, 1919: 04; YA, Anglican Church Records,
COR 249-15, Letter from M. Black to Bishop Stringer, April 9, 1919; DDN, June 18,
1919: 04.
367 *The Iola Daily Register* (Kansas), August 29, 1919: 04.
368 YA, Anglican Church Records, COR 249-15, letter from M. Black to Bishop Stringer,
July 5, 1919.
369 Ibid.

RIOTS AND DISCONTENT

370 Morton, Desmond. "'Kicking and Complaining': Demobilization Riots in the
Canadian Expeditionary Force, 1918–1919," *Canadian Historical Review* Vol. LXI,
No. 3, 1980, 335.
371 Morton, "Kicking and Complaining," 341.
372 Ibid., 342.
373 Information regarding the Kinmel Park camp riots came from two sources: Morton,
"Kicking and Complaining," and Putkowski, Julian. *The Kinmel Park Camp Riots 1919*.
Clwyd, Wales: Flintshire Historical Society, 1989.
374 *Winnipeg Free Press*, April 19, 1919: 01.
375 YA, Anglican Church Records, COR 249-15, letter from M. Black to Bishop Stringer,
July 22, 1919.
376 LAC, RG 13 Vol 243 file 1919-2870.
377 Ibid.
378 Another returning Yukoner remembered, a short time later, that of the original one
thousand members of the PPCLI, one remained at the end of the war. DDN, July 7,
1919: 01, 04.
379 "Exploits of Heroic Yukon Battery Recalled," *Vancouver Province*, May 20, 1919.
380 Ibid.

381 "Yukon Soldier Boys at the D.A.A.A. Tonight," DDN, April 9, 1919: 04; "Yukon Boys Are Seen on Silver Screen," DDN, April 10, 1919: 04; "Dawson Lad Is Wounded in France," DDN, September 5, 1918: 04.

382 For example: "Old Timers Get In by Small Boat," DDN, June 11, 1919: 04; "First Steamers Get in from Whitehorse," DDN, June 13, 1919: 04; "Yukon Vets Back from the Battle Front," DDN, June 28, 1919: 04; "Soldier on Selkirk," DDN, July 9, 1919: 04; "Yukon Vets Get Back from Front," DDN, July 18, 1919: 04.

383 "Pioneers Show Honor to Departed," DDN, November 25, 1918: 04.

384 "History Dawson G.W.V.A. and Ladies Auxiliary," DDN, August 18, 1919.

385 "St George's Day Observed in Dawson," DDN, April 23, 1919: 04; Bourke was still being lionized in Dawson on this day as late as 1923, "Toasts Proposed at St. George's Day Banquet," DDN, April 26, 1923: 04. In fact, he earned the DSO on April 23; the VC came May 9–10, 1918.

386 "Dawson Will Observe the Day of Peace," DDN, July 18, 1919: 04; "Dawson Has a Big Peace Celebration," DDN, July 21, 1919: 04.

387 "Capt. Black on Yukoners in Great War," DDN, August 9, 1919: 04.

388 "Dawson Shows Honors to Her Soldiers," DDN, August 12, 1919: 01, 04.

389 Ibid.

390 "Eagle Memorial Day Observed Yesterday," DDN, August 18, 1919: 04.

391 "G.W.V.A. Holds a Meeting of Importance," DDN, August 21, 1919: 04; "Money to Be Refunded to Yukon," DDN, September 27, 1919: 01; "Meeting Held by the Yukon Patriotic Fund," DDN, October 10, 1919: 04; "Ottawa Grants $10,000 for Yukon Soldiers," DDN, February 9, 1920: 01.

392 "Whitehorse Wants Names on the Roll," DDN, September 23, 1918: 04.

393 "Shrine to Yukoners Is in Position," DDN, October 26, 1918: 04. One man, G.T. "Mickey" Monson, was incorrectly identified as dead. George Black was to write the *Dawson Daily News* that "Mickey may have slipped a few times, but he didn't fall. You do him an injustice. 'Mickey' came home unscathed and re-enlisted in the R.C.M.P." "Capt. Black Writes of Error on Shrine," DDN, January 3, 1923: 04.

394 According to military historian Cameron Pulsifer (personal communication) this dimension refers to the inside diameter, or bore, of the barrel.

395 WS, November 10, 1989: 06.

396 Ibid.

397 WS, November 10, 1989: 13.

398 "Dedication Is Held in the Public School," DDN, November 12, 1920: 04.

399 Ibid. I could confirm the death of only one son of Sergeant Major Bowdridge, Cyril Anthony, who died November 1, 1916.

400 "Dawson Men Who Served in War Honored," DDN, December 19, 1921: 01, 04.

401 "Pleasing Address on the War Memorial," DDN, February 2, 1924: 04; also an additional article on pages 2 and 3.

402 "Unveiling of Yukon Soldiers' Monument," DDN, September 26, 1924: 04; "How The Funds Were Raised For Monument," DDN, September 27, 1924: 02; also YA GOV 1667 file 33844, Yukon Memorial Committee.

CLOSURE

403 "Domesday Book of C.E.F. Been Compiled," DDN, January 2, 1925: 01; Coates and Morrison (1988: 312, footnote 61) state a similar number—2,327—without providing a source for that figure.

404 See Jones, Preston. *Fires of Patriotism: Alaskans in the Days of the First World War 1910–1920.* Fairbanks: University of Alaska, 2013, for more information about Alaska in World War I.

405 Berton, Laura Beatrice. *I Married the Klondike.* Toronto: McClelland & Stewart, 1961, 143.

406 A "sourdough" is said to be a seasoned veteran of the North, someone who has remained in the Yukon valley from freeze-up of the river in the fall, to the breakup of the ice in the spring. By comparison, a "cheechako" is a newcomer, greenhorn or tenderfoot.

407 Berton, Laura Beatrice. *I Married the Klondike*, 151.

408 "Many Women at Meeting Last Evening," DDN, November 30, 1921: 04.

409 *Edmonton Journal*, May 23, 1922: 01.

410 Black, George. Striking Gold in Klondyke… was my Greatest Hour." *John Bull*, December 24, 1932: 22.

411 Taylor, Leonard. *The Sourdough and the Queen.* Toronto: Methuen, 1983, 369.

412 *Ottawa Evening Journal*, December 18, 1915: 14.

413 Armstrong, Nevill A.D. *Yukon Yesterdays: Thirty Years of Adventures in the Klondike.* London: John Long Ltd., 1936, 238.

414 *Yukon News*, January 15, 2015: 33.

415 WS, July 29, 1938; DDN, August 4, 1938: 06.

416 "Dedication Is Held in the Public School," DDN, November 12, 1920: 04.

417 "Jack Suttles Writes to Dawson News," DDN, January 16, 1923: 02.

418 Kula, Sam. "There's Film in Them Thar Hills!" *American Film*, Vol 4, No. 8, 1979: 141–148.

419 "Old Timers Pass on from Northland," DDN, August 24, 1937: 04. Although it is stated in the newspaper account that he was sixty-five years old, his wartime enlistment papers indicate that he was not yet sixty-four years of age.

420 "War Veteran and Pioneer Passes Away," DDN, October 7, 1938: 08.

421 "Veteran of Great War Answers the Last Call," DDN, November 04, 1938: 02.

422 "R.L. Allen Passes Away at Victoria," DDN, April 20, 1939: 04.

423 See: www.collectionscanada.gc.ca/microform-digitization/006003-119.01-e. php?PHPSESSID=8gduimj71909091ullmvoq2a21&sqn=238&q2=36&q3=2847&tt=1359.

424 "Yukoner Buried Last Wednesday," DDN, February 23, 1950: 01.

425 Coates, Ken, and William Morrison. *Land of the Midnight Sun: A History of the Yukon.* Edmonton: Hurtig Publishers, 1988, 185.

426 "Dawson Shows Honors to Soldiers," DDN, August 12, 1919: 04.

427 Ibid.

BIBLIOGRAPHY

Anderson, Torchy. "Noted Princess Pats Sniper, 'Uncle' Christie, a Warrior, Gentleman and Fine Friend," *Windsor Star*, July 22, 1939: 11.

Armstrong, Nevill A.D. *After Big Game in the Upper Yukon*. London: John Long Ltd., 1937.

———. *Yukon Yesterdays: Thirty Years of Adventures in the Klondike*. London: John Long Ltd., 1936.

Berton, Laura Beatrice. *I Married the Klondike*. Toronto: McClelland & Stewart, 1961.

Berton, Pierre. *Vimy*. Toronto: McClelland & Stewart, 1986.

Black, George. "Great Fight Made by the Yukon Boys." *The Gold Stripe*, Vol 1, Wednesday, December 25, 1918.

———. Striking Gold in Klondyke... was my Greatest Hour." *John Bull*, December 24, 1932: 22.

Black, Mrs. George (Martha Louise). *My Seventy Years*. As told to Elizabeth Bailey Price. Toronto: Thomas Nelson and Sons, Ltd., 1938.

Christie, J.M. "The World's Biggest Bear Story." *Vancouver Province Sunday Magazine*, June 17, 1933: 1, 4.

Coates, Ken, and William Morrison. *Land of the Midnight Sun: A History of the Yukon*. Edmonton: Hurtig Publishers, 1988.

———. *The Sinking of the* Princess Sophia: *Taking the North Down With Her*. Toronto: Oxford University Press, 1990.

Cook, Tim. *At the Sharp End: Canadians Fighting the Great War, 1914-1916*. Toronto: Penguin Canada, 2007.

———. *Shock Troops: Canadians Fighting the Great War, 1917-1918*, Volume 2. Toronto: Penguin Canada, 2008.

Cowan, Edward J. "The War Rhymes of Robert Service, Folk Poet." *Studies in Scottish Literature*, Vol. 28, Iss. 1, 1993: 12-22.

Dobrowolsky, Helene. *Law of the Yukon: A Pictorial History of the Mounted Police*. Whitehorse: Lost Moose Publishing, 1995.

Elections Canada. "A History of the Vote in Canada." www.elections.ca/content.
aspx?section=res&dir=his&document=chap2&lang=e.

Ellis, John. *The Social History of the Machine Gun.* New York: Pantheon Books, 1973.

Foster, Charles Lyon. *Letters From the Front: Being a Record of the Part Played by Officers of the Bank in the Great War.* Canadian Bank of Commerce, n.d.

Gaffen, Fred. *Forgotten Soldiers.* Penticton, BC: Theytus Books Ltd., 1985.

Gates, Michael. *Gold at Fortymile Creek.* Vancouver: UBC Press, 1994.

Grafton, Charles Stewart. *The Canadian "Emma Gees": A History of the Canadian Machine Gun Corps.* London, Ontario: Canadian Machine Gun Corps Association, 1938.

Hill, Captain George A., D.S.O. *Go Spy the Land.* London: Cassell and Company, 1932.

Hodder-Williams, Ralph. *Princess Patricia Canadian Light Infantry 1914–1919,* 2nd edition. Toronto: Carswell Printing Co., 1968.

Johnson, Linda. *With the People Who Live Here: The History of the Yukon Legislature 1909–1961.* Whitehorse: Legislative Assembly of Yukon, 2009.

Jones, Preston. *Fires of Patriotism: Alaskans in the Days of the First World War 1910–1920.* Fairbanks: University of Alaska, 2013.

Junger, Ernst. *Storm of Steel.* London: Penguin Books, 1961.

Kula, Sam. "There's Film in Them Thar Hills!" *American Film,* Vol 4, No. 8, 1979: 141–48.

Lee, David, and Edward F. Bush. "George Black, last commissioner of the Yukon." Historic Sites and Monuments Board of Canada agenda paper 1991-50, 1991.

Library and Archives Canada, War Diaries of the First World War. www.collection-scanada.gc.ca/archivianet/02015202_e.html.

Logan, Major H.T., Captain M.R. Levey, Major General R. Brutinel, Major W.B. Forster, Lieutenant W.M. Baker and Lieutenant P.M. Humme. "History of the Canadian Machine Gun Corps, C.E.F.," 1919. University of British Columbia Archives, Harry T. Logan fonds, D547.M3 L63 1919a. Transcribed by Ron Edwards, Les Fowler, Brett Payne and Dwight Mercer, December 17, 2015.

Mackay, James. *Vagabond of Verse. Robert Service: A Biography.* Edinburgh: Mainstream Publishing Company, 1995.

Mallory, Enid. *Robert Service: Under the Spell of the Yukon.* Surrey, BC: Heritage House Publishing Co., 2006.

Merrill, Anne. "Mrs. Black and the Yukon 600," *The Canadian News,* March 15, 1917: 69.

———. "Yukon M.P.'s Wife Real 'Sour-Dough.'" *Maclean's,* May 1, 1922: 64–65.

Moore, Mary MacLeod. "War and War Work in the Arctic Regions," *Canada,* March 17, 1917: 305.

Morton, Desmond. "'Kicking and Complaining': Demobilization Riots in the Canadian Expeditionary Force, 1918–1919," *Canadian Historical Review*, Vol. LXI, No. 3, 1980: 334–60.

Nicholson, Col. G.W.L. *Canadian Expeditionary Force 1914-1919*. Ottawa: Queen's Printer, 1962.

Pakula, Hannah. *The Last Romantic: A Biography of Queen Marie of Roumania*. London: Phoenix Giant, 1984.

Parliament of Canada. "Women's Right to Vote in Canada." www.parl.gc.ca/Parlinfo/ Compilations/ProvinceTerritory/ProvincialWomenRightToVote.aspx.

Princess Patricia Canadian Light Infantry. *Princess Patricia's Canadian Light Infantry: Nominal Roll of Officers and Non-commissioned Officers and Men*. Ottawa: King's Printer, 1914.

Putkowski, Julian. *The Kinmel Park Camp Riots 1919*. Clwyd, Wales: Flintshire Historical Society, 1989.

Reddick, Don. *Dawson City Seven*. Fredericton, NB: Goose Lane Editions, 1993.

Rodney, William. *Joe Boyle, King of the Klondike*. Toronto: McGraw-Hill Ryerson, 1974.

Service, Robert W. *The Complete Poems of Robert Service*. New York: Dodd, Mead & Co., 1960.

——. *Harper of Heaven*. New York: Dodd, Mead and Co., 1948.

Smyth, Stephen. *The Yukon's Constitutional Foundations, Volume 1: The Yukon Chronology*. Whitehorse: Northern Directories, Ltd., 1991.

Taylor, Leonard. *The Sourdough and the Queen*. Toronto: Methuen, 1983.

Tsukamoto, Suyoko. "Soldier Survives Grizzly Bear Attack in Yukon," *The Brandon Sun*, January 16, 2015.

Tuxford, Brig. General G.(eorge) S. "The Trail of the Midnight Sun," Volume 2, George S. Tuxford Memoirs, Vol 1–4, Saskatchewan Archives Board, University of Regina, Microfilm R 2.247, n.d.

Williams, Jeffrey. *First in the Field: Gault of the Patricias*. St. Catherines, ON: Vanwell Publishing Ltd., 1996.

——. *Princess Patricia's Canadian Light Infantry*. London: Leo Cooper Ltd., 1972.

Winegard, Timothy. *For King and Kanata: Canadian Indians and the First World War*. Winnipeg, MB: University of Manitoba Press, 2012.

INDEX

MICHAEL GATES was formerly the curator of Collections for Klondike National Historic Sites in Dawson City and pens the popular column "History Hunter" for the *Yukon News*. He is the author of *Dalton's Gold Rush Trail: Exploring the Route of the Klondike Cattle Drives* (Harbour Publishing, 2012) and *History Hunting in the Yukon* (Harbour Publishing, 2010). He lives in Whitehorse, YT.